Egyptian Magick

> "where do we start, on the threshold, before a door.
> Here it is - simplified so we can see its complexities...
> doors are very potent symbols."

Disclaimer

Take appropriate precautions and keep your wits about you. The information in this book should not be used as a substitute for professional advice. Neither the author or publisher can be held responsible for any loss, claim or damage arising out of the use, or misuse of the suggestions made.

By same author

Tankhem: Seth & Egyptian Magick
The Bull of Ombos (Seth & Egyptian Magick II)
Demonic Calendar Ancient Egypt
Seth and the Two Ways

Egyptian Magick

A Spirited Guide
By

Mogg Morgan

Mandrake

Copyright © 2021 Mogg Morgan

All rights reserved. No part of this work may be reproduced or utilized in any form by any means electronic or mechanical, including *xerography, photocopying, microfilm,* and *recording,* or by any information storage system without permission in writing from the publishers.

Published by
Mandrake
PO Box 250
OXFORD
OX1 1AP (UK)

Contents

Preliminary invocation 8
Drawing down the plough 9
1 North 10
Thoughts on that preliminary rite 10

2 Heka & Hekau 25

3. Power of the Gods: The magical-religion 87
Not temple 100
The Egyptian Magick of Abramelin 102

4. The Temple or Imaginarium 173
The Temple of Seti I 195
A description of the Temple 197
Simple way of using this model 206

5. Initiation 212
The Classical Mystery Cult 212
Initiation 215

6. Books of the Nightworld (duat) 224
The Book of Gates 227

7 The Ritual Year 238
Timings for ritual 243
1st Month – Tekhy (July-August) Set 245
2nd Month (August-September) Min 257
3rd Month (September – October) Hathor (or Isis) 261
4th Month (October – November) Sokar or Osiris 268
5th Month (November – December) Neith 278
6th Month (December – January) Nwt 284

7th Month (Jan – Feb) Wepwawet/Anubis 289
8th Month (February – March) Renenutet or Meretseger 300
9th (March – April) Khonsu "The wanderer" 306
10th Month (April – May) Khentykhet – (Horus) 312
11th Month (May – June) Ipet Hippo goddess 316
12th Month (June – July) RaHorakhty or Ra 320
13th Month (July – August) Thoth 330

8. Taboo Magick, Sacrifices etc 336
Eating magic 337
Seven spells or utterances of Nekhbet 361
Sex and Death 371

The Egyptian Liturgy 383
Opening: (revised version) 384

Final Words on Egyptian magick 389
Select Bibliography 403
Glossary 409
Index 417

"Within its own 'world view' Egyptian (Heka/ḥekȝ) was of far more exalted significance than its Coptic descendant or Western approximation.

Amoral and quintessentially effective (Akh/ȝḫ), a power to which gods, men, and all nature were subject, it was still the same force whether used by god, king, priest, private individual, rebel or foreign enemy, whether hostile or beneficent, sanctioned or suppressed."

Robert Ritner, *The Mechanics of Ancient Egyptian Magic*: 247

PRELIMINARY INVOCATION

The 'Abydos Arrangement'

'Before me in the East Nephthys
Behind me in the West Isis
On my right hand in the South is Seth
And on my left hand in the North is Horus
For above me shines the body of Nuit
And below me extends the ground of Geb
And in the centre abideth the 'Great Hidden God.'

DRAWING DOWN THE PLOUGH

Whenever I have need of you
I draw down the plough
Standing under the night stars,
The canopy clear above me
Searching the heavens for your sign,
An ox moving withershins,
Tethered to a mast of flint
In the northern part of the sky

First I rouse your mate
Who lies sleeping in the earth beneath
Stamping the ground,
So Bat for Bata will awake
Tremors below rising through me
A conduit for the seething cauldron
As the power rises to my belly
My arms upwards piercing the barrier
Separating I and thou

And down it flows
that thing
into me,
or my cup
or via me to my companion
Dizzy now with the elixir
I follow your movements backwards
to the nameless aeon
when none ruled but I

1 North

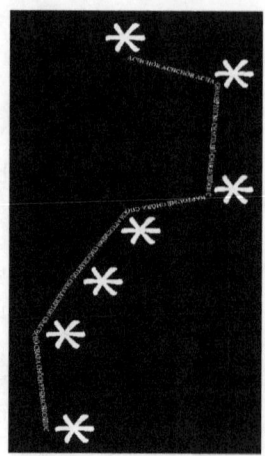

THOUGHTS ON THAT PRELIMINARY RITE

If you completed the preliminary rite above you might appreciate some background information. You may be familiar with Aleister Crowley. For those not so, I'd point out that in Crowley's grimoire *Magick – Liber ABA*, much of the really important instructional material is contained in appendices to the main text. Appendix II in *Magick* is entitled 'One Star In Sight' and is 'a glimpse of the structure and system of the great white brotherhood A∴

> A\ A\ is often fleshed out as Argenteum Astrum, or Order of the Silver Star. This term A∴ A∴ occurs as the name of an order in ancient Greece and there are conflicting opinions on the exact meaning of the term. This text sets out the magical work appropriate to the eleven grades of the A\ A\ as envisioned by Crowley. I don't really intend to go into that

here, if interested you can read the appendix for yourself. What interests me, as indeed it has interested others such as Kenneth Grant, is connecting this idea of 'one star in sight' with an actual constellation.

What led me to this material was a long time interest in the mythology and magick of the Egyptian deity Seth, who is supposedly the dark or opposing force in this ancient holy family of Isis, Osiris, Horus (or Anubis), Nepthys and Seth. All were born from Nuit who with her consort Geb and their father Amon completes the pantheon. Incidentally this eightfold pantheon is represented in the Temple of Seti I at Abydos as the seven shrines, connected by the eighth which is the overarching Nuit: 'above Nuit, the mother of us all unfolds'

I don't really expect you to accept the existence of these deities. I think we use these terms as some sort of symbolic language for discussion of what is in the psyche. As is well known, ancient Egyptian religion was very stellar, i.e. they liked to make correspondences between things they could see in the night sky and the kinds of god forms that moved around in their heads. Each of the eight important gods had a stellar equivalent. The two most important constellations were the Great Bear (known also as 'the Imperishable Stars') and Orion. Both were regarded as deities. The Dog-star Sirius or Sothis was chief of all stars because it was the herald of the inundation and its reappearance before dawn at the summer solstice was celebrated as a religious festival. It was dedicated to Isis and there is a legend that the tears she shed at the annual death of Osiris caused the inundations.' (Murray *TSTWE* p. 189)

It is widely believed by some of the magi, that there is some link between Sothis/Sirius and Seth. In the Osiris cult, Osiris was drowned by Seth – a possible parallel with the way in which the vegetation of Ancient Egypt was overwhelmed and 'killed' by the annual flood, at the same time refreshing the land and making way for new growth. It seems an obvious step to make the star Sirius that signals the beginning of the flood, some kind of personification of Seth, the storm deity who ultimately causes the flood. There are however problems with this idea – during the time of the popularity of the Osiris cult, direct rain and its personification Seth, was not necessary for the ecosystem and neither was it welcome. The flooding of the Nile and the use of irrigation refreshed the ecosystem. In fact the ancient Egyptians made a correspondence between Seth and the Constellation *Ursa Major*. The ancient Egyptians knew this constellation under the name Meskhetyu, the Bull, although in later times its name changed to the Great Bear. Both totemic beasts occur in later Invocations with veiled Setian undercurrents. Although Ursa Major is always visible in the night sky, it does in the course of twenty-four hours, 'dance' around the pole star and as well as rotate on its own axis. This outer lip of the 'gourd' always points to the Pole Star, currently Polaris (just to confuse matters Polaris in found in the constellation *Ursa Minor* - although four thousand years ago the Pole-star was located in the constellation Draco).

To the ancient Egyptians, the constellation we call *Ursa Major was* Seth. It is as well to remember that in the cycle of the year, Osiris is not the only sacrificial victim – whilst at the summer solstice Osiris is sacrificed by water, at the winter solstice Seth was sacrificed by fire, so the two great constellation/dragons, revolve and replace each other over and over again?

Whether I've got this cycle quite right – the fact is that elements of this mythos have traveled quite widely, and are found in many other parallel mythologies. The clearest connecting link is the appearance of the constellation Ursa major in several outwardly diverse magical systems – its is a secret link if you like – here are some examples:

The Setian connection with the cult of Mithras as revived, (not created in the Greek and Roman world) is seen in *Mithras liturgie* (H D

Betz –The Greek Magical Papyri In Translation – PGM IV line 700) This is an ancient magical 'grimoire' dated from several centuries before the birth of Christ.

> 'Now when they take their place, here and there, in order, look in the air and you will see lightning bolts going down, and lights flashing, and the earth shaking, and a god descending, a god immensely great, having a bright appearance, youthful, golden-haired, with a white tunic and a golden crown and trousers, and holding in his right hand a golden/ shoulder of a young bull: this is the Bear which moves and turns heaven around, moving upward and downward in accordance with the hour.'

In this cult the central mystery revolved around the sacrifice by Mithras (a god with qualities very like the Egyptian Horus) of the Bull, (although as in ancient Egypt, this bull was not a full grown adult, but a young and more manageable bull calf, of which the foreleg, which resembles the constellation Ursa Major, was offered.

Another example comes from the Leyden Papyrus:

> '(1) And you set up your [planisphere?] and you stamp on the ground with your foot seven times and recite these charms to the Foreleg, turning {?} to the North seven times (2) and you return down and go to a dark recess.'

This is the beginning of a 'spell' for divination by use of a lamp. The constellation is the easiest way to fix the northern point for any ritual work.

Yet another example comes from the Book of Job (ix.9), often regarded by the magi as giving an insight into the real nature of the dark initiator Shaitan, who tests Job's faith in Jahweh.

Job says:...

But how can a man be just before God?
If one wished to contend with him,
One could not answer him once in a thousand times.
He is wise in heart and mighty in strength
- who has hardened himself against him and succeeded? -
He who removes mountains and they know it not...
Who alone stretched out the heavens and trampled the waves
Of the sea;
Who made the Bear and Orion,
The Pleiades and the chambers of the south.

These last few lines mark out the four directions of space using stellar coordinates. And finally here's another important example, this time from Taoism,

> 'To dance the eight trigrams requires some tricky technical information. As maybe you'll want to do a ritual along these lines one day, I'll give a brief synopsis of the principle of the ceremony and hope that this is not too complicated a task. Plenty of Taoist rites make use of the dance of Yü. First the eight signs are projected on the ground. Look at the illustrations now and you can see that the order of the dance is made up out of the appearance of numbers in a magical square. In the ordinary arrangement, the dance of Yü begins in the north and ends in the south. The dance pattern can be applied to the circle of early and later heaven, that is, the dance steps remain the same but the signs visualized in each direction differ. When you use the circle of early heaven you begin with the receptive and end with the creative, using the circle of later heaven the dance begins with dark water and ends with bright fire. So far this is a fairly simple matter. Some

found it too simple and introduced complications. There are several schools of thunder magic that were developed to counter and combat the malevolent sorceries of the Tao of the left with its violent spirits. In the performance of thunder magic the dance of Yü is a key element. Not the simple version of the dance but a variety that was invented around the fifth century to introduce a bit of exclusive secret knowledge and confusion. In the circle of the eight signs, Ken, The Mountain represents not only a cloud covered peak but also (look at the shape of the sign) the entrance of a cave. In this aspect, the sign receives the title "The Gate of Life" and becomes a crucial focus of power. In the usual arrangement of the chart of the later heaven, the sign Ken is in the northeast. The thunder magicians, however, decided that the position of the gate is not fixed but changes every few hours. In their system the gate of the otherworld has to be found. The position of this gate depends on the constellation known as the Great Bear (Ursa major), also called the Big Dipper or the Great Wagon. If you look at it as a wagon, you can see that the shaft points in a certain direction. As the wagon moves around the polar star, the direction of the shaft keeps changing. If the shaft points at the east, for instance, the gate to the otherworld is also in the east. This means that the eastern trigram functions as the gate. As the wagon keeps moving, there is a new gate every couple of hours. It is part of the complications in ritual thunder magic Taoism to calculate the direction of the gate. In practice, the gate shifts from trigram to trigram as the Great Bear moves around the centre of heaven. The gate represents the weakest and most dangerous point in the circle, as it seems strong on the outside but is weak further in. You might argue that the sign Kun, the receptive, is a lot weaker than Ken. Though this is true, a Chinese strategist would not dream of attacking at a spot where an attack is expected. Weak as Kun is, it might conceal an ambush. Ken, looking strong but being weak, is a much better choice. At this sign, the otherworld is closest. The dangerous Chia spirits use it to come to earth, so do various disease spirits, and generally, people fear to lose their vital Ch´i energy through this gate. The deceased leave earth through this doorway, but they also use this gate to escape from hell and to ascend to heaven. It is also the point where the thunder magic Taoist begins and ends the dance of Yü, and from which the power of the thunder-breath is summoned. Sealing this dangerous place is among the first priorities of the practising ritualist.'

(Jan Fries, *Living Midnight – three movements of the Tao*)

I could go on but maybe you've got the picture. Almost any text, which mentions this constellation the Great Bear, will have an interesting magical undercurrent and very often will yield a lost and obscure element of the ancient magick of the Setians, from which the magi descend. It is for this reason that I suggest we always honour this constellation and use it as much as possible as a connection in our magick. Anyway to finish, there follow another example of a very old invocation of the same Northern Constellation, this one taken from the Egyptian magical papyri.

A Great Bear rite

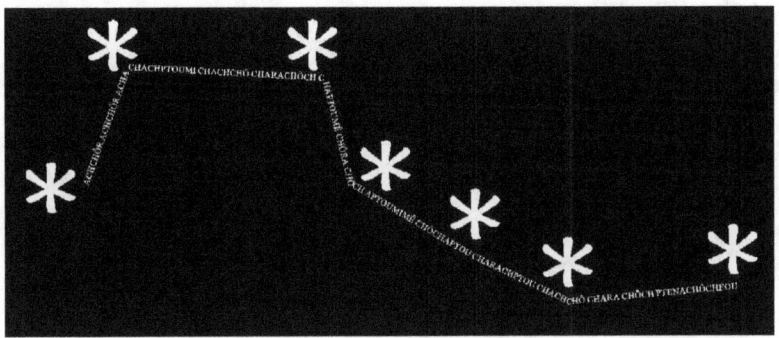

Opening Rite
Seven are the sacred sounds of the void

A E Ê I O Y Ô,

I call upon you, the greatest power in heaven,
in the name of the bear.
You appointed by the lord god to turn with a strong hand
the holy pole'

NIKAROPLÊX. [Polaris in the lesser Bear]

'Listen to me, Amon Ra, hear the holy [prayer].
You who hold together the universe and bring to life the whole world.'

THÔZOPITHÊ
EUCHANDAMA
ÔCHRIENTHÊR
OMNYÔDÊS
CHÊMIOCHYNGÊS
IEÔY
(perform a sacrifice)

THERMOUTHER
PSIPHIRIX PHROSALI
KANDTHIMEÔ ZAZZEMIA
ÔPER PEROMENÊS
RÔTHIEU ÊNINDEU
KORKOUNTHO EUMEN MENI
KÊDEUEA KÊPSEOI
(add the usual)

THÔ ZO PTAH,
'Bear, greatest goddess ruling heaven, reigning over the pole of the stars, highest, beautiful-shining goddess, incorruptible element, composite of the all, all-illuminating, bond of the universe.'

Have the following square:

A	E	Ê	I	O	Y	Ô,
E	Ê	I	O	Y	Ô	A
Ê	I	O	Y	Ô	A	E
I	O	Y	Ô	A	E	Ê
O	Y	Ô	A	E	Ê	I
Y	Ô	A	E	Ê	I	O
Ô	A	E	Ê	I	O	Y

'You who stand on the pole,

you whom the lord god appointed to turn the holy pole with a strong hand':
THÔZOPITHÊ (formula)

Petition to the sun at sunset:

Formula
'THÊNÔR,
O Atum,
SAN THÊNÔR,
'I beseech you, Lord, may the play and the lord of the Bear devote themselves to me'
(while petitioning sacrifice armara. Do it at sunset.)

Offering for the procedure:

4 drams of frankincence, 4 drams of myrrh, 2 ounces each of cassia leaf and/ of white pepper, 1 dram of bdellion, 1 dram of asphodel seed, 2 drams each of amomon, of saffron, of terebinth storax, 1 dram of wormwood — of vetch plant, priestly Egyptian incense, the complete brain of a black ram/ Combine these with white Mendesian wine and honey, and make pellets of bread.

Phylactery for the procedure:
Wear a wolf's knucklebone, mix juice of vetch and of pondweed in a censer. Write in the middle of the censer this name:

'THERMOUTH* EREPSIPHIRIPHI PISALI (24 letters),
and in this way make an offering.

The hundred lettered name of Typhon

---

* *Thermutis or Egyptian Rennutet, Egyptian harvest goddess and Fate*
Based on PGM IV,1275 -1322

Curved as a star and bind it in the middle of the core with the letters showing

ACHCHÔR ACHCHÔR
ACHACHACHPTOUMI
CHACHCHÔ CHARACHÔCH
CHAPTOUMÊ CHÔRA CHÔCH
APTOUMIMÊ CHÔCHAPTOU
CHARACHPTOU CHACHCHÔ
CHARA CHÔCH PTENACHÔCHEOU

Result

In the desert I burn your incense, placing my candles in the shape of the constellation. Across time the greatest of all your ancient priests appears to me, his face an embalmer's miracle – Sethos. I am your servant, teach me the ancient ways of he/she who upholds Polaris. It is good, I hear you say.

It was, fate that led me to Abydos, this unpromising place in the desert. Abydos, such a place, the most sacred on earth. The very name is a word of power. It was, and perhaps always was, a place sacred to Osiris/Orion – give him his due. Although the most ancient sacred enclosure of that god, is not where I planned to build my temple. The first temenos of Osiris is a good mile away across the desert. But in my day this was an old place and becoming very overcrowded. There was, you see, a need for a new sacred enclosure to the god and this task fell to me, the scion of a new dynasty. Throughout my life I worked to undo the harm done by the worshippers of the one god – Aten – I shall not name them, you know who they are. As a Setian, I am tolerant of all the gods, although for one in particular, I have a greater love, that is natural.

But the disasters that befell us when we turned from the old polytheistic ways are surely the real reason why I hate Akenaten and his family so much. If it had worked for us, then so be it, even the wanton acts of vandalism on the shrines of the 'god of existence' Amon, could be tolerated, if nature had not rebelled against us. Even now I doubt if I shall be able to undo the damage wrought by them, and they say I am a fearsome General. I doubt if even my warrior sons will be able to restore order and stop the tide of Assyria and their treacherous Hebrew cohorts. They are building an empire, or so they think, and when you have land on your mind, honour goes out the window. But history has a bitter lesson in store for them, if they think they can play footsy with the Assyrian and not end up with spike through their heels! But I digress.

I am a man of Seth, as are all my family. Born to holy orders in his service. And yet I was pharaoh.

'Some say you were the greatest pharaoh that has lived.' I interject.

'Thankyou – I have heard this said also. My life shows that anyone may become sovereign.'

Magick

The force that through the green fuse drives the flower
Drives my green age; that blasts the roots of trees
Is my destroyer.
And I am dumb to tell the crooked rose
My youth is bent by the same wintry fever.

Dylan Thomas

A privileged moment from the 21st dynasty Papyrus B of Her-Uben in the Cairo museum. She was a chantress of Amon-Ra and second prophetess of Mut. Most women served as priestesses in such a cult. This short pictorial papyrus presents the key scenes she must witness in her post mortem journey. Here she sees the boat of Ra steered to safety thanks to Seth's spearing of Apophis the demon of 'non-being' (Piankoff 1954). The original is 2m long, ¼m wide, painted in black, red, white, green and brown.

2 Heka & Hekau

The Egyptian word usually translated, as 'magick' is *Ḥekʿu* (hereafter given in anglicised form). It can be difficult to work out whether the action involves gods, men or both. This above ambiguity arises from the failure of Egyptian scribes to use an appropriate determinative, when writing about Hekau. Perhaps this omission was deliberate? It is clear that Hekau has three connotations:

A quality something might possess

A rite to be performed.

words or spells to be spoken aloud (ah) –

These rites are seldom confined to words but require actions and substances – for example the burning of bryony to overcome Apophis. Internal repetition of words is seldom enough.

Thoughout this chapter, we will make good use of the *Setna* cycle of stories. See *The Bull of Ombos* for versions of both. This series of interlocking stories was popular in Ptolemaic times when Egypt was ruled by the Greek successors to Alexander the Great. The first tale concerns the quest of Setna for the legendary magical *Book of Thoth*. The second tale is a sequel set when Setna has settled down to raise a family of his own. But his first child is wise beyond his years and turns out to be the reincarnation of a famous sorcerer from Egypt's past, who has returned to defend Egypt from one of its traditional enemies, the sorcerers of Nubia. Nubia, modern day Sudan, is one of Egypt's ancient enemies. Although set in 1200BCE the stories are actually composed around 200BCE.

In the second story, Setna provides a classic example of the efficacy of *spoken* spells. The narrator tells how one of the protagonists Panishi, '*uttered the words* of a spell and a flood of water appeared from the south, and put out the flame in an instant'.[1]

Practitioners of magick are called *ḥeka*, the same word as the god *Ḥeka*, which we can distinguish in English by the use of a capital letter, no such facility exists in the Egyptian language. The word *ḥeka* survived into the Coptic period and language as HIK. It occurs in chapter eight of the Coptic version of *New Testament*, 'Acts of the Apostles', in an account of the sorceries of Simon Magus. There is probably a connection between the word Heka and Ka, the essence of a human being, especially at the birth of the king. Heka as the magician is one of 14 Ka(s) of the king, just as the magician is one of the seven Ba(s) or external manifestations of Ra. Could *Ḥeka* be one of the secret names in the *Litany of Ra*?

There is even some indication that at least some Egyptians saw Seth as the counterpart of Ra. Te Velde says this conflation of *order* and *chaos* had only one known example. Even so the contemporary Temple of Seth have amplified the idea with their archetype of Kephra. Rather confusingly they render this *Xeper*, the 'X' being the Greek letter 'kh', a distinction perhaps lost on most readers.

One possible meaning of *Ḥekau* is derived from Ahau or *akhu* meaning 'to shine'.

> 'So Setna went to the Necropolis of Memphis with Inaros, his foster brother. They spent three days and three nights searching among the tombs of the Necroplis of Memphis, reading the inscriptions on the stones and deciphering the formulae carved

on the doors of the tombs. At last, on the third day, he found the place where Nanefer lay. When he had made certain that it was, indeed his tomb, Setna was able to descend into the place where the mysterious book [of Thoth] was kept, it was as light as though in full sunshine, because the radiance coming from the book lit up the surroundings' (Divin 1969: 106).

Setna Khemwaset uses magick to break into Nanefer's tomb in search of the legendary book, which in turn radiates its own light. Setna then uses the book to light his way out.[2] The story doesn't end there, Nanefer vows to hunt Setna down: 'Let your heart not grieve, I will make him bring that book back here, with a forked stick in his hand and a lighted brazier on his head'.[3] The forked stick or *stang* is a sign of Setna's repentance.

The purpose of Egyptian magick

'Ten measures of magic have come into the world. Egypt received nine of these, the rest of the world one measure.'
Talmud b. Qid 49b (quoted by Ritner)

The above quotation neatly encapsulates the ancient world's attitude to Egyptian prowess in magick. But what is the purpose of Egyptian magick? Bodily resurrection would on the face of it, appear to be one major aim. But I contend there is an older, perhaps in some ways more profound magical aim. That aim is good rebirth. That reincarnation is a central belief of the Egyptians is well illustrated by the second tale of Setna Khemwaset. Composed around 200BCE it is roughly contemporary with Indian discussion of the doctrine as evidenced in texts such as the *Caraka Samhita*. It is clear that the doctrine of reincarnation is extremely old and pervasive. It makes sense of much of the literature before that time. Pharaonic funeral rites, although supposedly based on the cult of Osiris and the ideal of bodily resurrection. Actually they contain a heck of a lot of birth imagery. That is to say *new birth* rather than *resurrection* of the old body. This feature is often hidden from view or overlaid by the much more showy aspects of the funeral.

It leads me to consider the difference between underworld and stellar deities. We perhaps all want to 'come forth by day', to be in the sun, but after that, you maybe have a choice between a starry Otherworld and the caverns of the night accompanied by the doll-like Osiris. I say this not out of rudeness, but merely as an observation on the two dimensional nature of the Osirian archetype. The passive nature of Osiris is pretty much all we see of him, for example in the famous ritual drama of Abydos (see *Bull of Ombos*). Whereas all the other parts are played by actors, the role of Osiris is literally a puppet or manikin. Osiris may rule in the caverns of the night, but when the sun god Ra passes through on his nightly journey, the gods that remain behind with Osiris groan when Ra departs.

Lucky are those gods, such as 'The Elder Magician', who along with Isis are the two major exponents of magick in Egyptian religion. They get to accompany and guard Ra on his journey. Men of earth may also perform the magick and stay with Ra until the birth of a new day. The magician's quest for good rebirth is achieved by accompanying the sun god Ra in his solar barque. Their presence there was dependent on knowledge rather than faith.

Religious texts such as *Amduat* and *Book of Gates* show Heka, the god of magick, in the divine barque of Ra as one of the personifications of his power. In the *Amduat* he appears even before Hu (logos) hence his title as the 'Elder Magician'. The great scholar of this mythology, Herman Te Velde, thinks the 'Elder Magician' is another synonym for *Heka*. Heka was perhaps one of those primordial seven shamans who pray the universe into life. Heka is perhaps interchangeable with Shu, Atum's eldest son, the first of all offspring. Heka was the local god of the fourteenth Upper Egyptian nome, although nothing remains of ancient Qis/Kusai, near modern el-Qusiya.

There is a very close association between the Egyptian god Seth and Egyptian magick. Another distinguished scholar Hornung thought this 'elder magician' was in fact Seth. Hornung was the commentator on the *Book of Gates*, the same text inscribed on the alabaster coffin of Sety I. If Hornung is correct that this 'elder magician' is in truth another form of Seth, he is seen here as the helmsman of the solar barque. Seth's role as ferryman continues in the guise of Nemty, the ferryman god in the *Contendings of Horus and Seth*, (see *Bull of Ombos*). Heka's name is unusually written with a hieroglyph that represents the hinder parts of a lion or leopard. The leopard is yet another beast with strong Sethian associations by reason of its spots, said to be marks of branding. The hind legs of a leopard or lion are its powerhouse, hence magick or Heka signifies 'physical strength, sexual or creative power'!

Perhaps what is obvious from all this, is that magick is an activity of the Gods. The title *ah hekau* meaning 'great of magic' being one of the most common adjectives used of the gods, more so than men. Humanity must, if anything, assimilate to the magic-working gods in order to copy them. Ritner thought this was a strong indication of how much magick is seen as a part of nature. According to Te Velde, the power of magick is especially necessary during the seventh hour of the night, a crucial moment just after midnight.

If you think about the above, you might see how it disposes of those theories that see magick as evidence of decline from religion. All of these activities are performed by priests as the techniques of religion,[4] Egyptian 'magic' cannot be opposed to religion and the western dichotomy of 'religion vs. magic' is thus inappropriate when describing

Egyptian practice.'[5] The same point was made by Sir Alan Gardiner back in 1915. It has taken a long time for the message to get through:

> 'That magic should have been regarded as an attribute of a deity and *a fortiori* as itself a deity, destroys at one blow the theories of those who discern a fundamental distinction between what is religion and what is magical.'
>
> Gardiner (1915) p 262 quoted in Ritner (1993).

It has to be said that Egyptian magick has not been well served by extant theories of magick (who has?), i.e. Frazer, Malinowski and Evan-Pritchard, all of which crumble as theories, when used outside of their original locus and are confronted by Egyptian material. R K Ritner adopts what is a new approach in Egyptology, by focussing on magical *activity* rather than some western definitions of magick such as 'obtaining a goal outside of the natural laws of cause and effect' etc, etc.[6] This emphasis on magical *activity,* rather than the futile quest for an essential *definition* of magick, is one used in the study of Hinduism. It's one I've used myself in this area, which I in turn learnt from the works of Gupta, Hoens, & Goudriaan T, *Hindu Tantrism.*[7]

> 'The practical mechanics of magic may provide a focus not only for the pertinent materials (magical essences) and attendant spells (magic words) of any magical procedure but also for the fundamental meaning of the procedure itself. It is in the rite – and not the spell – that the essence of Egyptian magic is to be sought.' (Ritner 1993: 67).

This is not to minimise the importance of the words spoken in a ritual. It's just that many other important lessons can be missed if you ignore the mechanics of a rite. The 'importance of ritual yields new knowledge of cultures, although the rubrics were often omitted by earlier

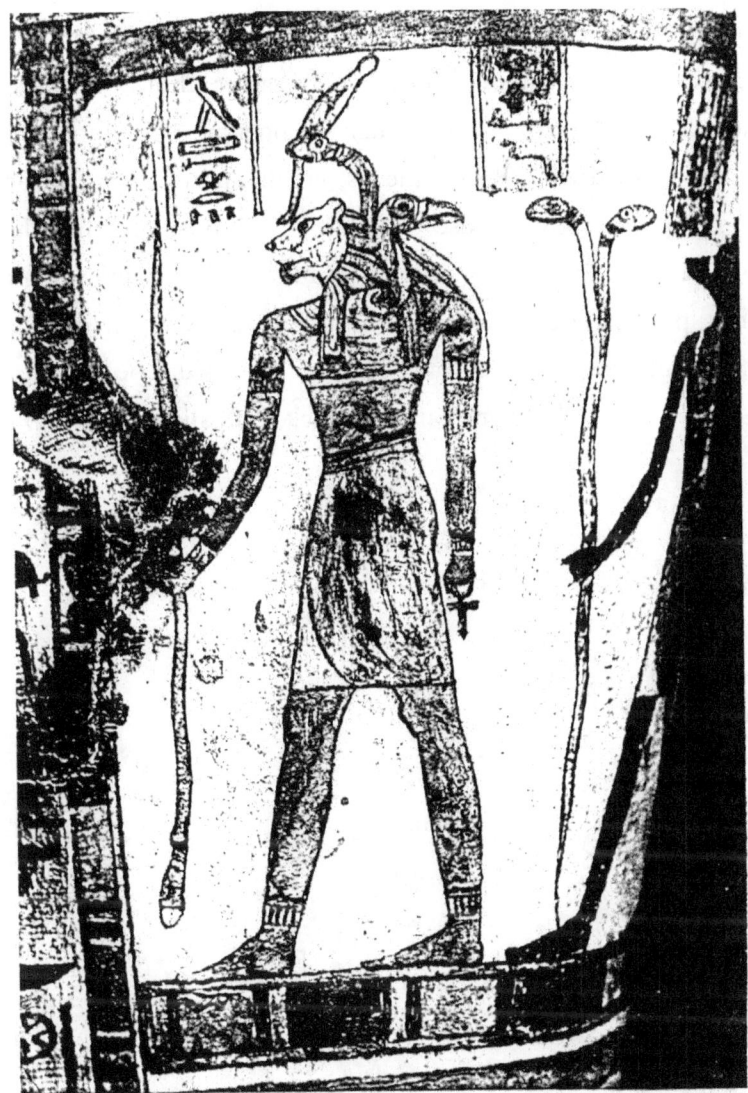

The god 'Ash' from a mummy-case in Brighton Museum (JEA, II 1925, 78f). He appears on sealings of Peribsen and Khasekhemui and thus is associated with Seth (Mercer 1949: 189). The *Book of the Dead* has a spell 'I am the Terrible One in the Thunderstorm. I am refreshed by this "Ash"' (BD XCV). By the 26th dynasty, he has three heads – lion, snake and vulture. Margaret Murray discusses the possibility of the continuation of his worship as a medieval Frankish demon/deity 'Ash' consulted by King Marcomir. The latter also has three heads – lion, toad and eagle (See Murray 1973: 223).

scholars.'[8] Ritner is referred to the fact that papyri with *too much* practical information were often ignored or censored by earlier scholars. *The Papyrus Salt*, source of the 'Abydos Arrangement' being a prime example.

By 'magical activity', Ritner means, circumambulations, spitting, blowing, licking, swallowing, use of images, superposition, trampling, binding, use of red, breaking, use of sand, burning, numerological symbolism, piercing, decapitation, reversal, burial, use of the dead and oracular consultation. Wouldn't you agree that it would be strange to omit these from any presentation of magick, but this is how it once was?

Notes
1. Divin 1969 : 140.
2. Lichtheim 1980 : 133.
3. Lichtheim 1980 : 135.
4. Te Velde 1973 : 8.
5. Ritner 1993 : 2.
6. Ritner 1993 :1.
7. Gupta, Hoens, & Goudriaan, 1979.
8 Ritner 1993 : 67.

Magical activities

'To ascribe feelings to nature as in "The Cruel Sea" is only a fallacy to those who do not understand the power of metaphor.'

The Book of Shu

Words and speech (words spoken out loud)

Earlier I mentioned the seven creative utterances that are hypostasized as the seven sages or shamans of the primordial cow, those who utter the seven creative words or spells that bring the world into being. This also provides us with a key axiom of ancient magical praxis – magick revolves around the power of the word that must be uttered or spoken to be effective.

The ancient hieroglyph particularly connected with this activity is, not surprisingly, a picture of the human mouth -

– vocalised as 'er' – quite a primal sound. This is fully expressed in the archaic 'voice' offering alluded to in the famous Egyptian formula: *peret kheru* – 'a voice offering' which can be appended to the votive *bread* and *beer*, or stand alone as a word offering or song.

In the *Contendings of Horus & Seth*, Isis uses verbal magick to take the form of a beautiful young girl, and thus disguises herself from Seth. Apart from these chthonic sounds – as language developed, spells were constructed by a play on words, that can only occur if the words are spoken aloud. So for example the construction of an amulet often relies upon a word play, such as where the name of a semi-precious green stone (*wadj*), which coincidentally also means 'to flourish' (*wadj*). Both words may be written differently but sound the same. This principle applies to all languages, so you might want to compile your own list of useful synonyms, for example a prolific synonym such as *rose*.

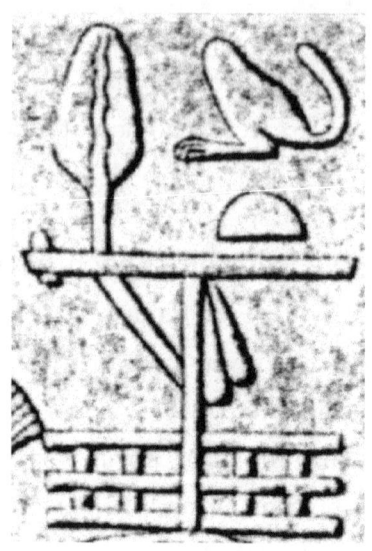

Left: The god Heka from the Papyrus of Khonsu-Renep in the Cairo museum. He was a scribe as well as one of the 21st dynasty clergy of Amon-Ra (Piankoff 1954). **Right:** The hieroglyph of the God Heka seen here (upper right) in ensign of the 14th Upper Egyptian Nome (Qis/Kusai), from the second courtyard scene of the Temple of Sety I at Abydos, drawn by Amice Calverley (1933).

Take this a stage further, and we reach the kind of intimate relationship between medicine and magic – where the word *pechart* – is used for both. Taken even further, it leads to the use of certain medicaments, for example, a head wound is treated by an ostrich egg compress, because of its apparent similarity (pun) to the human skull. Now it might be objected that this kind of word play is hardly likely to be the basis of a very effective medicine. I've argued elsewhere[9] that many effective medicaments have in fact found their way into the pharmacopoeia via this strange route. In European medicine, a related doctrine of 'signatures' led some early physicians to experiment with aconite for eye disease, purely on the basis of the eye-like flowers of the mature plant – a visual pun. They did in fact discover an effective medicine via this intuitive method. And so it turns out that according to a modern trauma surgeon, ground ostrich shell would make quite an effective filler for a head wound. This highly valued substance was transported to Ombos from the Africa motherland.

To sum up, speech and sound provide us with one of the primary means of working magick. Sound and vibration provide the matrix from which the entire cosmos is made. This doctrine is comparable to the sophisticated speculations of Tantrism, where sound is also seen as the primary material, and is manipulated by an archaic proto-language known as mantra yoga. In Egypt, especially in later times, any speech whatever by Thoth is *ipso facto* a vocal spell.[10] It brings to mind the vibration of the rune *Uroz* in the invocation of Seth. This highly effective technique grew out of the kind of word play alluded to above. Coming right up to date it is worth exploring Surrealist word games such as the *Exquisite Corpse*.

Texts

Where you have the spoken word, the next step is the text. Most of the surviving examples of texts with recognisable magical intent fall into the category of execration i.e. texts intended to do harm to an enemy. There are at least a thousand extant examples of execration texts. The text is again in the form of a picture – as indeed are all of the earliest hieroglyphs. Arguable one of the oldest such hieroglyphs is the image of a bound figure, representing one's enemy. Even in more literary constructions of later times, the proto image survives as a grammatical component of the text – the bound figure either becomes a so-called 'determinative' – i.e. a sign that determines the meaning of the foregoing sound signs and defines their meaning in a general way. Or the bound figure becomes the object on which the rest of the text is written. Next time you look at an Egyptian freeze, try not to see it as a text with a large incidentally illustration. Remember that an image, however large, is actually part of the text. To take an example that is familiar to some, the otherwise undistinguished *Stele of Revealing*, has a winged disk at the top. In the Egyptian language, this is rendered 'Horus Behadit' – the winged solar disk Horus of Edfu (Behadit). Crowley misheard the translation and wrote this as Hadit – thus are new gods born everyday.

Curse objects are most often made of pottery. Here too the substance is no accident but a deliberate choice for magick; the god Khnum, is the divine potter who forms the foetus from clay. Lead, a Sethian metal is also widely used.

In later times it is Seth who become the prototype for this bound figure. That is to say, the characteristic posture and features of this motif stem from the mythology of Seth. Several famous images illustrate this point. Furthermore thirteen pins or miniature flint or iron knives may pierce an object. Leave aside whether the number thirteen has lunar connotations, which I think is also a Sethian feature. Knapped flint power objects are amongst some of the very oldest human artefacts. They are a very distinctive feature of Ombos and the cult of Seth. They never loose this heavy ritual significance. Iron, as has already been noted, is another extremely significant magical substance. Before the so-called age of iron, it was only known from meteorites and was strongly, perhaps exclusively, associated with Seth. Now there is still a mystery here concerning how the cult practices of ancient times, that would have only positive connotations, are later used in negative way against *those same people*?? What do you think – is it a kind of perverse compliment? Perhaps the conflict of ancient times was never as total as in the modern mind. My teacher once told me that the notion of *total* war, as in for example nuclear destruction, was actually quite alien to the ancient mind.

Encircling

The third major component of ancient Egyptian magick is to *encircle*. One modern commentator suggested that the word 'sorcery' might contain a similar notion. In Egypt, a common word used in this context is *pechart,* whose root is a hieroglyph[3] meaning 'to go around or encircle'. The image is a representation of the intestines. In one account, the god Osiris is encircled by goats, which in the Ramessium papyrus are the traditional enemies of Osiris and are sacrificed in the Temple of Seth at Sepermeru. On a micro level the practice features in the writing of a king's name, the so called cartouche, nothing more than a symbolic double encircling of the critical name, by a rope-like line of ink. The practice is so old; it is not possible to say when it began. This form of magical activity is said to be coeval with Egyptian civilization. The circumambulation of *mastaba* or tomb is a feature of the earliest funeral rites. Later we find examples of encircling in the first Setna story, when the hero eventually get his hands on the *Book of Thoth*, and is able to repeat one of the spells:

> 'He put the book into my hand and I read aloud the first formula which was written. I [circled] the skies, the earth, the world of the

night, the mountains and the waters: I understood clearly what birds were saying, as well as fish and the four-footed beasts. Then I read aloud the second formula that was written, and I saw the sun appear with its escort of gods. I saw the moon at its rising and all the stars of the sky in their places. (see Lichtheim 1980: 128-131).

After this reading of the second formulae, the magician joins the sun god Ra at the centre of a circling universe. What may have begun in the remote past as a funeral spell or rite, is reused for the benefit of the living? This reminds us of yet another important feature of magick, the centrality of funeral rites in its activities.

Spitting/Ejaculating, Licking and Swallowing

Now we come to three related magical processes. Spit as a magical substance, survives in modern folk attitudes from all over the world. We say 'spitting image' or in French 'c'est son père tout craché' –Spit is also a common euphemism for semen. In ancient physiology, both spit and semen were thought to originate in the bone marrow.[12]

> 'I have appeased Suty with the spittle of the earth and blood from Geb's marrow.' (BD spell 96§5).

The spitting mouth[13] is a common grammatical determinative as opposed to image of a pot to designate washing or purifying.

Spittle can thus be seen as a form of excrement, hence detoxification is a dominant component of Egyptian medicine. In one of the most important Egyptian creation myths, spit and semen are interchangeable. Here we are again at the beginning of an exceptionally rich vein of magical ideas. From these foundations are built the entire edifice of tantrik body magick. In the myth, the mysterious demiurge Atum or Amun-Ra creates the first pair of beings from either spittle or more commonly by an act of masturbation or autogenesis. The results are the cosmological deities Shu (atmosphere, space) and Tefnut (moisture). Here is the divine precedent that is evoked in a great deal of later magick, the so-called 'histeriola' or divine precedent for a spell.

For example, the *Legend of Isis and the Secret Name of Ra* appears as the 'histeriola' for a spell designed to heal scorpion stings. The story of how Isis extracts Ra's secret name by the use of her bodily fluids, is recounted in greater detail in several places.[14]

Spittle or semen also plays a part in the otherwise miraculous birth of both Seth and Apophis. Hence the demotic proverb 'He who spits at heaven'. Even the oceans are said to be salty because of the accumulation of Seth's spit.[15]

The use of the substance is an activity with mythic elements, that go right to the core of Egyptian theology, and is far from being *small tradition* stuff. Spittle is a substance that never loses its malign and indeed curative power. See for example, how in later times it is used by the New Testament magician Jesus to accomplish many famous miracles.[16]

Licking

The power of spitting is part of a complex of magical techniques that stem from the occult qualities ascribed to human bodily fluids. This includes sexual fluids, sweat, blood, saliva and even the breath. All these things were often considered taboo, which is perhaps part of their power.

But we need not view this as the whole story. It is an important occult doctrine, that human beings are able to imbue things with magical power, perhaps because bodily fluids contain hidden or microscopic qualities. Later, I will explore one of the key magical techniques, by which these taboo substances are used for magical ends. Following on from the above discussion of spitting, is the lick – a physical practice magically sanctioned by the Egyptian love goddess Hathor and her obvious cow-like qualities. Thus:

'I kiss your head, I lick your limbs with the pleasant tongue which has come forth from my mouth, you being born daily from the head of your father Amon'
Sethe 1930 p.238 II 1-4 quoted in (Ritner 1993: 93).

In later erotic texts, licking in the relaxed manner of a cow is recommend for acts of cunnilingus. Licking something has a dual role of activating it by the power of the spittle. Also it is an important way in which we investigate our world, sensing things via the sense of taste, also absorbing things into our own bodies. The Egyptian magical technique associated with this sense combines it with the power of the hieroglyphic language. A picture representing the person's desire is painted in henna or red ochre and licked each day, enabling it to transition to the otherworld where it can do its work of change. In my contacts with the god Seth, he actually suggested the following technique, which combines licking with sexual magick. I found myself desirous of protection from persons or person unknown. My partner and I painted the appropriate hieroglyph on our bodies, using red ochre. The sign we choose for the protective component of the rite, was coincidentally that of Hathor in the form of the horned mirror. This is an excellent way to reflect back any bad vibes.

Incidentally, painting the hieroglyph of a particular deity on the shoulder, chest or forehead, was also the way in which ancient magicians did what is known in modern parlance as 'assume the god-form'. In Crowley's *Liber Al*, Nuit enjoins her companions, to come before her in a single robe, wearing a rich headdress. I think this may also be accomplished by the above painting technique, as an alternative to the more literal interpretations utilising a nemys (or bath towel and headband). Suitable attired my partner and I performed our ritual, which culminated in a bit of play of the love god. By the close of the ritual, all of the signs painted on our bodies had disappeared, either licked off or otherwise erased. The effects were very dramatic, revealing the culprits and giving them a very uncomfortable night!

If you do some investigation of your own you will soon find many other examples of licking spells from diverse magical traditions. Why not try one of the magical techniques used by the Bard Taliesin and known as Imbas Forosna. See the works of Jan Fries for much more background to Celtic licking spells. Not surprisingly the canine god Anubis has many spells of healing that involve the licking of wounds. And the classical *Mithras Liturgy* contains an important licking spell:

> 'Now the encounter with the great god is like this: Having obtained the above mentioned herb (*kentritis*), at the conjunction of [of the sun and the moon] occurring in the Lion [FN says this is the new moon] take the juice and, after mixing it with honey and myrrh, write on a leaf of the persea tree the eight-lettered name, as given below . And having kept yourself pure for 3 days in advance, come at morning to face the sunrise; / lick off the leaf while you show it to the sun, and then he [the sun god] will listen to you intentively. Begin to prepare [the scarab] on the new moon in the lion, according to the god's [reckoning].[17]

Now this is the name: "I EE OO IAI" Lick this up, so that you may be protected; and rolling up the leaf/, throw it into the rose oil. Many times have I used the spell and have wondered greatly.' (Betz 1986: 53).

Sleep magick

'We reason in our dreams the way primitive man did when awake'   Carl Jung

Rituals to send a dream, whether to oneself or *to another*, were a common feature of ancient magick. If waking consciousness fails you in a task, for example, that of devising some further variations on the above techniques of eating magick, then I suggest you use sleep magick. Ask the gods to send you a dream with an application of the technique. Mark the appropriate sign on your body before going to sleep. One of the core practice of the tradition, asks you to visualise the first journey through the Temple of Sety I to the shrine of Amon-Ra (see chapter 4). The night time retiring of the magician to an astral temple is something I first encountered in the esoteric novels of Dion Fortune. When you go to bed, you fall asleep and your spirit spends the night safely tucked up in your astral temple. You will no doubt be rewarded with a visionary dream containing a variation of your own upon this technique.

Ancient dream manuals tell us that Seth is the source of evil sleep i.e. nightmares. The riding of the 'dreamy night air' is especially appropriate for the hidden god Seth, who has many associations with dream control. Dream control of one sort or another was a common element of ancient magick. As a counterpart to this there are manuals, many dating from quite early times, to help one interpret such dreams when they come. An example in Webb has:

'The god in him is Seth ... he is a man of the people ... He is one dissolute of heart on the day of judgement – discontent in his heart. If he drinks a beer, he drinks it to engender strife and turmoil. The redness of the white of his eye is this god. He is one who drinks what he detests. He is beloved of women through the greatness [a lacunae in which you might like to add you own bit] the greatness of his loving them, though he is a royal kinsman, he has the personality of a man of the people . . . he would not descend unto the west, but is placed in the desert as a prey to rapacious birds . . . he drinks beer so as to engender turmoil and disputes . . . he will take up weapons of warfare . . . he will not distinguish the married woman from ... As to any man who opposed him . . . massacres arise in him and he is pleased in the Netherworld.'

(Webb says it's a 19th dynasty dream manual – from Papyrus Chester Beatty c1800BC).

Swallowing

The next stage takes in swallowing or eating, which by extension could be said to include cannibalism. Cannibalism is perhaps divisible into two kinds – what we might call the *elective* consumption of the corpse, either in whole or part by one's surviving relatives. The other, much less common variety is compulsory, the involuntary consumption by an enemy.

This is as good a point as any to introduce a discussion of so-called 'occult' crime. As I write this, a self-styled 'satanist' is in the news at the conclusion of his trial for the slaying his girlfriend. It is unlikely to be the last time such as crime is in the headlines.[18] Psychopaths exist in all societies. Restricting the discussion of taboo issues such as sacrifice and cannibalism will not, in my opinion make the world a safer place. Afterall we've had the way of restriction for a long while now and the results are everywhere to be seen. So called 'occult' crime has its own causes, one of them being ignorance. That's why I'm particularly keen to discuss this material in an informed way. The stream of thought we are about to follow leads to the contemporary magical conclusion that there is no need for *violent* sacrifice. The most powerful of all magical sacraments is freely given and does not involve harm to the donor.

But before revealing that, we need to look at the origin of cannibalism. Once again we find a religious precedent for both these practices. It comes from one of the oldest religious texts ever discovered, so far at least, those carved onto the walls of 5th dynasty pyramids, and therefore known as the pyramid texts, circa 2500BC. One of these texts is known as the *Cannibal Hymn* :

> 'The King is one who eats men and lives on the Gods. . .
> The King eats their magick, swallows their spirits.'
>
> Pyramid Texts 273-74

The so called 'Cippi' (no pun intended) of Horus use this technique. This child god is sometimes called *Shed* – who appears to be a later form of Horus as saviour. *Cippi* are clay plaques depicting the triumph of Horus over the crocodiles, and other desert beasts. This particular incident occurs during the sojourn of Horus and his mother Isis in the Delta, hiding from Seth during the infancy of the future divine king. Water, passed over such images that depict the above scene, was then drunk as a prophylactic.

Another fine example comes from the first story of Setna.

> 'He put the book into my hand and I read aloud the first formula which was written. I encircled the skies, the earth, and the world of the night, the mountains and the waters: I understood clearly what birds were saying, as well as fish and the four-footed beasts. Then I read aloud the second formula that was

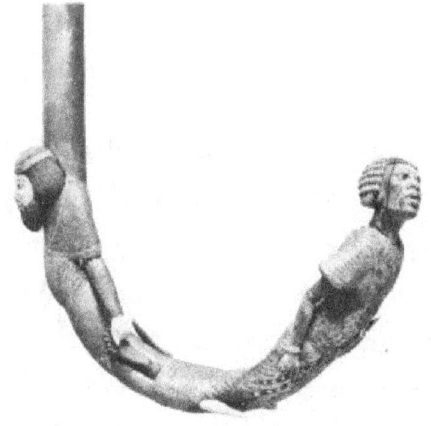

Above: Nubian and Asiatic prisoners bound on King Tutankhamun's walking stick. Nubian, Asian, Libyan and Egyptian were the four 'races' acknowledged in ancient Egyptian 'anthropology'. **Below**: a version of the 'Mehen' game found in one of the Ombos graves, a version of which survives in modern Sudan. Mehen is the serpent who guards the boat of Ra on his journey through the caverns of the night. This ancient game had mysterious funerary significance. Its fall from favour coincides with the decline of the cult of Seth. The slots that 'cut' the serpent perhaps added to the unlucky association. One version of the game found by Petrie had 545 divisions. I have an intuition this might be a 'bead game', for example guessing the permutation of glass beads in the opponent's hand, the lion shaped pieces used on the board to keep score. For more information see Decker 1992.

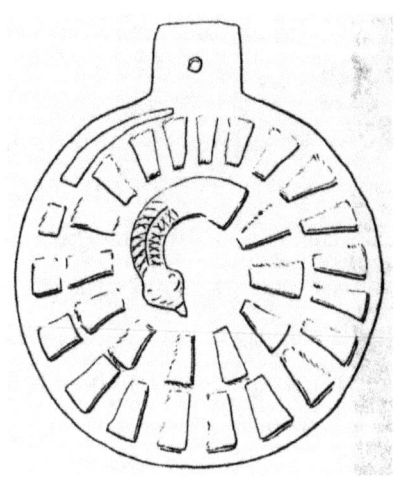

written, and I saw the sun appear with its escort of gods. I saw the moon at its rising and all the stars of the sky in their places.

I wanted to absorb these marvellous formulae, and as I did not know how to write, I had to rely on Nenofer, my brother and my husband, who was a skilled scribe and a very learned man. He sent for a piece of papyrus, and on it he carefully copied all the words that were in the book. Then he moistened the papyrus with beer (see glossary) and dissolved it all in water. When he was certain that it had melted, he drank, and in this way contained within himself all that was in the book. And then he did it all again for me.' (Divin 1969: 114)

Key incidents in the 'sethian' *Tale of Two Brothers* also involve magick connected with the drinking of water:

'And this is what shall come to pass, that I shall draw out my soul, and I shall put it upon the top of the flowers of the acacia, and when the acacia is cut down, and it falls to the ground, and thou comest to seek for it, if thou searchest for it seven years do not let thy heart be wearied. For thou wilt find it, and thou must put it in a cup of cold water, and expect that I shall live again, that I may make answer to what has been done wrong.' (Petrie)

So the eating of something is an ancient method by which magical substance is passed back into the body to make it powerful. In the examples given so far, what is eaten has been water, ink, maybe paper, but the precedent is a form of cannibalism, in the sense that either your own or another's bodily fluids are eaten. Could it be that the elective funeral cannibalism practiced by our Neolithic ancestors, was where they first learnt the technique? There is some contemporary research that indicates that memories can be passed from one organism to another by this eating process. Now you may well have heard that eating your own relatives can be a dangerous practice – in the modern world, it it said to be the cause of brain disease. Well in the Neolithic the person would be long dead before such a disease could manifest. There are even some, who say that the phenomenal human brain is some sort of mutation brought about by the cannibal habits of our ape ancestors. Perhaps things are not as simple as they at first appear.

Returning to the topic of eating spells, the Egyptian technique seems to have passed lock, stock and barrel into the Hebrew holy books. One of those obscure passages rarely mentioned by Sunday school teachers reads as follows:

Adultery curse from Bible, Number 5: 23-24

'Then the priest shall write these curses in a book and wash them off into the water of bitterness; and he shall make a woman drink the water of bitterness that brings the curse, and the water that brings the curse shall enter into her and cause bitter pain.

And the priest shall take the cereal offering of jealously out of the woman's hand and shall wave the *cereal offering* [my emphasis] before the Lord and bring it to the altar; and the priest shall take a handful of the cereal offering, as its memorial portion and burn it upon the altar, and afterward shall make the woman drink the water.

And when he has made her drink the water, then, if she has defiled herself and has acted unfaithfully against her husband, the water that brings the curse shall enter her body and cause bitter pain, and her body shall swell, and her thigh shall fall away, and the woman shall become an execration among her people. But if the woman has not defiled herself and is clean, then, she shall be free and shall conceive children.'

It goes without saying, that had such a passage been found in *any other* literature, it would be sufficient for scholars to dismiss the *entire* text as superstitious magick. But if you think about it, it is yet another example of how magick and religion are two sides of the same coin. The above passage may even have entered into the transmission of the third chapter of the *Book of the Law*, the moment at which a very powerful 'new' technique of magick re-entered our tradition. I'm talking about the famous *Cakes of Light* ritual. As is well known, Crowley was very familiar with the Bible. Could it be that in the process of channelling a mystical Egyptian text, he also released an obscure cell of memory?

Notes

9. Morgan (1999) *Medicine of the Gods*, Mandrake of Oxford.
10. Ritner (1993: 67).
11. F46 in Gardiner's sign list.
12. Ritner (1993: 80).
13. D26 in Gardiner's sign list.
14. Morgan (2005).
15. Ritner (1993: 101).
16. Ritner (1993: 76).
17. Betz (1986: 53fn) says this 'new moon of god' means 'according to the heavens', whereas 'new moon of man', is 'according to the calendar'.
18. See for example *The Guardian*, UK 22.1.5.

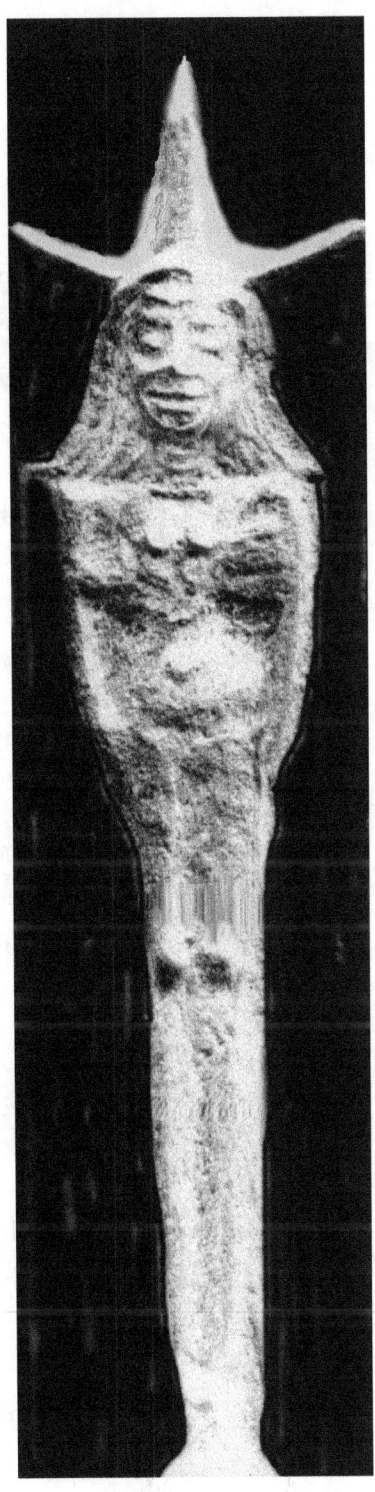

'Edible Astarte', with horns, product of a mould - used to create some form of *shew* bread - or cake of light - offered in her rites. Original height 8ins. Based on object found at Nahariya, now in Israel National museum. (see Patai 1978: 65).

Cakes of Light

The following is a modern ritual technique, that nevertheless manages to key into an extremely old form of 'eating magick'. Dare I say it, there is even an element of *elective* cannibalism, that ultimately derives from the nameless aeons of the Neolithic. The baking of a magical cake or loaves we might call *eucharist* magick. Archaeologists have found many clay bread moulds from all over the Middle East especially Palestine. They produce a bite-sized image of the ancient goddess Astarte for consumption by the celebrant. It is perhaps another of those well kept secrets of the ancient Hebrew religion, that there was in fact an image of this goddess, who was worshiped alongside Yahweh in the Solomonic temple.[19] To explore this issue in more depth, I recommend *The Hebrew Goddess* by Raphael Patai or Othmar Keel and Christoph Uehlinger's, *Gods, Goddesses and Images of God in Ancient Israel.* It seems likely that the Christian eucharist (literally: thanksgiving) stems from this same tradition.

I am indebted for the following analysis to the work of Alex Bennett, whose fuller document on *Eucharist Magick* can be viewed online. The *locus classicus* for this technique is the third chapter of the *Book of the Law*, usually considered the most difficult and controversial of this entire holy and *prophetic* text:

Liber Al, Chapter III vs 23-25

> 23. For perfume mix meal and honey & thick leavings of red wine: then oil of Abramelin and olive oil, and afterward soften & smooth down with rich fresh blood.
>
> 24. The best blood is of the moon, monthly: then the fresh blood of a child, or droppings from the host of heaven; then

of enemies; then of the priest or the worshippers; last of some beast, no matter what.

25. This burn: of this make cakes & eat unto me. This hath also another use; let it be laid before me, and kept thick with perfumes of your orison: it shall become full of beetles as it were and creeping things sacred unto me.

If you want to work with this, you are going to need some Abramelin oil. It is possible to buy this from various suppliers, but the quality varies radically. You might find that the only alternative is make your own blend of the oil, something that is difficult, but does have its own rewards. I have been fortunate in knowing several good blenders over the years, so I'm never short of a good supply. I was also fortunate enough to be able to obtain supplies from *Id Aromatics* in Leeds, and when that went, from *Amphora Aromatics* in Bristol. Both shops are said to have connections with Chaos magick, who did much to widen interest in the use of good essential oils and incenses, long before the mainstream commercialisation of the art. If you do intend to do it yourself the recipe can be found in several books, including David Rankine's *Becoming Magick*.

The Abramelin oil and incense are essential to the modern Cakes of Light ritual. Its presence it not merely as a highly evocative magical fragrance, but equally as importantly as a preservative, allowing the cakes to be consumed over many weeks, perhaps even years. They can therefore be stored and used in the several rituals as you have need of them.

But the other important ingredient is the blood. This is perhaps one of the most misunderstood passages in magical literature. Aiwass, Crowley's spirit guide, gives the entire doctrine, warts and all. The spirit begins by emphasising how the best blood does not involve any permanent harm. It is funny how the blood that causes the very least harm, is freely given, is also in many cultures the most taboo. It tells you quite a lot about mainstream values. Even amongst Neo-Vampires – there can be some acceptance of drinking of a partner's venous blood – but consider for a moment how you'd feel drinking the menstrual variety? Do you detect a mental knot there?

Aleister Crowley is often accused of feeding the media frenzy over human sacrifice. This is the old 'blood libel.' levelled against all religions at some time in their development – the false accusation that they are stealing children to eat in their secret rituals. The Old Testament stories of Abraham preparing to sacrifice his son Isaac are usually seen as the moment at which, Judaism moved away from the older blood rites in favour of animal sacrifice. The *Book of the Law* continues a tradition whereby, even animal sacrifice is downgraded, as it was more than a century before in the occult tradition, when Francis Barrett proposed fumigations of incense, as an alternative to the sacrifice of a chicken.

Blood, so say the experts, should be fresh, for this is still a sacrifice. 'It is no good preparing this ingredient before making the Cake of Light. Every type of blood no matter what, must come directly from its source. The other ingredients should be prepared before making the sacrifice.'

The blood types in descending order of strength are:

1. Blood of the moon, monthly (menstrual blood). I have already mentioned how taboo, and also how progressive a notion is enshrined in the type of blood.

2. The 'fresh blood of a child' is usually said to be placental blood. Again very taboo, although in the modern world it is increasingly popular for the placenta to be used by the parents, perhaps in the form of pate consumed at the child's naming ceremony as a powerful protection rite.

3. Droppings from the host of heaven are taken to mean semen. Again freely given, it can be viewed as a type of blood.

4. Of enemies – this speaks for itself. It would be a bit po-faced to suppose that mortal enemies are not part of your possible universe. Personally I would have no moral qualms about using blood magick against an evil despot like Adolf Hitler etc. The use of magick against the Third Reich during WWII. is part of the *foundation myth* of modern witchcraft.

5. Of the priest or of the worshippers, i.e. blood taken from the veins, as self sacrifice either from you or other celebrants.

6. Of some beast, no matter what i.e. blood taken from any animal whether it be from the veins, menstruation or semen. It is possible to envisage such a usage, that does not involve the physical death of the animal. It would be rash to deny the power of this kind of sacrifice, but in the new covenant, it is placed at the bottom of the scale in terms of efficacy.

The blood, Abramelin oil, etc, are blended together and cooked as a Cake of Light. This is then used in a future ritual; one is burnt on the altar, whilst an additional Cake is eaten by each of the participants to the rite. In the *Book of the Law*, the purpose of the rite is to hasten the development of the Aeon of Horus. But there is no pressing reason why the Cakes should not be used in other rituals of your choice. It is also common practice for the Cakes to contain the blood of two (or perhaps more) participants in their making. I'm talking about *Tankhem* or tantrik rites here, where two lovers contribute their bodily fluids to the creation of these very powerful magical talismans, otherwise known as Cakes of Light. I would remind you that a close reading of the *Contendings of Horus & Seth* (see appendix IV), reveals not an act of anal sex, but in fact more eating magick! When viewed through the Osirian lens, Seth's intentions seem abusive. But what actually happens, is an act of frottage which, leads to Seth eating the semen of Horus. Seth then gives birth to the golden moon god Thoth. There is an older technique hidden in this late version of the myth. It concerns the mysteries of 'dolphin sex' not to be written of in this place.

Image magick

The most famous of all Egyptian magical techniques, we might call image magick, which is in reality a more graphic extension of things discussed above. It is known in modern versions as the 'voodoo doll' or 'wax image spell'. Incidentally the term 'voodoo doll' is highly misleading, as voodoo is one religion from which the practice is unknown. Furthermore the surviving Egyptian examples mostly use clay although wax is specified in *The Book of Overthrowing Apophis*. In examining these kinds of thing one should not overlook the symbolic importance of the clay, mythologically considered the substance from which the god Khnum fashioned human beings. The doll must have hands bound and be pierced with thirteen needles. Binding has very negative associations in Egypt.

This spell is probably as old as Egyptian civilization itself. This image harkens back to the so-called 'bound prisoner' motif – an image always found in religious contexts in ancient Egypt and which, therefore cannot be dismissed as simple militarism. The second story of Setna provides another good example. In it an older Setna visits the underworld in the company of his precocious and otherworldly son, and he is shown the fate of the wealthy 'sinner' in 'hell'. Bound in the traditional manner, his eye socket provides the pivot for one of hell's many doors! This highly evocative and gruesome image might well be called to mind with one of your own enemies!

This mindset is expressed so well in the *Book of the Law*:

> ... Trample down the Heathen; be upon them, o warrior, I will give you of their flesh to eat! (AL III:11)

Trampling down one's enemies was a fairly ubiquitous Egyptian activity. Amongst the grave goods of King Tutankhamum, were slippers whose soles were decorated with the image of nine bows. The 'nine bows' represent the nine tribes of Nubia, one of Egyptian's most feared ancient enemies. This image later becoming a cipher for any of Egypt's foreign enemies.[20] Once on the lookout, this type of image magick is everywhere. The so-called 'Golden Horus' name is a hieroglyph that depicts Horus as a falcon perched on a golden necklace. For various reasons, it is quite likely that the golden necklace was understood by the ancient Egyptians to represent Seth – 'He of Nubt' literally the 'City of Gold'. From Egyptian prehistoric times, this town was probably a central point of access to the gold fields of the Eastern desert and Nubia. As with so many things, it is always Seth that provides the archetype for bound power.

The following text, extraordinary in so many ways, comes from the masterful anthology of the *Greek Magical Papyri* edited by Hans Dieter Betz.[21] Their discovery is itself rather a good story, which at the risk of boring you I shall repeat:

> 'We know from literary sources that a large number of magical books in which spells were collected existed in antiquity. Most of them, however, have disappeared as the result of systematic suppression and destruction. But not everything was lost. At the end of antiquity, some philosophers and theologians, astrologers and alchemists collected magical books and spells that were still available.'

Buried in clay pots and tombs, these secret caches remained hidden until the nineteenth century when they fell into the hands of a diplomat 'at the court in Alexandria a man who called himself Jean d'Anastasi (1780?-1857). Believed to be Armenian by birth, he ingratiated himself enough with the Pasha to become the consular representative of Sweden. It was a time when diplomats and military men often were passionate collectors of antiquities, and M. d'Anastasi happened to be at the right place at the right time. He succeeded in bringing together large collections of papyri from Egypt, among them sizable magical books, some of which he said he had obtained in Thebes. These collections he shipped to Europe, where they were auctioned off and bought by various libraries.'

> 'Unfortunately, we know almost nothing about the circumstances of the actual findings. But it is highly likely that many of the papyri from the Anastasi collection came from the same place, perhaps a tomb or a temple library. If this assumption is correct, about half a dozen of the best-preserved and largest extant papyri may have come from the collection of one man in Thebes. He is of course unknown to us, but we may suppose that he collected the magical material for his own use. Perhaps he was more than a magician. We may attribute his almost systematic collections of *magica* to a man who was also a scholar, probably philosophically inclined, as well as a bibliophile and archivist concerned about the preservation of this material.' (Betz 1986: xii-xiii)

The term 'magick', is Persian in origin, and was used by the xenophobic Romans with a pejorative sense.[22] The Egyptian tongue has no word for either superstition or indeed religion. Whatever the Romans did not like they ascribed to foreigners. Magick was banned in the empire by various edicts from Augustus to Theodosius. Rigid classification with Latin words like 'religion' and 'magic' is really alien to the Egyptian point of view.[23] Other magicians make the best guides, as in for example Giordano Bruno, centuries ahead of his time, had the 'revolutionary' idea of interpreting magick in its own terms. In modern anthropological parlance, Bruno took an *Emic* rather than an *Etic* approach.

As the public religion was driven underground, the use of cipher become more common.[24] Some techniques such as bowl magick, scrying into a bowl of burning herbs, were still conducted in private by cautious Egyptian priests; Heryheb or Lector priest the most likely agent. One famous account of such an episode is found in Porphyry's *Life of Plotinus*.[25] Plotinus (AD 205-270) was a Neoplatonic philosopher, born in Egypt at Lycopolis:

> 'An Egyptian priest who had arrived in Rome and, through some friend, had presented himself to the philosopher, became desirous of displaying his powers to him, and offered to evoke a visible manifestation of Plotinus' presiding spirit. Plotinus readily consented and the evocation was made in the Temple of Isis, the only place, they say, which the Egyptian could find pure in Rome.
>
> At the summons a Divinity appeared, not a being of the spirit-ranks, and the Egyptian exclaimed: "You are singularly graced; the guiding spirit within you is none of the lower degree but a God." It was not possible, however, to interrogate or even to contemplate this God any further, for the priest's assistant, who had been holding the birds to prevent them flying away, strangled them, whether through jealousy or in terror.'

Itinerant magicians probably existed in ancient Egypt, though even a humble scorpion charmer might be schooled in the *House of Life*. Priests would be called out to extending an index finger, *mudra* like, to protect the people from crocodiles during a canal crossing.[26]

Amongst the *magica* is the following papyrus:

'PGM.IV. 296-466

Wondrous spell for binding a lover: Take wax [or clay] from a potter's wheel and make two figures, a male and a female. Make the male in the form of Ares fully armed, holding a sword / in his left hand and threatening to plunge it into the right side of her neck. And make hers with her arms behind her back and down on her knees. And you are to fasten the magical material on her head or neck.' (Betz 1986: 44).

The god Ares, can be viewed as a substitute for Horus. The posture of the female figure is a clear derivative from Egyptian originals in which the victim is Seth. This spell was written at the end of the classical era (circa 2nd century BC to 5th century AD), when in many ways, the original prototypes were forgotten hence Seth's significant change of gender. Like a great deal of later 'sethian' magick, the tone is abusive. It's amazing to think that the purpose of this elaborate spell is to attract a woman! Compulsion is a strong characteristic of the ancient mind - and this is extended to the object of desire as well as the gods themselves. The magical relationship of the ancients to their gods seems alien to the modern mind.

After some instructions on magical names to be written on the head, right ear, left ear, face, right and left eye, right and left shoulder, right and left arm, the hands, the breast, heart, lower belly, pudenda, buttocks, sole of the right and of the left foot. This division of the body again plays upon the notion of divinisation but also dismemberment, a motif that can be traced backwards to prehistory, the forwards through the cult of Osiris. We might boldly follow this notion to its eventual home in the erotic speculation of Hindu tantrism, whereby the body is divided into erogenous zones through which, the hidden inner moon moves throughout the month.

The spell continues:

'Take thirteen copper[27] needles and stick 1 in the brain while saying, "I am piercing your brain, NN"; and stick 2 in the ears and 2 in the eyes and 1 in the mouth and 2 / in the midriff and 1 in the hands and 2 in the pudenda and 2 in the soles, saying each time, "I am piercing such and such a member of her, . . . so that she may remember no one but me." From elsewhere in the rubric it can be seen that these are thirteen points of connection that are the object of his desire 'head to head . . . lip to lip . . . belly to belly . . .thigh to thigh and fit black to black [?], and let her . . . carry out her own sex acts / with me

And take a lead tablet and write the same / spell and recite it. And tie the lead leaf to the figures with thread from the loom after making 365 knots while saving as you have learned, "ABRASAX, hold her fast!" You place it, as the sun is setting, beside the grave of one who has died untimely or violently, placing beside it also the seasonal flowers.'

The above is yet another clear example of how funeral rites are reused in this 'binding spell' for the benefit of the living. The operant beseeching the 'chthonic gods' PERSEPHONE ERESCHIGAL etc, and ANUBIS who, by this stage in his history is said to 'hold the keys to Hades, to infernal gods and daimons, to men and women who have died untimely deaths, to youths and maidens, from year to year, month to month, day to day, / hour to hour. I adjure all daimons in this place to stand as assistants beside this daimon. And arouse yourself for me, whoever you are, whether male or female, and go to every place and into every quarter and to every house, and attract / and bind her.'

The spells continues at great length in this tone: 'Let her be in love with me, . . . Let her not be had in a promiscuous way, let her not be had in her ass, nor let her do anything with another man for pleasure, just with me alone, etc, etc etc. And finally there is a prayer to be recited at sunset, while holding the magical material from the tomb, saying:

'Borne on the breezes of the wandr'ing winds,
Golden-haired Helios, who wield the flame's
Unresting fire, who turn in lofty paths
Around the great pole, who create all things
Yourself which you again reduce to nothing,
From whom, indeed, all elements have been
Arranged to suit your laws which nourish all
The world with its four yearly turning points.
Hear, blessed one, for I call you who rule
Heaven and Earth. Chaos and Hades, where
Men's daimons dwell who once gazed on the light,
And even now I beg you, blessed one,
Unfailing one, the master of the world,
If you go to the depths of earth and search
The regions of the dead, send this daimon,
From whose body I hold this remnant in my hands,
To her, NN, at midnight hours,
To move by night to orders 'neath your force,
That all I want within my heart he may
Perform for me; and send him gentle, gracious
And pondering no hostile thoughts toward me,
And be not angry at my potent chants,
For you yourself arranged these things among
Mankind for them to learn about the threads
Of the Moirai, and this with your advice. /
I call your name, Horus, 72 which is in number
Equivalent to those of the Moirai,
ACHAIPHO THOTHO I'HIACHAAIE EIA IAE EIA
THOTHO PHIACHA.

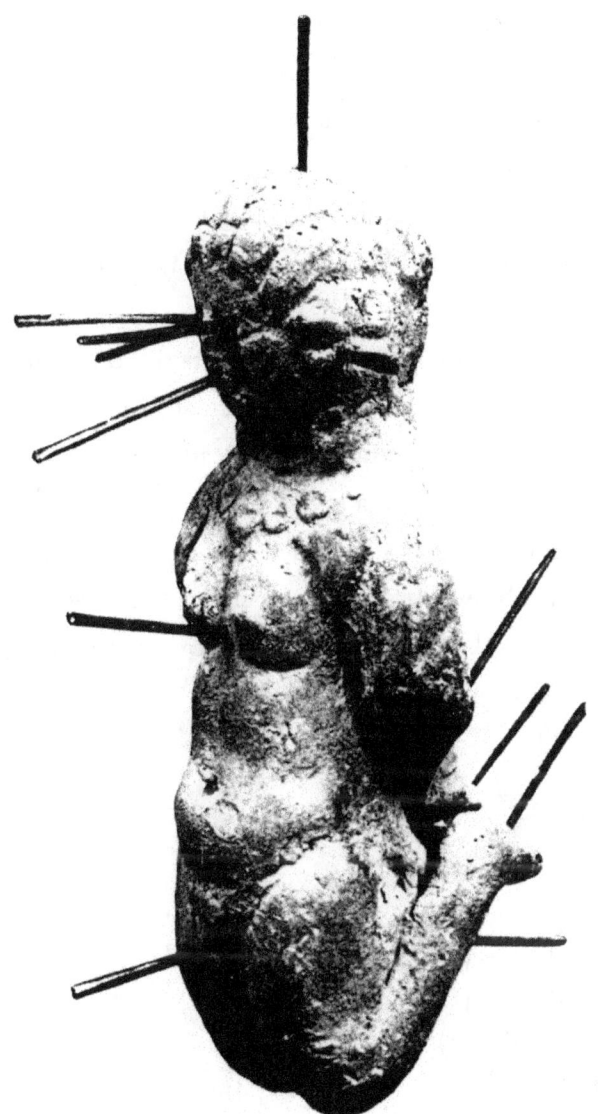

Figurine found by archaeologists, together with a lead tablet containing an inscription *nearly* identical to the 'love spell' discussed in section on *Image Magick* below. See S. Kambitsis, "Une nouvelle tablette magique d'Egypte, Musée du Louvre, Inv. E 27145, 3C/4C siecle," BIFAO 76 (1976): 213-23 and plates.

> Be kind to me, forefather, scion of
> The world, self-gendered, fire-bringer, aglow
> Like gold, shining on mortals, master of
> The world, / daimon of restless fire, unfailing,
> With gold disk, sending earth pure light in beams.
> Translation by E.N.O'Neil in (Betz 1986).
> Reproduced courtesy of University of Chicago Press

As if to prove that this spell was probably fairly common currency in the classical world, the picture above is actually of a *similar* figurine found by archaeologists, together with a lead tablet containing an inscription *nearly* identical to the above.[28]

The use of image magick is extended to the vivifications of divine statues (splendours) by what is known technically as *phi-neter*. Under the patronage of the god of magick Heka, the now sentient image could be used for sorcery or oracular consultation.

Notes
19. Patai (1978 : 65).
20. Ritner (1993 : 123).
21. Betz (1986).
22. Cheke: 2004.
23. Ritner (1993 : 241).
24, Ritner (1993 : 218).
25. Mackenna (1917: 11).
26. Ritner (1993 : 227).
27. A metal associated with Venus, Isis and perhaps Hathor.
28. See S. Kambitsis (1976).

Magick as use and misuse of the funeral rite

Several times now I have alluded to the fact that, a great deal of Egyptian magick is essentially derived from funeral spells used for the benefit of the living. There is any number of options here:

Performance of your own funeral as a kind of dry run. This provides the more 'gnostic' side to magick – not so much bound up with mundane results, but more about the preparation of the Self for the journey across the abyss. It also links in with those magical techniques, such as the postmodern *Liber Samech* whereby one seeks contact with beings of the 'inner planes' as a means to higher knowledge.

Performance of someone else's funeral for their benefit or indeed as a way of getting rid of them.

Performance of the funeral rites of a particular ethnic or national group as a way of deriding Egypt's troublesome enemies.

Performance of 'outmoded' versions of the funeral rite as a way of harming or controlling others.

Performance of the funeral rites of the past, in a deliberately distorted, reversed or contradictory manner as a way of harming or controlling others.

All these things and more are features of Egyptian magick, and indeed occur in many other subsequent cultures. Now you might be asking yourself – whose funeral? If it's not already obvious, the rubric for all of the above practices is provided by the ancient and indeed the normal Sethian way of death. All magick, especially that with a negative purpose, implicates Seth. It is therefore a way, by deconstruction, of viewing the original Sethian cult that lies behind it, albeit in distorted form. Is this an affront to Seth, or does it go with his territory? The difficulty of resolving this question, is perhaps the reason why Seth is sometimes said to be a hazard to the unwary – a demonic initiator.

The Mirgissa Deposite & Human sacrifice

Mirgissa is a 12th dynasty (c 2000BCE) fortress situated on Egypt's southern frontier, above the second cataract of the Nile. The time leading up to the so-called second intermediate period, was one of political instability, when many external enemies seriously threatened Egypt's existence. Most powerful amongst these, was the coalition of nine Nubian tribes, represented by the hieroglyphs of the bow, hence the phrase 'nine bows' to designate Egypt's enemies. Much of this ancient territory falls within modern day Sudan. Complex societies have existed in Sudan for at least as long as they have in Egypt. The high culture of Sudan is roughly contemporaneous with that of Egypt, although this is a recent discovery, and for most of the last four thousand years, this has been hidden from history.

Amongst the neglected remains of Mirgissa, archaeologists found a virtually intact execration burial. Unlike normal burials, this is an elaborate ritual assemblage whose purpose, seems to be to ward off enemies on this dangerous frontier. The Mirgissa deposit provides the first indisputable evidence of human sacrifice in pharaonic Egypt.

Curiously it resembles one of the burials from Ombos as described in detail elsewhere. Although it was once the normal mode of burial for the ancient Ombites, the practice was discontinued by the time this so-called execration burial was unearthed. It also has many similarities with the burial practices of Egypt's Nubian enemy. Indeed it might well be, that the people of Ombos, were once migrants from Nubia.

This deposit contains the remains of a human sacrifice, which not surprisingly turns out to be one of the Nubian enemies, probably a captive. The skull and skeleton are found in different locations, and when the possibility of disturbance is ruled out, human sacrifice seems the most likely explanation. The head and jaw were removed from the skeleton, and deliberately buried with the rest of the assemblage in what seems to be a reversed position. The upper jaw of the inverted skull is flush with surface.

Near the skull were found the remains of the ritual that accompanied these actions, included a melted beeswax figurine dyed with red ochre – providing yet another example of the quintessentially Sethian wax image spell discussed above. In fact, everything about this burial brings together all of the magical techniques discussed before. Even the burial in sand should be seen as a ritual substance, symbolic of the desert necropolis. Sand is associated with Seth – placing something under sand is significant – and probably represents the image magick of *separation* of the two parts during burial.[29] Mention of sand may also bring to mind geomancy – divination by marks in sand. Examples of the crooked hippopotamus tusk wand, shows signs of wear from repeated use to draw signs or sigils, probably in prepared sand. Could the phrase 'vision in the feet', sometimes applied to Seth, be a reference to a geomantic practice, whereby footprints in sand were interpreted as an oracle?

The burial also includes incineration, figurines, word magick, broken pottery, invariably in multiples of seven. Noticeable too is the use of flint knives, which is traditional for ritual slaughter. Traces of similar rites have been found in other parts of Egypt, and indeed Nubia, modern Sudan. It is plain from the above rubrik, that the ethnicity, real or symbolic, of the victim, can be changed depending on the intention of the magician.

Flint Knives

> 'My nails like knives of flint are against the faces of them that do these (things) against thee.'   BOTD spell 172

The preparation of flint artefacts, along with the collection of red ochre, is one of humanity's oldest activities. Amongst all of the many flint power objects found at ancient Ombos, the flint knife was plainly the most treasured. Such a knife may have a talismanic function. The contemporary 'throwing knives' of Southern Sudan play a similar role, the blade and handle representing the two domains of the bearer's world.

Next consider the fishtail knife that Seth, in canide form, wears strapped to his tail! The examples found at Ombos by Petrie are amongst the very finest knapped flint weapons ever devised. These objects were the Ombite's innovation. This one was bought from a local dealer at Abydos by Petrie.

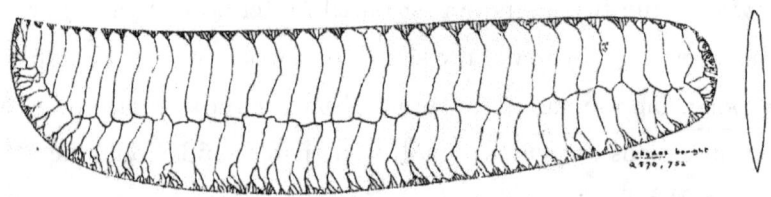

The possession of such a magical weapon was something no Ombite could abjure. It was the *must have* thing, even when superseded by more modern materials such as bronze. The flint knife was the weapon of choice for acts of magick, ritual slaughter etc. The confusion in contemporary magical practice, between the knife and the wand is relieved by meditating on the original sacrificial function of the knife. It is said to provide the precedent for the later practice of *bisecting* of *harmful* hieroglyphs. Images such as a hieroglyph have a latent power, that needs to be treated with care. Therefore a hieroglyph of a dangerous beast needs to be neutralised by bisection. At Ombos, the ubiquitous flint knives are almost always found broken in burials, and this is probably a deliberate magical act. This is the precedent for those examples of symbolic breaking of text and images in the pyramid texts. Despite the extreme antiquity of the Pyramid texts (c3500BCE), it happened first at

Ombos. Flint continued in agricultural use even to the present day – providing a cheap blade for sickles and scrapers.

In pharaonic culture, images of Seth were routinely neutralised in this manner. In a sense, Seth was stabbed with his own flint knife. Miniature flint knives in the form of nails or pins were used as an obvious substitute. The thirteen pins used in the 'wax image spell are a classical example of the practice. As the practice was internalised, Isis and Horus used copper against Seth. Contemporary magicians consider copper to be a 'venusian' metal. Cast your mind back to the 'love spell' discussed earlier, and you may recall that the thirteen pins were also of copper. Seth had his own metal, iron or lead, with which to ward off his old enemy Apophis, the demon of non-being.

Decapitation and reversal

The integrity of the corpse was something that became a taboo, for the later Egyptian followers of Osiris. Hence, the two greatly feared punishments of the Coffin texts were decapitation and reversal or otherwise jumbling, of the body parts. 'Coffin Texts' is a term reserved for those spells which are peculiar to the early coffins, and do not recur later, not at least until the Saite period, when some of them were sporadically revived. These Coffin Texts contain excerpts from the earliest Pyramid Texts, usurped by the nobility of the IX-XI dynasties for their own benefit.[30]

In some ways, we might see this fear of dismemberment after death as irrational. The whole process of mummification necessitates, what is essentially an elaborate dismemberment and then re-assembly. The integrity of the finished product must in many ways, be in the eye of the beholder. Egyptian sacred texts express a fear of the going down or reversal of bodily functions. This is linked with other disruptions to the normal order of things, such as, the eating of excrement and urine, something normally only reserved for the damned in *hell*. This taboo seems to have continued unabated even into the early modern and modern era. In his innovative study of the *Archaeology of Magick and Ritual,* Ralph Merrifield describes the incidence of deliberate reversals of such things as 'witch bottles'.[31] The rite of Mirgissa is pretty much identical with that prescribed for enemies of Horus in the Amduat. In late period texts such as *Papyrus Jumilhac,* such a fate is reserved for Seth. And again, we must point out the odd paradox here: reversal and decapitation may have been part of the funeral rites of the original pre-dynastic Egyptians, the residents of Ombos, the people of Seth.

Burning sand

Fire is universally considered a threshold between one realm and another. We find the fullest development of this important idea in Hinduism. Fire of various varieties, the physical fire of the cremation or cooking pyre, or the internal fire of the stomach, is the main nexus of transition from one state to another. For the Egyptians, the burial in sand, a Sethian substance, was a practice loaded with meaning and therefore power. In the Mirgissa deposite, burning and burial were final acts of an elaborate execration rite. The burial was especially effective, if done in an existing necropolis otherwise, the burial was *de facto* a creation of same. Ritner maintains that this sends the object or talisman into the realm of the dead – the underworld. The sandy pit is the equivalent of the abyss. Canopic jars or glass coffins, made ultimately from sand, provide an alternative. The *Papyrus Salt* has a parallel rite to protect the 'House of Life' or temple scriptorium. That rite forms the basis of what I call the 'Abydos arrangement'. The canopic jar is another form of *encirclement*. Later spells amplify the Sethian component, written *defixiones* or spells for the benefit of the living are placed in the mouth of the corpse.[32]

Breaking the Red Pots

> 'Hail [Osiris NN] this is the Eye of Horus. Take it so that you may be strong and that he may be terrified of you – break the red pots.' PT spell 244, 249

To continue with this necromantic theme, we come to one of the most common magical techniques of the ancient Egyptian world. The breaking of the red pots was associated with the funerary offering meal.[33] Once again Seth is involved. A distinctive feature of the Sethian mode of death was a vast funeral feast. To give some idea of possible scale, in nearby Nubia, which had similar burial practices, one assemblage had the remains of 5000 cattle, presumably slaughtered for the funeral feast. It is quite likely, that communal feasting was the method by which, surplus wealth was redistributed amongst the more communitarian

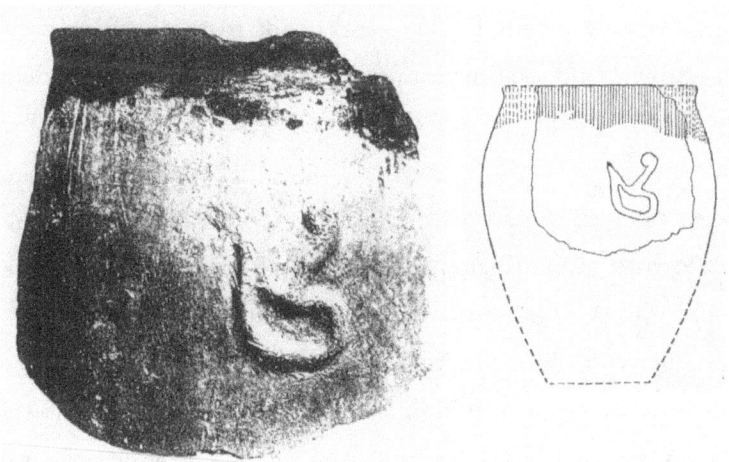

This same example was reproduced above in connection with proto Egyptian kingship. This pot is also a good example of Naqada's black top redware much favoured in the later rite of 'breaking the red pots.' Its fragmentary state may show the 'Sethians' use of the same type of magick.

people of the Neolithic. Some of these practices continue in changed form right into dynastic Egypt. The culture has moved away from what Dr Jude Currivan calls its 'shamanic' roots, to the more familiar 'geomantic' culture of the King and his followers.[34] Hence the beautiful red pots associated with archaic Sethian worship, become objects to be broken releasing their great magical power. This practice is reinforced in the Coffin Texts. The timing is circa 2000BCE, just after the first intermediate period, notable again as a time of crisis and civil war.

In Osirian religion, the breaking occurs simultaneously with the slaughtering of a bull in the temple slaughterhouse. The bull and the pot are substitute figures for the repulsed enemy i.e. Seth. The bulls, the pot, the colour red, the clay, all possess well-known and ancient Sethian associations. The breaking pot ritual is extended by the priests, to breaking of hieroglyphs in order to counteract their power. In the twilight of Egyptian culture, the Coptic Christians turned the same technique against Egyptian religion. Before desecrating and looting the great shrines of Abydos and elsewhere, they were careful to nullify the power of the images by breaking – hacking the faces and hands from the stone.

I don't know about you, but for me just the thought of breaking a pot already carries quite a lot of charge. Try visualizing it, start by imagining a ceramic pot with the most pleasing shape and decoration. Try to make it one you would really like to own. Perhaps you see one you already do own and treasure. Or maybe call to mind a favourite exhibit in an art gallery or museum. Imagine the process of manufacture or creation, either with slabs of clay or on a wheel.

The use of pots still plays an important role in modern sorcery. My friend, the cunning man Jack Daw, has fired many a 'clay virgin', in a simple outdoor kiln made from discarded house bricks. For fuel, he uses a packing of sawdust, which most sawmills are glad to give away. Having moulded the pot without a wheel, he fires it in a simple brick kiln. By controlling the airflow, the sawdust once lit smoulders for several days. Although not as hot as a professional kiln, the results are impressive. It's quite possible for the average person to make quite a fine pot. You might find you are even more attached to those you make for yourself. You can use your emotional connection. (see www.cornishwitchcraft).

The breaking of the red pots, may appear to you as a deliberate act of desecration, practiced only by the followers of Osiris. Although that is a tempting mindset, it is probably not really justified by the evidence. In truth, all of these practices are so old there is no way of knowing when they began. All that's needed is a pot, and the Sethians made many innovations in pottery design and creation. It is just as likely that, in some circumstances, the Sethians also broke the red pots as a magical act. Their emotional attachment makes the activity even more redolent with magical power. The breaking of such a beautiful object, specially crafted for the event, is indeed a very acceptable form of sacrifice.

The breaking of green faience in the *Book of the Dead* (125C) re-enacts the destruction of Osiris by Seth. This may also influence the choice of a broken potsherd for a written spell.

Letters to the dead

> Then Thoth said to the Master of the Universe: Cause a letter to be sent to Osiris, that he may pronounce judgement upon the two youths.
>
> *The Contendings of Horus and Seth*

Writing to the dead was a magical act used by the Egyptians, almost as soon as they discovered hieroglyphs. Precedent for this can be taken from the above letter to Osiris, lord of the dead. This was often combined with the kind of magick described earlier in the section on breaking the red pots. Examples of specially made and consecrated bowls can be viewed in various museums, including the 'Oxford Bowl' now in the

Pitt Rivers museum.[35] Broken pieces of pottery, known as ostracae, are also much favoured for this kind of work. I'd remind you that, the red clay from which they are made, is a substance with strong sethian associations, as indeed is the breaking and burial. Their substance and condition remind us of the realm of the earthy underworld. The inclusion of a large number of valuable pots interred with the deceased, is a practice as old as the potter's art. It is very likely that these always functioned as 'letters to the dead', or contained coded messages to the ancestors. Is it also a kind of prayer? You might think prayer is the technique favoured by many of the enemies of magick. I would suggest to you that, it is a useful magical technique worthy of reclamation. It is another example of how, the illustrious dead can still work on behalf of the living. What could be simpler than taking a piece of broken red pot, scratching a message or sigil addressed to an ancestor, thereafter burying that in a grave, preferably their grave or if that isn't possible, a recently made one, on the principle that the newly dead will deliver the message for you.

The Harem Conspiracy

You might be wondering how effective was Egyptian magick? To answer that, it is probably worth a look at the so-called Harem Conspiracy.[36] The conspiracy took place during the reign of Ramesses III (c1182-1151BC). His failure to nominate an heir from his many children (and wives) fuelled a conspiracy led by the formidable royal wife Tiye. The attempted coup d'état involved several dozen key individuals including an army commander, the royal prince Pentawere, the overseer of the priests of Sekhmet (specialists in medicine), a magican called 'Prekamenef' and scribes in the temple library. What was once a single book roll, subsequently broken up by antiquities dealers into six manuscripts, is the only surviving ancient record, of the conspirators trial for sorcery. The magician, known only by the deliberately 'mutilated' name Prekamanef (Ra blinds him), was charged to 'prepare magical texts for the purpose of confusing and disturbing. And to make waxen (figures) of some gods, and some potions for disabling the limbs of the people'.[37] He also began 'a ritual of consulting the divine oracle (pekh-neter) so to delude people. He reached the side of the harem of that other great expansive place, and he began to use the inscribed wax figures in order that they be taken inside by the inspector Adi-ran'.[38] Magick was used to pacify and spellbind the guards, so that messages could be taken in and out.

The wax figures are of precisely the kind discussed earlier. The 'harem' was the secure residence of the many wives of the King. The ultimate aim was, to coordinate an assassination attempt on the king using magick, with a coup d'état by supporters of Queen Tiye's son Pentawere. Ramesses III was indeed murdered, although the coup d'état failed and the succession passed to another prince, who became Ramesses IV and, presumably organised the trial of the conspirators. Which shows the truth of the old saying 'he who wields the knife cannot wear the crown.' Here then is clear evidence of the practice of lethal magick in the ancient world. Many of the magical techniques already described were used. The records show that magick was perfectly legal, although attempting to kill the king was obviously not. This sorcerous act against the king is what is condemned, not the act of sorcery. The conspirators, including the hapless guards were variously exiled, mutilated, executed, or forced to commit suicide.

Notes
29. Ritner (1993: 167).
30. Gardiner (1927:13).
31. Merrifield (1987 : 168).
32. Ritner (1993 : 179).
33.. Ritner (1993 :145).

34. Lecture, Pagan Federation Convention, 27th Nov 2004.
35. Gardiner (1928).
36. Redford (2002).
37. Translation Redford (2002: 18).
38. Translation Redford (2002: 19).

Re-emergence of the Hidden God

'The 47th spirit Uvall, or Vual or Voval. He is a Duke, Great Mighty and Strong; and appeareth in the form of a Mighty Dromedary at the first, but after a while at the command of the Exorcist he putteth on Human Shape, and speaketh the Egyptian tongue, but not perfectly.' (The editor adds the humourus note to the effect that this spirit now converses in colloquial Coptic.)

Goetia L W de Laurence (1916 : 37).[39]

Throughout, I've digressed much to introduce some interesting aspects of the mythology and magick of Seth the 'Bull of Ombos'. He is a mysterious, archaic entity, whose has a demonised cult, but isn't all demon. Seth represents the way of initiation and magick. Seth's constellation is *Ursa Major,* although one of his early *consorts* was associated with Sothis. Seth and Hathor make an interesting, more sensual pairing than the usual suspects.

As in my earlier book *Tankhem*, I wanted to draw attention to the lunar aspects of his magick, and the powerful doctrine of the *kalas* and associated body magick. About 93% of modern magick derives from the so-called Hermetic tradition of Egypt. With the disastrous and devastating rise of Christianity, this current was forgotten. It lay dormant and dreaming beneath the sands of the desert, or perhaps found a new home in Hindu Tantrism. The priests of Koptos took it there, as they fled across the desert to the Red Sea, where they took sail to South India. For an exploration of this theme see my *Isis, Goddess of Egypt & India*. During the last 100 years, the magick of the Hidden God has reawakened after 2000 years of 'stony sleep'.

There is no obvious beginning to the cult of Seth the 'Hidden God'; neither is there a complete explanation of his character. Perhaps, that is what makes him such an interesting archetype with which to work. He is a powerful spirit, that despite his outwardly frightening form, teaches initiation and liberation.

Crowley states that we, the *mystoi*, should be one pointed and focussed on one overarching aim – in the words of our holy books, 'one star in sight'. That star represents the inner abiding spirit or genius that, according to occult theory, is within each of us: 'every man and every woman is a star'.

In Crowley's tarot deck, his *Book of Thoth*, one card above all others seems to stand out. It is even the subject of a special message – 'Tzaddhi is 'Nuit' the Star'. This card shows the constellations known by the ancient Egyptians as 'the imperishable stars'. One in particular stands out as the 'Son of Nuit' – The Plough, *Ursa major*, the star of Seth. Hence the prayer from the Coffin texts where Nuit stretches herself over the gods:[40]

> 'Oh my mother Nuit,
> spread yourself over me,
> so that I may become one
> of the imperishable stars
> that are in thee,
> and I shall not die.'

It is the first axiom of *Tankhem* magick that, such a star or group of stars, *points the way*, just as the constellation known variously as Ursa Major, The Starry Plough, Big Dipper points the way to the centre of the universe, our own centre. The first step in opening the door to the Hidden God, is to go out under the stars and draw down the plough.

In the oldest Egyptian magico-religious texts, this constellation was known, as Meshketyu or Khepesh (Meshkhet = Bull's Leg).[41] From the time of the Egyptians, this image of the Bull's Leg recurs time and again, in many diverse religions. It finds its way into Mithraism and even into the final book of the Christian *New Testament*. I hazard a guess that, there is no religious or magical current in the Northern Hemisphere where this image does not play a role. It is said that this constellation contains the soul of the Stellar god Seth. And hence whatever the religion, the Hidden God is there, if you know his signs.

This information comes from the so-called Pyramid texts, sacred writings carved onto the walls of the very first pyramids and therefore approximately four and half thousand years old. But even as they were copied they contain their own internal evidence of being much older, of being copied from very ancient originals indeed.[42]

Mercer[43] tells us that Seth was the 'indigenous god', i.e. the first whose worship was general among the indigenous people of ancient Egypt. Red is the primary colour of Seth and any deity with Sethian affiliations. See for example his estranged consort Nephthys, who retains an underworld connection, and appears in a spell to enable a man (or perhaps a woman) to attract to himself a lover.[44]

Like all classical and ancient magick, the mindset is quite different to our own. There is an element of compulsion, both of the God and indeed of the object of desire. The piety of the ancient Egyptian magicians, was maybe more sanguine than our own. They were unafraid of compelling their deities to do their work – and in return, those deities seem to accept the bargain? Once such spell involves the use of 'the red veil of Nephthys'. This is probably a strip of fabric once used to clothe the image of the deity in a local temple, subsequently sold as a relic. Such a cloth could function as a gateway to further understanding of the lost mysteries of Nephthys. In Middle Egyptian times, Nephthys was the consort of Seth. I have argued elsewhere, that she may not have been his original choice or Nephthys her original name. Like many of the later goddess names, it really addresses her as a piece of temple furniture. Nephthys is enticed away to become the lover of Osiris. This must have some relevance to the way the spell works.⁴⁵ Seth often occurs in love spells of this kind.

Seth, the Egyptian god of ambiguity was associated with foreign lands, and the adversary of the god Osiris. Seth was usually depicted in human form with a head of indeterminate origin. He had a curved snout, erect square-tipped ears, and a long forked tail. Sometimes he was represented in entirely animal form, with a body similar to that of a greyhound. He was said to be the son either of Nuit and Geb, or of Nuit and Ra, and therefore brother of Isis, Osiris and Nephthys. Nephthys was sometimes given as his consort, although he is more commonly associated with the foreign, Semitic goddesses Astarte and Anat.

Egyptian religion is completely permeated by sex and sexual magick, to an extent that an older generation of scholars felt this information needed to be suppressed. There are strong parallels between the Egyptian worldview and that of Hindu Tantrism. Ancient Egyptian society is also surprisingly like our own – they drank beer (Egyptian for beer is Hnkt, perhaps pronounced Heineken),⁴⁶ they used contraception and they practiced sexual magick. The sexual and sensual aspect of ancient Egyptian religion, is something that took a while to filter through to modern books.

Seth, who is a great lover of men and women, was very jealous of Isis's new addition to the holy family. Isis believed Seth meant to harm her child, so she fled to the Nile delta and gave birth to Horus at Chemmis near Buto. With the assistance of other deities, such as the goddesses Hathor and Selket, Isis raised Horus until he was old enough to challenge Seth and claim his royal inheritance.⁴⁷

If Seth represents the Indigenous God, i.e. one of the gods known of in Egypt before the cult of Osiris came to the fore, and before the followers of Horus came on the scene. You can see why, some feel that

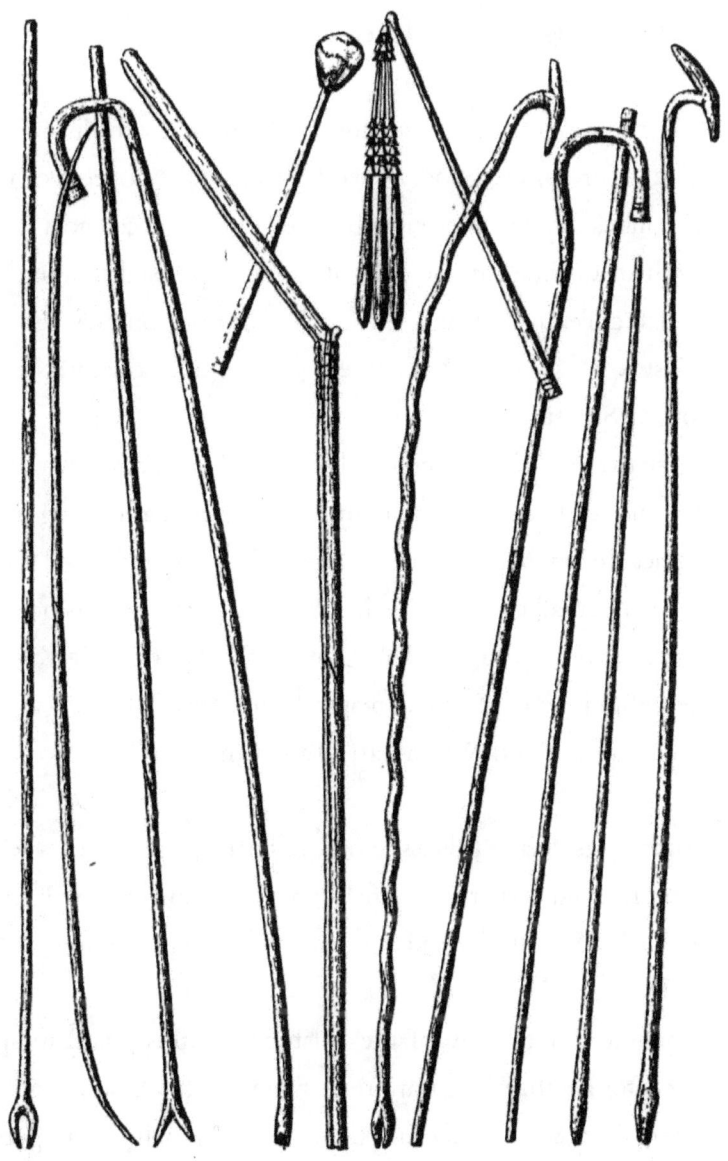

A selection of wands deposited in the pyramid of Senwosret I at Lisht. The *Was* and *Djaam* scepters are first and fifth from the right respectively (Gautier 1902: 76). There is no consistant distinction as to use, both bestow 'well being' on the bearer, both are seen holding up vault of heaven.

Seth represents an original or indigenous spirituality, that was demonised by later *incomers*.

Many in the modern world see initiation and individualism as the new evil. The nature of the good, so we are told, is the collective good. In modern politics, the collective is subsumed under the category of the state. So Sethian qualities are seen as all things opposed to the state, and opposed to collective religion. The ancient opposition between Seth & Horus/Osiris is essentially the same – it's the individual versus the new religion of Statism.

It is these two gods in particular – Horus and Seth, along with their associated family and consorts, that appear to be re-manifesting in the modern magical realm. You might think that what I've so far said is only relevant to a very small group of dedicated occultists. But it is possible to show that, what I've called 'The Cult of the Hidden God' is the secret force behind many, if not all magical currents of the new age. In that, I include Wicca and Witchcraft, Tantrism, even the Northern tradition.[48]

It's worth considering this issue of the guardian spirit for a while. Occult theory maintains that individuals have a guardian spirit allocated to them at birth. We find this idea in many differing cultures of the ancient world.

Most people don't know of the existence of this guardian spirit until near or after death. Some important magical rituals, deriving from ancient Egypt, were able to activate this knowledge whilst the person was still living. The Egyptian god form Seth was often connected with such operations.

It's the often-levelled critique of Seth, that he wants his own way. And this is seen as a very human failing, we want our own way. So it's another example of how, Egyptian Seth is a very important piece in the puzzle of the human psyche. Stephen Flowers says that 'Seth represents the individual will, in contradistinction to the collective will of the Egyptian state.[49] Like many powerful 'night-side' spirits, Seth clearly has a beneficent side. His ferocity may be a mask, that tests our true desire for initiation.

Myths of dismemberment

I discussed the most ancient burial customs in Egypt, the dismembering of the body, especially the head and also burning. Then some kind of reassembly, wrapping in a leather bag or exposure as carrion. The 'Osirians', who *may* have been immigrants into the Nile valley, preferred their bodies to remain whole and indeed one of the spells in the 'Book of the Dead' is designed to prevent decapitation in the afterlife.[50] This later taboo about decapitation is an obvious bone of contention between the followers of Seth and Horus (defender of Osirian faith). Seth's companions, the *smaiut n seth*, are punished by decapitation, and Seth is sometimes called the 'headless demon'.[51]

There is also said to be a secret method by which, the phases of the moon are somehow 'controlled' or predicted by Seth's northern constellation Ursa major. But the primary lunar reference comes from the fact that in myth, Seth dismembers the first king Osiris into fourteen pieces (one vital part omitted). The Egyptians, when talking about the inner nature of a person, use this lunar number fourteen. We too talk of someone as divided into various parts: mind, body, spirit, soul, ego, consciousness, memory etc. All peoples seem to have done such a thing. Just exactly how the ancient Egyptian did this is a bit sketchy, as there is no surviving work of what you might call Egyptian anthropology. In ancient Egypt, the individual is said to be a conglomeration of *seven* parts Viz: Heart, Sekhem (power), Ka, Ba etc.[52] The Ka, is some kind of childlike double, that takes hold of the person at birth. An individual can have anything up to 14 Kas of doubles attached.[53]

The Egyptians celebrated a bewildering number of festivals. One of the commonest was the celebrations for the new and full moons – the moon was called Yael, represented as the latest Egyptological opinion, is that what the Egyptians called the 'half-moon festival' is the full moon – written as a five pointed star with half moon:

Pronounced either as *semedet*, or more recently in a reading based around the number fifteen *mededint*.[54] The fifteenth day of the moon was known as the 'day of rams', when the moon begins to wane and thus loses its virile powers – it was on this day that the ritual of filling the eye was performed.

In Babylonian astronomy, the cycle of the moon is divided into two halfs of 14 days each – so it seems likely that what we are seeing here is a very ancient system of correspondences between the parts of the moon and the human body.[55] I've argued elsewhere that the contention found in several authors, including Kenneth Grant's of some kind of parallel between the Tantrik doctrine of the Kalas or lunar phases, and its earlier Egyptian model, is essentially correct. In fact, it seems highly likely that many of the secret body magick techniques of the ancient Egyptians were transferred or certainly only survive in India, after the systematic destruction of the Egyptian religion and sacred technologies by Roman Christianity.

The term 'kala' as found in the works of Kenneth Grant, is a Sanskrit term meaning part or digit. There is a maxim in Hinduism that 'Man is a microcosm of the universe – as above so below'. Sound familiar? This is pretty much identical with the Hermetic doctrine of the so-called Emerald Tablet. The physical moon can be described as have thirty different parts or phases throughout the month, half waxing, half waning.[56] These parts are also reflected in the subtle anatomy of every human being.[57]

These parts are most noticeable in the doctrine of erogenous zones (chandrakala)– zones of sensitivity that migrate around the body through the course of a month. We might also compare this with the thirteen 'puncture' points used in the wax image spell. Throughout the above I've aimed to introduce some interesting aspects of the mythology and magick of Seth. I wanted to draw attention to the lunar aspects of his magick and the powerful doctrine of the Kalas and its associated body magick. Nine tenths of modern magick derives from the so-called Hermetic tradition of Egypt. With the disastrous and devastating rise of Christianity, this current lay dormant and forgotten. It remained dormant and dreaming beneath the sands of the desert, and also in its new home in Hindu Tantrism. The priests of Koptos took it there, as they fled across the desert to the Red Sea, where they took sail to South India. For the last 100 years, the magick of the Hidden God has reawakened, after 2000 years of 'stony sleep'. Seth is this 'Hidden God'. There is no obvious beginning to his cult, neither is there a complete explanation of his character – perhaps that's what makes him such an interesting archetype with which to work. He is a powerful spirit that despite his outwardly frightening form, teaches initiation and liberation.

Notes
39. quoted in Ritner (1993).
40. Pyramid Text 777a, b.
41. The phoneme ms (msh) is an apron of foxes skins – meaning uncertain but may have some connection with birth rites.
42 See Budge BOTG, xxxiii for example. Also Edwards Pyramids of Egypt.
43. Mercer (1949: 48sq).
44. PDM lxi 100-105: The Red Cloth of Nephthys: "Pre arose; he

sent for the Seket boat (morning boat of Re) of heaven; the water under the bark of Pre has dried up. The gods and the two crowns (of the south and the north) complain until NN is brought to NN. If not doing it is what will be done, the gods whose names I said will bend down so that they fall into the fire ... I am the one who said it, she will repeat it 'Be destroyed, impious one!' She is the one who said it; / she is the one who heard it [and][repeated it." [It is] very good when he says it. (Betz p. 289).

45. PDM Lxi 100-105 is a spell of compelling that contains much Sethian imagery. Quoted in Betz p. 289.
46. See 'Beer' in glossary.
47. Edited from Anthony C. DiPaolo, M.S. (internet).
48. See for example the eightfold festivals and miracle play of Abydos.
49. Flowers (1995 : 75).
50. Budge (1901 : xxviii)
51. See Crowley's *Liber Samech*.
52. Is the ordinal seven (sefekh) linguistically connected with Seth. His name may mean 'to cut' or 'pierce' and begins with same consonant (O34) bolt. This sound may originally have been distinguished from (S29) which Budge says in his dictionary entry is same consonant as Hebrew Shin.The Heart (ib) The name (ren) – axiom of magick being that knowing the name gives one power over something. Linked with sound – a spell must be spoken ie via mouth.The power (sekhem)/The magical power Khu/Heka /The Double (ka)/'soul'or 'life force'(Ba) , personified as a bird, agent of sexual activity in afterlife./The Shadow (Khaibit). Three parts of (from Flowers) social self/physical self/psychic / spiritual self (sahu). See Mailer (1983) for interesting realization of all this).
53. Mercer (1949 : 43).
54. Collier & Manley (1998:76).
55. Fourteen in the 'Solar' zodiac, the observation of the more abstract 'Lunar' zodiac of 16 lunar days (tithis) may have been beyond most people's powers of observation. Classical magick made a distinction between a 'new moon of god' ie. 'according to the heavens', and 'new moon of man', 'according to the calendar' Betz (1986: 53fn).

56 See for example the Picatrix where its Indian origin is acknowledged. see Chapter 4 p19sq. Ghayat Al-Hakim, *Picatrix: Goal of the Wise*, vol 1, Oroboros Press 2002.

57. The system appears in some but by no means all grimoires. One of the earliest is the *Sworn Book of Honorius the Magician* in which it appears as a mere listing of the angels of the mansions of the moon. It also appears more fully in the work of Cornelius Agrippa. Another important instance is Barrett's *Magus* in which the system broadly derives from Agrippa. See book ii p.165.

The Body Magical

3. Power of the Gods
The magical-religion

"Ancient Egypt is an intellectual and spiritual world that is linked to our own by numerous strands of tradition."
Jan Assmann, *The Mind of Egypt*

Phi-Neter, means 'Power of the Gods'. In hieroglyphs this is represented by the hind-quarters of a leopard, the driving force of this powerful predator.

This is followed by the sign usually thought to be a flag, although it might also be some kind of wrapped fetish or *packette* of a kind commonly found in Vodou or the African based religions of the Americas. So to continue our exploration of magick (*heka*), we now look at the casting of spells (*akhw*) and various other means to set in motion the divine powers of the ancient Egyptian Gods.

The Latin term *magick* is useful but also loaded with Roman bias that has haunted any discussion of its techniques for the last 2000 years. The Egyptian magician wields a power that was ultimately created by the Gods for the use of anyone who wishes to do their work. It's the same underlying power whether manipulated by Gods, priests, aristocrats, the common people or even the criminal. Same power, different ends.[58]

I first learnt of this via the Hermetic Order of the Golden Dawn, probably the most famous occult sodality of modern times. Founded in 1888 it had largely ceased activities by the early 1920s. Even so there are a number of contemporary groups who claim to be successors to its mantle and there is hardly any modern initiate who has not either heard of or used some of its techniques and ideas.

It was for this reason that in 1981 a small group of novice initiates in Oxford formed their own Golden Dawn Occult Society as homage to the late 19th century original. My fellow initiates were of the opinion that one of many valid successors to the Golden Dawn was the celebrated magus Aleister Crowley. No doubt more traditional Golden Dawn aficionados would turn a jaundiced eye on such a suggestion; especially given the fact that many blame Aleister Crowley for the premature death of the esteemed order. Controversially, Crowley published the principal rituals of the Hermetic Order of the Golden Dawn in his journal *The Equinox*. Later, Israel Regardie, one of Crowley's most gifted students, completed the process with the publication of a *Complete Golden Dawn System of Magick*, the source of much subsequent work with these ideas. Perhaps one can see that, as pretentious as the Oxford initiates might appear, there was some method in their madness.

Over the years these ideas have been revised and supplemented in the light of my own journey of more than two decades into the magick of ancient Egypt. I am not claiming any special insider knowledge or initiation. Neither am I any longer interested in reviving the old sodality

---

58. Robert Ritner (1993) *The Mechanics of Ancient Egyptian Magical Practice*, Chicago University Press

in any organizational sense. I am an outsider. Even so it pleases me to return to the original optimism I had when first starting out in magick. I hope it will cast an interesting light on the inspiration of those eminent Victorian adepts who did so much to set the current occult revival in motion.

I have come to believe that the real 'Golden Dawn' is an experience rather than an organization. Apart from poetic insights, this chapter is in the main a short and simple excursion into the ancient Egyptian magical religion. My aim is to offer a workable summary of freeform Egyptian magick supplementing material already revealed and/or presented in earlier works from which I will extract vital bits of information as needed.

You may wonder why I use the term 'freeform'. Contemporary guides to Egyptian magick imply that it is anything but *freeform*. Isn't Egyptian magick very formal and theatrical? Pretty much all contemporary books present it as so. Consider this – if an ancient Egyptian were to teleport to contemporary London during the opening ceremony for the 2012 Olympics – would they be witness to a neo-pagan ceremony? Well in part maybe, especially Patrick Hetherington's *Olympic flame*. Viewing this spectacle changed my mind and showed me how such mass gatherings can be magick. Ancient Egypt had similar mass events but in my view the core of the tradition transpired on a much more personal and human scale. Monumental public spectacles of ancient Egypt were nourished by the personal and the private. So try to put aside what you know and approach the surviving records of ancient Egyptian magick with a fresh mind.

Egyptian magick and Hermeticism?

> 'The Gods rejoice when invoked according to the rites of the Egyptians' – Iamblicus, *On the Mysteries of Egypt*

"Hermeticism is a set of philosophical and religious beliefs based primarily upon the writings attributed to Hermes Trismegistus, ...a wise sage and Egyptian priest, and who is commonly seen as synonymous with the Egyptian God Thoth. These beliefs are central to the Western magical traditions. The Hermetic cult even gets a mention in the *Koran* as the Sabians " (*Wikipedia*)

The Greek sounding name "Hermes Trismegistos" was designed to cast a veneer over an Egyptian matrix. In a nutshell the Greek rulers of Egypt appropriated the magical wisdom of ancient Egypt whilst at the same time operating a system of cultural apartheid that eventually led to its complete suppression.

Until quite recently most scholarly commentators would say Egyptian wisdom is an oxymoron. Consequently the eminent Egyptologist Sir Alan Gardiner, recalls that when Herodotus toured Egypt shortly after 450BCE., "he thought claims that 5th century philosophers like Thales and Pythagoras derived much of their wisdom from Egypt were *undoubtedly fictitious.*" He also warned his readers to be sceptical about similar claims made for Democritus and Plato.

Standing as we do on the cusp of the new 21st century, all these issues are subject to widespread reappraisal. Eminent academic authorities such as Jan Assmann have challenged many old assumptions and transformed the way people see the Egyptian past:

> "[T]he basic concepts of the Hermetic doctrines are in fact deeply rooted in ancient Egyptian religious thought, which was still alive among Egyptian priests in the Roman period."

Until recently there were very few textual sources for the Hermetic tradition; the principal one being the so-called *Corpus Hermeticum* – a collection of short, late-Egyptian treatises, contemporary with early Christianity.

One of the important principles of the *Corpus Hermetica* concerns the cosmic significance of sound and vibration. Treatise XVI purports to be a letter, written in Greek by Asclepius, a student of Hermes Trismegistus, to King Ammon. The strange thing about this letter is that it begins with an explanation that the Hermetic mysteries only really make sense in the Egyptian tongue! This is taken to mean that "The very quality of the sound and the (intonation) of the Egyptian words contain in themselves the energy of the objects they speak of." It is the sound that matters, the language or the handwriting is incidental.

Like many of the so-called Hermetic axioms it reminds me of the ancient Hindu world view, which lionises the creative power of sound. Esoteric Hinduism can be seen as a synthesis of the Egyptian power of the word with the *Orphic* power of sound. Hence the later Hindu culture famously makes great use of special sound patterns called "mantras" to *manipulate* reality. It is one of many parallels between the Egyptian magical religion and esoteric Hinduism.

The Egyptian priests were pragmatists. At the end of Egyptian history, in Roman Egypt, during the rise of Christianity, times were hard. The Romans had removed the traditional livelihood of the Egyptian priestly intellectual. This was the culmination of a long period of colonial exploitation, by the Persians, then the Greeks and finally the Romans.

To make ends meet "Egyptian priests played on the expectations of their customers, taking on the role of the exotic specialist..." A game familiar to the modern practitioner who often finds it easier to live up to the expectations of the uninitiated.

As colonial subjects you'd expect they would reject the magical ideas of the Greeks. But this didn't happen. In fact many interesting aspects of Greek magick were combined with the Egyptian original. This is the origin of the so-called *Greek Magical Papyri* – also known as the *Theban Magical Library*. In truth the spells of the Theban Magican Library are multicultural and multilingual – "the result of a desire to collect and combine ritual texts of different origins."

We know that the language of magick and medicine is international. Much of its terminology comes from the Egyptian temple. Not surprisingly Egyptians often had a Greek personal name for public use and a native one for private.

Hermetic prayer & rubrik

"As they left the sanctuary, they began praying to God and, turning to the south (for when someone wants to entreat God at sunset, he should direct his gaze to that quarter, and likewise at sunrise toward the direction they call east) and they were already saying their prayer when in a hushed voice Asclepius asked: 'Tat, do you think we should suggest that your father tell them to add frankincense and spices as we pray to God?"

When Trismegistus heard him, he was disturbed and said "a bad omen, Asclepius, very bad. To burn incense and such stuff when you entreat God smacks of sacrilege. For he wants nothing who is himself all things and in whom all things are. Rather let us worship him by giving thanks [a voice offering], for Gods find mortal gratitude to be the best incense.

"We thank you, supreme and most high God, by whose grace along we have attained the light of your knowledge; holy name that must be honoured, the one name by which our ancestral faith blesses God alone, we thank you who deign to grant to all a father's fidelity, reverence and love, along with any power that is sweeter, by giving us the gift of consciousness, reason and understanding:

Consciousness, by which we may know you; reason, by which we may seek you in our dim suppositions; knowledge, by which we may rejoice in knowing you.

And we who are saved by your power do indeed rejoice because you have shown yourself to us wholly. We rejoice that you have deigned to make us Gods for eternity even while we depend on the body. For this is mankind's only means of giving thanks: knowledge of your majesty.

We have known you, the vast light reserved only by reason.

We have understood you, true life of life, the womb pregnant with all coming-to-be. We have known you, who persists eternally by conceiving all coming-to-be in its perfect fullness.

Worshipping with this entire prayer the good of your goodness, we ask only this, that you wish us to persist in the love of your knowledge and that we never be cut off from such a life as this.

With such hopes we turn to a pure meal that includes no living thing."

The Egyptian magical religion

No systematic book of Egyptian theology has ever been found. One has to rely on inference and so-called "implicit" theology to reconstruct core beliefs and see how much they resemble our own. The modern discipline of Egyptology developed out of the European occult tradition and speculations about the lost mysteries of Egypt. So-called "scientific Egyptology" began as a reaction to the occult approach and therefore focussed more on technical linguistics rather than religious speculation. As a result many Egyptian "occult" texts endured a twilight existence, sidelined as "pure witchcraft". Thus you may well have heard of *The Book of the Dead* and *Pyramid texts* but not the *Books of the Underworld?* I have often used them as the basis of much of my own "Egyptian Liturgy".

There is also many neglected "folk magick" aspect of Egyptian magical religion whose importance is difficult to exagerate.

Egyptian religion is sometimes defined as 'Realising Maat'. Maat, the principle of truth, justice and cosmic harmony was personified as a Goddess. But this is the big picture, religion considered in a wider sense. Jan Assmann suggests we could also consider Egyptian religion in another but equally important sense concerned with one's personal contact with the Gods and individual piety.

The Pagan theologian Iamblicus, wrote that religion in ancient Egypt was focused on two things:

1. The cult of the sun, and the continuation of the Sun's course
2. Protecting the mysteries of Abydos –
   the cult shrine of the God Osiris.

Solar mythology is therefore pretty central and our world is viewed as the unfolding (Kheperu) or emanation of the Sun God. The 19th dynasty of Ramesses and Sety circa 1350BCE is of particular significance in the development of this theology. The king's names were often written with the Kheper or Kheperu component.

A third more heterodox aspect to Egyptian religion is folk orientated and to do with the cult of the ancestors. We might call this the "left eye of Ra" – ie the realm of the moon, which is a secret key.

In the ancient world the Egyptians were considered to be very pious. We have already discussed the *Corpus Hermeticum* and its reference to Egypt as "the temple of the world". Modern Egyptians still love this explanation of the popularity of their country. Whereas in surrounding countries, the Gods, having completed their earthly tasks, were said to have withdrawn from the earth to the sky. For example in Israel, the priests "handed back" the keys of the Solomonic temple to angelic guardians before its destruction by the Babylonians.

In Egypt this process was delayed, in part because of the ancient and continued maintenance of religious activity. These activities come in three kinds:

1. Cultic – local or civil manifestation.
2. Mythic – i.e. stories of the Gods, often fabulous
3. Cosmic – divine action of Gods as in the myth of extra (epagomenal) days on the year.

1. Local or cultic dimensions

The 'concept of the city deity was one of the most ancient elements of Egyptian religion." Egyptian cities seems to have developed out of primary mounds, perhaps the remnants of ancient tribal gathering places. Due to peculiarites of Egyptian geology, the well known annual Nile flood actually resolves itself into forty-two enormous "temporary" lakes. The primevel first settlements began with the raised mounds of unflooded ground as their focal point. This is also the basis of the provinces known by the Greek term "nomes" (Egyptian : *sepat*).

Such places must have presented themselves as the natural choice for a temple. Mythology and geography are then unified in the form of a building. The ground plan of all temples is derived from the first primeval temple. Temples are very special buildings, to borrow a term from Giordano Bruno, they are "Theatres of Memory".

In later times the Egyptians sought to preserve the *atmosphere* of the first temple. Thus the Ptolemaic (Greek) temple of Horus at Edfu adheres very closely to an ancient paradigm. It was built towards the end of Egyptian history when the ideas were under threat. The architects went to enormous lengths to reify the core elements of Egyptian culture in this design.

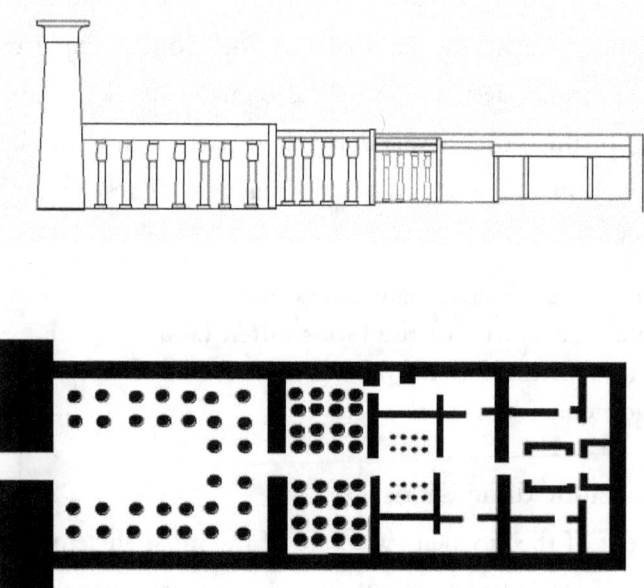

Whereas secular dwellings were largely constructed in mudbrick, sacred architecture enjoyed a virtual monopoly on the use of stone. The ancient cityscape was based around this very visible dichotomy.

The temple is an "image of the celestial horizon" (*akhet*) – the sky above, earth, with plants growing upwards. The temple either settles the Gods in the land or cuts out a piece for them to possess. The God within is a universal God – a conception that makes its first appearance during the time of the Ramesside kings, whose family affiliations were actually to the God Seth. The distinctive eastern façade of the temple looks like the notch on the eastern horizon, the "doors of heaven" from whence the Sun God makes his first appearance at dawn.

Thus the temple is an image of the cosmos. And Egypt is "the temple of the world". Right from the very beginning a temple records and teaches us details about its mythological origin. This can be via actual texts such as those carved on the walls at Edfu. Or more esoterically as in the "secrets" memorialized in the shape of the building. This tradition continues through time and can be seen in the design of medieval cathedrals and churches.

Which raises the question of the origin of religious experience? Is it, as some say, in those cult acts beside the grave of a loved one? Or do its roots lie in something even more mystical, even shamanic? The extreme antiquity of temples and shrines suggests that from the very beginning religious activity was collective. Some will even argue, as does Jan Assmann, that collective experience came chronologically prior to the individual variety. People made special artefacts found in even the simplest grave or tomb. These objects are then given life or a soul, a "Ba" by the Gods, becoming a permanent part of the tribal memory.

One of the most archaic of such rites comes down to us as "The Ceremony of Opening the Mouth". This ritual still forms the secret basis of some modern magick. In times of yore, the principal actor in this archaic funeral rite were the surviving children or heirs. To secure an inheritance one was required to sleep by the deceased, awaiting a vision in a dream. As we shall see in connection with the Ring spell, the same rite was used on statues, amulets and rings. So the final act in the consecration of an object would be confirmation via a dream.

It is a moot point as to what or who was the original subject of the ritual. Was it something done for the dead and then later extended to other "inanimate" objects? Or did it perhaps begin as an act bringing a magical object or fetish to life? The ceremony of opening the mouth was also performed as a temple dedication. This rite is the "finishing touch" to any cult object, the moment the spirit or "Ba" of the particular God is encouraged to take up residence.

Magick continues to use some of these techniques either in name or deed. Sometimes the mere calling to mind of the name of the rite (eg "Ouphor") is enough to invoke its power (*baraka*).

The power to *animate* or *entice* a spirit into a statue is also described in the *Corpus Hermetica*. This technique was one the early Christian theoreticians found particularly repellant. The passage on making statues may even have been deleted from selections of *Corpus Hermetica* used in Christian communities. The second of the ten commandments specifically forbids the making of idols. Herein lies the origin of the widespread Abrahamic taboo and indeed fear of this kind of magick.

The False Door

I have found the image of the Egyptian 'false door' an evocative entry point into the tradition. The image is based upon ancient examples. I have simplified it in order to bring out its complexity, its geometrical and "liminal" elements..

(The manner in which I reduced it to its "seed" meaning owes much to the visual techniques of the Hermetic Order of the Golden Dawn. The Order made creative use of "flashing colours", colours such as red and green. It also popularized heavily contrasted "sigils" in matt black and white as a means of evoking magical consciousness in the viewer. The source of these techniques undoubtedly lies in the visual culture of ancient Egypt.

To experience a flashing colour, get some coloured construction paper. Cut out a blue circle four inches in diameter and place it on a red square of similar dimensions. Lay them out on a table top and view by candle light. The image will oscillate and move around. Close your eyes and look at the after-image!

A door is a very potent symbol. Knowledge of the whole of the Egyptian magical religion is latent in this ancient image of a door. Experts on the Egyptian "false" or *Ka* door[59] usually discuss it in conjunction with an object known as a stele – a stone or wooden slab of varying size, inscribed with text and pictures and most commonly used at the threshold of a tomb, as a votive offering in a holy place or as part of a personal shrine in the home. The stele and the false door have much in common.

The door is "false" only in the sense that it bars the way for the physical body but allows the spirits of the living and the dead to pass through. It is the interface between our world and the Otherworld. I recommend calling this image to mind in meditation or ritual as a portal to an ancient Egypt which still exists in the imaginal realm. I will return to the motif of the false door in more detail below.

It would be useful at this point to call to mind the idea of the astral temple within the Western mystery tradition. One important refinement, discussed in the next chapter, is that one should base one's astral temple on an actual building, even if only the archaeological plans.

The other is to "sleep" in the temple. This is facilitated by having a representation of the "false door" in your bedroom, positioned such that it is the last thing you see before sleep. Sleep as absolutely the most important arena of Egyptian magick.

---

59. šebȝ Kr, šh-Kʿ, šh Neter

Not temple

Thinking about magical doors inevitably brings to mind the issue of location for Egyptian magick. A temple is the place but less obvious but in my opinion of equal importance is the space *outside* the temple.

By "not the temple" I mean everything that happens in magick that is outside of the formal temple space. This could literally be just outside the temple walls, perhaps outside the back wall of the holy of holies. I kid you not, archaeological research has revealed that the places immediately behind the temple holy of holies was a hotspot of ritual activity. Take for example the Osireion at Abydos, one of the most important ritual sites in Upper Egypt. One makes one's approach to this shrine via a path that lies *outside* of the main temple *temenos* or sacred barrier.

One of my scholarly mentors told me that Egyptian magick was so powerful it was only really safe when practiced in the temple. She viewed the temple as a complex piece of ritual mechanics. She has a point – most people can still sense the power in surviving Egyptian temples despite their ruinous condition.

Existentially we are outside the temple whether we like it or not, so we have to make the best of it. And as it happens, for most Egyptians the elaborate temple was a "black box" from which the folk (the *Rekhyt*) were largely excluded. Apart from the outer courtyards, the interiors of Egyptian temples were peopled by priests and their aristocratic patrons. There are of course important moments during which the two spaces come together.

There is an ebb and flow between these groups and spaces. I'd remind you that with some exceptions, there was no permanent priesthood in ancient Egypt. All those qualified to do so, male and female, might serve as priest at some time in their lives. I like this model of how the priesthood should be organized. To my mind it is so appropriate for our contemporary magical world. The shifts or "phyle" of priests worked one month in every ten according to a rota regulated by a lunar calendar.

A long time ago I parted company on rather bad terms with one of my first mentors in Khemetic magick. He knew of my calling to the *Companions* of Seth and his final grudging advice was that I should investigate the temple of Sety I at Abydos. I did and over time began to view this as my *omphalos*, not exclusively for the ancient Egyptians but for much of the classical world of the time. Its physical fabric is nowadays much depleted; even so there is an *archaeological* memory from which we can still benefit.

In fact I learnt so much it became a central part of my vision of a *Khemetic* Golden Dawn. Most of those trained in Golden Dawn techniques work on the physical plane but also in the imaginal or astral world. One's first access to this "imaginarium" is facilitated by plans of an idealised temple. Often this is based on the legendary temple of King Solomon described in the *Bible, Book of Kings* 6 1-39; 7; & 8. For many this functions as an "astral" or imaginal temple, envisioned as being in the sphere of *Malkuth* on the Golden Dawn Tree of Life. But even this Solomonic temple has a hidden Egyptian componant: "The holy of holies . . . an enclosed, windowless cube of wood, with sides each measuring about 10 metres, appears to have been an adaptation of an Egyptian tradition about a chapel of the Gods." This being so then it also makes a lot of sense to return to older, primal models such as the temple of Sety I at Abydos.

Like everyone else my first magical exercises involved the visualisation of the primal doorway of the astral temple. Back in the day I was guided to create a sacred space or *temenos* using a ritual called the Lesser Ritual of the Pentagram, for another method, read on.

The Egyptian Magick of Abramelin

Since its English publication in 1897, *The Book of Abramelin* has been much celebrated by occultists. Scattered throughout this book are instructions for a ritual which will reputably open the doors of the unconscious and bestow great magical knowledge and power. Even a cursory examination of this book reveals a debt to Egyptian temple practice. The book provided the working methods for the Hermetic Order of the Golden Dawn, who broke it all down into graduated steps by which the initiate could pass through the door of ignorance and ascend to gnosis. To this day these techniques underlie pretty much all occult ritualism.

Book III Chapter 7 provides the basic description – the candidate begins his or her rite by rising early just before dawn. This is precisely the moment at which the ritual day began in ancient Egypt. The ritual year commenced on the first morning of Passover or Easter, also an important day. After performing ablutions and wearing clean clothes, the priest entered a special prayer room or *Naos*. He opens the eastern window then kneels in front of his altar and prays to "mister" that he send a messenger (HGA or Holy Guardian Angel) to instruct him in the secrets of the universe. This rubrik offers no traditional or formal words for the prayer – the priest must speak from the heart in his or her own language. When done, the priest closes the eastern window and leaves the room, returning after sunset to repeat the whole procedure. In the version published by MacGregor Mathers the rite continues for six months followed by three days of revelation. In the more recent Georg Dehn version the whole practice takes 18 months.[60]

Living and sleeping space is in an antechamber outside, although

---

60. *The Book of the Sacred Magic of Abramelin the Mage* translated by S.L. MacGregor Mathers (1897; reprinted by Dover Publications, 1975)

occasional, especially in the climax of this work, one may need to sleep in the prayer room.

Using details in chapter seven and later chapter eleven it is clear how the layout of the prayer room closely resembles the standard Egyptian temple space. The holy of holies is a cubic room. There should be a strong sense of cardinality – north-south, east-west. Few houses lend themselves to such a precise orientation but there again neither did those of Egyptian temples, which often had to cope with a *nominal* or virtual north based on the flow of the river Nile. Basically there is an entrance in the south, a false door in the north (the place of midnight) and two windows opening to the east and west. In the centre is a monolithic altar, or one conveniently constructed of wood. If one does sleep in the prayer room it should be near the southernmost entrance door.

Here follows a ground plan:

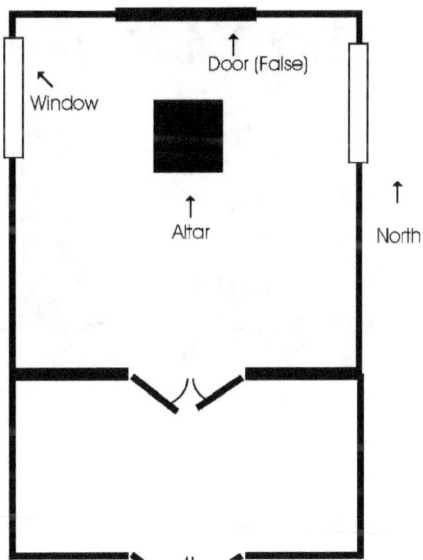

Temple floorplans often do end up echoing the inner structure of the mind and are for this reasons sometimes called "mind-maps". Even if you never undertake the "formal" Abramelin rite, just looking at the plan cannot fail to make you more aware of the primal wirings of your own mind. You could also consider it a precursor to something known in the East as *Feng Shui* – Chinese Geomancy. Not many people have the option to construct an ideal ritual space this way. Even so it may be possible to incorporate some small changes that will have a big impact on consciousness.

These geomantic ideas are common to Abramelin, ancient Egypt, the Orient, and not surprisingly Islam, from which some of it filtered back into Western magic. Look at this detail below which shows a typical floorplan of the "holy of holies" or barque shrine from the Temple of Sety I at Abydos. You should see the similarities

Abramelin belongs to a class of books called *grimoires*. Most grimoires are pretty nonsensical – or put it another way perhaps we are meant to be entertained. Back in the 15th century and maybe always –

people enjoyed a mysterious or scary story. Seen this way, the grimoire is the precursor to the novel. Abramelin certainly begins with an adventure story:

Take this example of raising the dead:

"All the high-ranking spirits take part in this work. All it takes is to do the following: as soon as the person dies, lay the word square on him after the fourth part of the day. As soon as he moves, and begins to sit up, dress him in new clothes. Inside the clothes sew a word square like was placed on his body. Whenever new clothes are worn, the word square needs to be placed inside.

It is not possible to extend the time past seven years. At exactly the point that the spirit again becomes one with the body the person will suddenly collapse. I myself saw an example of this when a dead duke — whose name I do not want to mention - who reanimated and was preserved on earth for seven years. Then, the young duke – his son - reached the correct age and was able to retain possession of the kingdom, which without this method would have fallen under the authority of foreign lands." [61]

Although part entertainment this need not preclude them containing genuine truths, of being "A fantasy but also true". In amongst all the

---

61 *Abraham Von Worms, The Book of Abramelin : a new translation being a complete and modern translation from various extant manuscripts, including a previously unpublished fourth part.* Compiled and edited by Georg Dehn, translation by Steven Guth (IBIS 2006)

62. Abramelin 2006 : 137. Mathers in his 1897 : 217 names the subject as Duke of Saxonia, perhaps Erik IV, who reunited the Saxe-Lauenburg lineage (1401–1876). In Mathers' version Abraham is said to have actually performed the miracle.

fantastic claims of magic power are philosophical nuggets such as "He who abandons his natural law or embraces another religion opposed to his own, can never arrive at the summit of the sacred science." [62]

Abramelin is a book of many parts. It begins with a magical journey from medieval Europe to ancient Egypt. Parallel to this it urges us to undertake an inner journey invoking one's "Guardian Angel". Together you will be able to raise and control the denizens of the demonic realm; the demon kings and their vassals and to do this in complete confidence and safety.

Abraham of Wurms was, according to Georg Dehn, a real 15th century magus. He studied with various teachers, mainly Kabbalists. He bequeathed his knowledge of the mysteries of Kabbalah to his oldest son; those of magick to his youngest (Lamech). To his daughters he left a handsome blob of money.[63]

Abramelin was the name of Abraham's Egyptian teacher. They met after Abraham's long pilgrimage across Europe to Constantinople and there on to Palestine, Arabia then to a place called Arachi or Araki near the Nile.

Al Araki is a small Upper Egyptian town near Qina just off a long route that in ancient times connected the western desert to the Red Sea. His route is therefore feasible. In his account he says he walked 3½ days from there into the desert. Is that symbolic? There is also a track near Al Araki across the mountains to Luxor via Thoth Hill. Here, deep in the mountains, in a very ancient spot on the northern face of "pyramid mountain" is the 11th dynasty tomb of Mentuhotep III.

Although the pharaonic remains on Thoth Hill are long abandoned, even in antiquity, they were reused as religious sanctuaries, and this was

---

63. Place the letter other way round and it spells malech, meaning King, an insight from MiryamDevi's little masterpiece *NakedTantra*

in part because they retained an odour of sanctity. Hence in the 4-5th century, Saint Paul the Hermit, built his small hermitage in the tomb. The tomb itself was built near an earlier pharaonic temple, which was itself built on even older temple ruins which has been aligned to the star Sirius. Which all goes to show how a story can have interesting connections.

In Egypt, even today, tombs can be places of contact with the local Genii, Djinn or Genius. There is even a special class of Djinn connected with ancient tombs – *Shaytan Faraon* (Pharaonic Shaytan)?[64]

It was perhaps in such a place that Abraham of Wurms met his teacher Abramelin. He may well have been an Islamic specialist in magick, perhaps a Sufi or Sheikh. When the training was finished, Abramelin allowed his student to make copies of the magical books in his possession, the rest is publishing history.

The Book of Abramelin views the spirits (or Djinn) as part of a hierarchy. At the pinnacle is the Sun-God and below that are four Kings:

Lucifer, Satan, Leviathan and Belial.

Next in line are eight Dukes:
Astoroth, Magot, Asmodee & Belzebub
Oriens, Paimon, Ariton, Ahaimon.

These princes rule over approximately 360 lesser spirits.

---

64. Hans Alexander Winkler (2009) *Ghost Riders of Upper Egypt*; Kees van der Spek (2010) *The Modern Neighbors of Tutankhamun, History, Life, and Work in the Villages of the Theban West Bank*.
65. Dehn (2006 : 257) The total number of spirits varies from one manuscript to another - Peter Hammer's published in Cologne in 1725 numbers them as 360. Bardon divided these 360 spirits into 30 groups of 12.

Georg Dehn draws our attention to the grouping created by Franz Bardon (1909-1958) in his book *The Practice of Magical Invocation*.[65] Following Bardon's lead, we might better use the Egyptian schema of decans or ten day periods. The entire Egyptian year consisted of 36 ten day weeks. This older Egyptian classification is also the key to their "daemons" and is undoubtedly the origin of the medieval list.

If we omit the names of the Dukes, a new list emerges. It is quite long and its utility might not be obvious at this stage. But for the record:

Abramelin daemons & egyptian decans

1. Morech, Serep, Proxone, Nablum, Kosem, Peresh, Thirana, Aluph, Neschamah, Milon,
2. Frasis, Haja, Malacha, Molabeda, Yparcha, Nudatoni, Methaera, Bruahi, Apollyon, Schaluah,
3. Myrmo, Melamo, Pother, Schad, Echdulon, Manmes, Obedomah, Iachil, Ivar, Moschel,
4. Peekah, Hasperim, Kathim, Porphora, Badet, Kohen, Lurchi, Falfuna, Padidi, Helali,
5. Mahra, Rascheä, Nogah, Adae, Erimites, Trapi, Naga, Echami, Aspadit, Nasi,
6. Peralit, Emfalion, Paruch, Girmil, Tolet, Helmis, Asinel, Ionion, Asturel, Flabiscon,
7. Nascela, Conioli, Isnirki, Pliroki, Aslotama, Zagriona, Parmasa, Sarasi, Geriola, Afonono,
8. Liriell, Alagill, Opollogon, Carubot, Morilon, Losimon, Kagaros, Ygilon, Gesegos, Ugefor,
9. Asoreg, Paruchu, Siges, Atherom, Ramara, Jajaregi, Golema, Kiliki, Romasara, Alpaso,
10. Soteri, Amillee, Ramage, Pormatho, Metosee, Porascho, Anamil, Orienell, Timiran, Oramos,

11. Anemalon, Kirek, Batamabub, Ranar, Namalon,
    Ampholion, Abusis, Egention, Tabori, Concario,
12. Golemi, Tarato, Tabbata, Buriuh, Omana,
    Caraschi, Dimurga, Kogid, Panfodra, Siria
13. Igigi, Dosom, Darachin, Horomor, Ahahbon,
    Yraganon, Lagiros, Eralier, Golog, Cemiel,
14. Hagus, Vollman, Bialode, Galago, Bagoloni,
    Tmako, Akanejohano, Argaro, Afrei, Sagara,
15. Ugali, Erimihala, Hatuny, Hagomi, Opilon,
    Paguldez, Paschy, Nimalon, Horog, Algebol,
16. Rigolon, Trasorim, Elason, Trisacha, Gagolchon,
    Klorecha, Irachro, Pafessa, Amami, Camalo,
17. Taxae, Karase, Riqita, Schulego, Giria,
    Afimo, Bafa, Baroa, Golog, Iromoni,
18. Pigios, Nimtrix, Herich, Akirgi, Tapum,
    Hipolopos, Hosun, Garses, Ugirpon, Gomognu,
19. Argilo, Tardoe, Cepacha, Kalote, Ychniag,
    Basanola, Nachero, Natolisa, Mesah, Mesadu,
20. Capipa, Fermetu, Barnel, Ubarim, Urgivoh,
    Ysquiron, Odac, Rotor, Arator, Butharusch,
21. Harkinson, Arabim, Koreh, Forsterton, Sernpolo,
    Magelucha, Amagestol, Sikesti, Mechebbera, Tigrapho,
22. Malata, Tagora, Petuna, Amia, Somi,
    Lotogi, Hyris, Chadail, Debam, Abagrion,
23. Paschan, Cobel, Arioth, Panari, Caboneton,
    Kamual, Erytar, Nearah, Hahadu, Charagi,
24. Kolani, Kibigili, Corocana, Hipogo, Agikus,
    Nagar, Echagi, Parachmo, Kosirma, Dagio,
25. Oromonas, Hagos, Mimosah, Arakuson, Rimog,
    Iserag, Cheikaseph, Kofan, Batirunos, Cochaly,

26. Ienuri, Nephasser, Bekaro, Hyla, Eneki,
    Maggio, Abbetira, Breffeo, Ornion, Schaluach,
27. Hillaro, Ybario, Altono, Armefia, Belifares,
    Camalo, Corilon, Dirilisin, Eralicarison, Elipinon,
28. Gariniranus, Sipillipis, Ergomion, Lotifar, Chimirgu,
    Kaerlesa, Nadele, Baalto, Ygarimi, Akahimo,
29. Golopa, Naniroa, Istaroth, Tedea, Ikon,
    Kama, Arisaka, Bileka, Yromus, Camarion,
30. Jamaih, Aragor, Igakis, Olaski, Haiamon,
    Semechle, Alosom, Segosel, Boreb, Ugolog,
31. Hadcu, Amalomi, Bilifo, Granona, Pagalusta,
    Hyrmiua, Canali, Radina, Gezero, Sarsiee,
32. Soesman, Tmiti, Balachman, Gagison, Mafalach,
    Zagol, Ichdison, Sumuram, Aglasis, Hachamel,
33. Agasoly, Kiliosa, Ebaron, Zalones, Jugula,
    Carahami, Kaflesi, Mennolika. Takarosa, Astolitu,
34. Merki, Anadi, Ekore, Rosora, Negani,
    Cigila, Secabmi, Calamos, Sibolas, Forfasan,
35. Andrachor, Notiser, Filakon, Horasul, Saris,
    Ekorim, Nelion, Ylemis, Calacha, Sapasani,
36. Seneol, Charonthona, Carona, Regerio, Megalogi,
    Irmana, Elami, Ramgisa, Sirigilis, Boria.

With the list rearranged this way we can perhaps make more sense of the frequent references to the number 72 in the text.

Eg: "Abramelin asked if I had any money. I answered 'yes'. He asked me for 10 gold guilders which he - as an obligation to Adonai – was required to distribute to 72 people."[66]

72 is one of those special magical numbers that occurs again and again in magical contexts. It is for example an important number in ancient Egyptian astro-lore, being the average number of days in the

yearly cycle a star is absent from the night sky. It is thus also the ideal number of days required to prepare a mummy to rise again. 5 x 72 = 360.

After the long performance of the ritual, either for six or more properly 12 plus six months is a religious experience in part ecstatic and part intellectual. The results are tabulated in the book's final section which deals with the *Magick Squares*.

Magick squares

Magick Squares are very much part of the mechanics of late Egyptian magick. Given the importance of puns and word play in their construction, it seems likely they are an Egyptian innovations with a long history.

In our time one of the most well-known is the SATOR-AREPO square which is early Coptic Christian magick based on older Pagan techniques. Writing in the *Classical Review* the eminent Egyptologist Gwynn-Griffiths identifies one of the words as an Egyptian personal name AREPO, translating the entire square as:

"The farmer Arepo pushes his plough"

SATOR,
AREPO
TENET
OPERA
ROTAS

---

66. Dehn (2006 : 16)

In addition there is a second, secret message or *spell* hidden in the square, one that was only discovered in the early 20th century. If one regroups all the letters one finds the embedded *acrostic* (crossword):

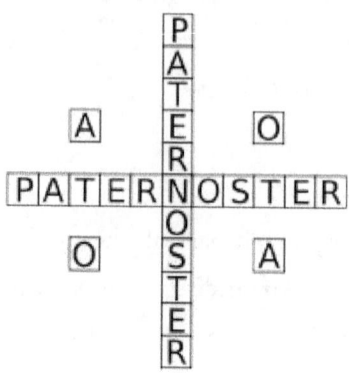

Paternoster ("our father") Alpha and Omega

Acrostics, Palindromes and other word games are all part of an old "daemonic" and hidden language used by spirits to communicate with us and we with them. The oldest examples are Egyptian circa 1400BCE.[67]

Anthony Peake in his book *The Daemon* has an interesting modern psychological way of looking at *daemons*. Peake starts from the premise that we each have not one but two personalities. The ancient would have called these the "Daemon" and the "Eidolon".[68]

Several books have pointed to experiences we all have at key points

---

67. Gwynn-Griffiths 1971 *The Classical Review* vol 21.i . Arepo is an Egyptian name (Hor-Hep). Other examples cited by Zandee are from time of Ramses II. See J Zandee (1966) *An Egyptian Crossword Puzzle*, Leiden.

68. Anthony Peake (2010), *The Daemon: A Guide to Your Extraordinary Secret Self*, Arcturus.

in our lives where this dual personality seems to be at work. For example "The Old Hag" or "Night Shadow".

> Evil Sleep - You're in your bed, it's dark, you hear footsteps coming up the stairs and into your room. There's someone there – a presence. They lie on you or beside you, perhaps even gripping you tightly, crushing you into the bed. You can't move. There may be a sound, a grunt or a strange smell. Time passes, you are paralysed with fear. Eventually the entity changes, perhaps expanding or contracting, moving away from you, sinking to the floor. With a great effort of will you manage to move the tip of your finger, then the hand until movement returns to your whole body and the experience ends. You have been visited by the old 'hag'. [69]

Magick explicitly aims to bridge the gap between both personalities, although the terminology "angel" or "daemon" is more common. The angel is perhaps the hidden, more powerful side of one's personality; otherwise angels and daemons are really very similar.

Occult lore stipulates that from the moment of your birth you are accompanied by a spiritual double. In modern speak: the brain has a dual-core processor. The organism is divided. Most people are unaware of this or if they are it is only through dreams or trance. The other personality, the "daemon", cannot speak directly but uses indirect methods to communicate in times of distress. Thus one must use some "occult" techniques to help things along.

The Book of Abramelin contains recipes for a unique perfume and incense for use in its experiments. Smell is the most primal of all the

---

69. David J Hufford, (1982) *The Terror that Comes in the Night: An experience centred study of supernatural assault traditions*

senses. One could perhaps look at several other occult techniques that in effect mediate this gap between the *labial* conscious self and the silent, inner daemon.

The use of a medium is another such method. Older texts suggest the use of a medium, often a "child". The first mediums were named after the Egyptian God Anubis, and because of a confusion of names, the idea arose that it had to be a child.[70] Even in 1930s Egypt, local children were used as mediums to talk to the spirits and search for buried treasure.

One's daemon may turn out to be of the opposite gender! In more class conscious ancient times, the higher one's social standing then the higher that of your "daemon". When the aristocrat "asks a friend" it might turn out to be a God.

When you die you are reunited with one's daemon, hence the Egyptians sometimes referred to death as "going to one's Ka". The magician is continually trying to bridge the gap with the angel and hopes to complete the process before they die. For, so 'tis said, the "daemon has special powers which you do not. The daemon dwells in the *liminal* world of the spirits, therefore it may know the future.

Crowley & his Daemon

Crowley was eventually put in touch with his *daemon* – Aiwass, an entity which some say was his own psyche. There is a famous photograph of Crowley posed with a magick book, a pentagram emblazoned on the front cover. What's in the book, nothing other than his complete collection of magick squares neatly drawn during his preparation for the Abramelin practice![71]

---

70. *inpu*

71. Frater Shiva (2012) *Inside Solar Lodge: Behind the Veil*, Desert Star Temple, p 773

The name of his angel lends itself to a bit of wordplay. Aiwass or "I Was" does indeed have a split personality, dictating a book that proposes entirely contradictory solutions to humanity's problems viz "The Law of the Jungle" versus "AL True Ism"? [72]

At the time of writing Aleister Crowley is still a force in modern magick. In so many ways he was the first modern magician.[73] 1904 was the pivotal year in Crowley's career. He was 29 years old and therefore well into what is popularly known as the "Saturn Return".[74]

Crowley had just got married although neither his or the bride's family were pleased with the match. He'd pretty much given up on the magick of his youth. The newlyweds were in Egypt – which

---

72. Mogg Morgan, "The Heart of Thelema: Morality, Amorality, and Immorality in Aleister Crowley's Thelemic Cult" *Pomegranate: The International Journal of Pagan Studies*, Vol 13, No 2 (2011)
73. Lawrence Sutin (2000) *Do What Thou Wilt: A life of Aleister Crowley* NY
74. Saturn takes approximately 30 years to orbit the Sun and return to point in the sky it occupied near one's birth. Astrological lore contends that the end of one's third decade on the planet is influenced by saturnine thoughts etc.

coincidentally is for magicians, an important rite of passage. Every self-respecting magician is almost *required* to go there and make contact with the "Secret Chiefs".

The prequel to this journey was Crowley's experiments with the already mentioned *Book of Abramelin*. Crowley had been advised by his magical teacher George Cecil Jones to fully master its techniques. He therefore scoured Scotland for a suitable house and bought one called Boleskine overlooking Loch Ness. Some say his arrival re-awakened the famous resident monster!

His embarked on the crash course version of the rite, allocating just six lunar months for completion. In the 15th century, Abraham began his retreat at Easter (Jewish Passover) itself a very important ancient feast connected with demons and angels of death. These myths make use of doorways of one kind or another, the ancient Hebrews supposedly inscribing magick signs on their lintels, a signal for the angel of death to *passover* the house.

The ritual continues from equinox to equinox – starting the day after Passover or at the nearest new Moon, continuing until the full Moon after the autumn equinox. The practice therefore makes good use of a specific astro-symbolic segment of the year.

It terminated on the old feast of Tabernacles or "Booths". The modern interpretation tells us this was originally a reminder of the temporary dwellings used by the early Hebrews during their flight from Egypt. Other than the Biblical and Koranic accounts, the flight from Egypt is not yet corroborated by any other textual or archaeological evidence. It may be pure myth. However the feast of Tabernacles was also the first festival celebrated after the resumption of religious activity following the Babylonian captivity.

Another possible purpose of this feast was to celebrate a successful harvest. There is an equivalent Egyptian feast of Min in month II of Egyptian year, and this involved portable shrines or *booths*.

Six months of continuous practice proved too much for such a mercurial figure as Crowley. He was soon distracted – magical war had broken out within the Order of the Golden Dawn and he answered the call to arms. It all ended in farce but that's another story.

As for *The Book of Abramelin*, the magical moment had passed and there was no point in returning to Boleskine until the following Easter. So Crowley travelled to Mexico and as often happens did not return for several years. When he did he was again distracted by his future wife Rose Kelly. They headed off on the *grand tour* via the Suez Canal. Stopping in Cairo on April 8th, 9th & 10th 1904 at precisely the right moment to restart the rite – the rest, as they say, is history.

The Khemetic version of the Lesser Ritual of the Pentagram (LRP)

The work of the magician often begins with the pentagram or more precisely the Lesser Ritual of the Pentagram or its equivalent. Almost every serious ritualist knows it. You can go most places in the world and transcend any language barrier with this rite. Even so its origin are a bit of a puzzle. The ritual first appeared in instructional papers on the Pentagram for the outer order of the Golden Dawn. Expert Nick Farrell writes that in the original papers, the *invoking* version was much more prominent than its *banishing* counterpart. In the so-called "lesser version" the magician traces pentagrams in each of the cardinal directions. The elemental quality of these symbols is determined by one's starting point and direction. Hence the lower left or fifth point of an upright pentagram is said to correspond with the Earth element. The topmost corresponds with Spirit. If you trace the pentagram beginning from Spirit anti-clockwise or *widdershins*, it is said to be invoking. On the other hand, should one need a banishing, one begins at the Earth point and proceeds in a clockwise or *deosil* direction.

Many post-Golden Dawn groups habitually use the banishing version, probably much more often than was originally intended. I must admit if I am asked to perform this ritual, I habitually favour the banishing version. However *intention* is probably more important than these subtle differences in technique. Even so what Nick Farrell says has persuaded me to think again.

The magicians of the Golden Dawn perhaps used the older Heptagram rite which they divided into two distinct parts. This Heptagram ritual is the precursor to the Pentagram and another Victorian ritual, the Hexagram. The *Heptagram* literaly means "seven characters" or sevenfold rite. A Khemetic Golden Dawn reinstates the older sevenfold version based on Egyptian sources. [75]

The Heptagram originates in an ancient papyrus, part of the library of a magician from Thebes in ancient Egypt. This library re-emerged in the 19th century and was translated into several European languages, as well as Latin. All these sources would have been available to MacGregor

---

75. Nick Farrell "In Defence of the Lesser Invoking Pentagram" Published in the *Hermetic Virtues Magazine*, Volume 2, Issue 3.

Mathers, the senior adept who compiled much of the Golden Dawn ritual material from sources in the British Library etc.

The Heptagram

Magick can be surprisingly physical. Before starting this kind of ritual it is a good idea to do a gentle *physical* warm-up; ie., all of your muscles from top to bottom. Begin with gentle neck rolls; loosen your shoulders, hips, thighs, knees and feet and anything else that needs doing.

This ritual is powerful and was used by magicians of ancient Egypt and transcribed in the Theban's magical library. I like to preface this with an exercise similar in intent to the Golden Dawn *Middle Pillar* but derived from another manuscript in the "House of Life" at Abydos. This is published in *Papyrus Salt*. I refer to this as the *Abydos Arrangement*:

> Face North and visualise the constellation
> *Ursa Major*. Draw down its power
> Now turn to the East and say:
> "Guardians of the House of Life at ....
> Before me in the East: Nephthys
> Behind me in the West Isis
> On my right hand in the South is Set
> And on my left hand, in the North Horus
> For above me shines the body of Nuit
> And below me extends the ground of Geb
> And in my centre abideth the 'Great Hidden God'. "[76]

This action roots one at the crossroads of the four cardinal directions. But also the three planes: the earth, the sky and the centre. One stands at a point of equipose between them. This sphere of

---

76. Lucie Lamy (1981) *Egyptian Mysteries: new light on the ancient knowledge*, Thames & Hudson. *Le Papyrus Salt 825* (B.M. 10051) : rituel pour la conservation de la vie en Égypte par Philippe Derchain (1964)

operation is sevenfold; seven is one of the most sacred and potent numbers in the magical tradition.

Before we consider the Khemetic Heptagram, I want to take a short diversion into the topic of sound within the Egyptian magical tradition.

Vowel song

> "It is highly significant, albeit extraordinary; that the device of the seven vowels was taken up in Demotic spells." [77]

> "They employ the seven vowels, which they utter in due succession as the sound of these letters is so euphonious that men listen to it in preference to the flute or lyre." [78]

The above and other antique sources inform us that in Egypt, the priests sang hymns and incantations in praise of their Gods. The number seven was always considered extremely powerful by Egyptian magi. "Vowel song", using the seven sounds, is in many ways beyond any particular language. It is part of the universal or international language of magick. We can also say that the nature of the vowels depends upon the structure of the human body, especially the vocal chords. Vowels *are* the sounds of nature. We can follow this idea backwards to the beginning of time or sideways into for example Hinduism, which also utilises "vowel song" in its science of mantra – the most famous example being the ancient mantra *Om*. Vowel song can become a freeform or improvised technique.

---

77. Hans Dieter Betz (1986) *Greek Magical Papyri in Translation: including Demotic spells*, Chicago, intro
78. Demetrius *On Style 71* quoted in J Dieleman (2005: 65)

An ancient Gnostic composed the following polyphonic chant in which the congregation takes on the form of seven heavenly choirs:

> "The first heaven utters the Alpha, the one after it Epsilon, the third Eta, the fourth, which is in the middle of the seven, utters the force (or sound) of Iota, the fifth Omicron, the sixth Upsilon, and the seventh, which is the fourth from the middle, expresses the Omega ... All these powers, he says, when lined to one another, sound forth the praises of him by whom they were brought forth. The glory of this sound is sent up again to the Forefather. The echo of this utterance of praise is brought down to earth, according to him, and becomes the shaper and parent of the things on earth."[79]

In ancient Egypt words were sacred. Any word is both a sign representing something but also a sound. Scholars say that the very first Egyptian hieroglyphs were very like those images seen in dreams.[22] The hieroglyphs are direct images of reality, with the proviso that reality for the ancient Egyptians included the otherworld of dreams. Not surprisingly, the Egyptians were among the very first known interpreters of dreams. Some of the earliest examples of dream manuals come from their temple libraries.

Greek magick, also popular in Egypt, was heavily influenced by the cult of Orpheus. Therefore some say it values sound over and above the signs or letters by which it is represented. The letters do service to the underlying sound which is seen as more archaic and primary. From

---

79. Jacco Dieleman (2005) *Priests, tongues, and rites : the London-Leiden magical manuscripts and translation in Egyptian ritual (100-300 CE)* Leiden : 66.

the time of Cleopatra (69-30BCE) both magical systems began to coalesce. Even predominantly Greek spells show evidence of an Egyptian user and vice versa.[80]

Returning again to the example of the seven vowels of magick. The ancient Egyptian language had its own vowels but, as in Hebrew, did not use any special characters to represent them. In this sense the vowels of the Egyptian tongue are *hidden* or secret.[81]

The Egyptian and Greek vowels must have been similar. In Cleopatra's time, the native Egyptian priests embraced the seven Greek vowels. In fact the Greek vowels were themselves derived from a common fund of Semitic semi-vowels (eg: Y becoming I) including those of the ancient Egyptian tongue.

These seven vowels can be seen as the 'soul' of the alphabet. These entities have power on many different levels. They are letters, numbers and musical notes. They and indeed the consonants, correspond with the twenty-five notes of the Lute, the seven fold musical scale, etc., etc.

A mnemonic device by which one can easily remember the seven vowels:

Father Get Game to Feed the Hot New Home.

So for example to vocalise A, sing the word "Father", repeat a

---

80. Quoted in David Frankfurter, "The magic of writing and the writing of magic: the power of the word in Egyptian and Greek traditions" *Helios - Journal of the Classical Association of the Southwest*, vol 21, no 2: 101

81. Jan Assmann (1987) *Moses the Egyptian : the memory of Egypt in western monotheism*, Harvard: 113, Dielemann (2005 : 146). Recent research has revealed that even the ancient Pyramid texts paid some attention to correct vocalisation – see Baines – lecture. E Doblhofer (1961 : 34) *Voices in stone : the decipherment of ancient scripts and writings*, London

couple of times with the emphasis on the A in Father. Next drop everything apart from the A, and you have the vowel.

The seven sacred vowels:

Alpha :	a	A	A
Epsilon :	e	E	E
Eta :	h	H	Ê
Iota :	i	I	I
Omicron :	o	O	O
Upsilon :	u	U	U
Omega :	w	W	Ô

Character name, then lower case, upper case and Roman transliteration respectively.

Cardinality

Combinations of these vowels are used to invoke the divine forces of the four directions. For some these correspond to the four elements – earth, air, fire and water. David Rankine and Sorita D'Este write that the "alchemist Zosimos of Panopolis [in Egypt] attributed the elements to the four cardinal points in his classic third century work "Upon the Letter Omega". The attribution of the four elements to the four directions remained constant for many centuries, with Fire in the east, Air in the south, Water in the west and Earth in the north. This can be seen through to at least the Eighteenth century, where the *Key of Solomon* records that, "the spirits created of fire are in the East and those of the winds in the South . . . It would be Eliphas Levi in the mid 19th century with his writings who clearly switched the attributions of Air and Fire, giving Air as being attributed to the East and Fire to the South . . . This attribution was picked up by the Hermetic Order of the Golden Dawn, and has become the standard attribution in nearly all of the Western Esoteric Traditions."[82]

Cardinal winds

If, as I do, you prefer a more wholely Egyptian presentation of the cardinal directions, then you might like to use another schema of four primary winds – ruled over by Shu, the God of the atmosphere, the air and winds.

The winds are:

North = Meheyet: Ram headed winged lion

---

82. David Rankine and Sorita D'Este (2008) *Practical Elemental Magick*, Avalonia

East = Iabet: Scarab with four rams' heads, yellow, also left side

West = Jimenet, Blue. Ram headed falcon with four wings. Also symbolises the right side.

South = Resey: Lion with four rams heads and four wings.

This ritual is given in liturgical form elsewhere. I am repeating it here in order to analyse its components.

The Heptagram (sevenfold) rite combines physical gesture with intonation, vibrating or singing of words of power.

The first gesture is called "Horus Fighting". Inhale and in one perfect movement, form both hands into fists and raise them up and to the left of your head.

Next stretch your right hand and arm in front of you and bring the left hand and arm to join it. As you finish the intonation, bring both hands back to the centre of your body. [You'll be glad you did the physical warmup recommended earlier!]

Combine the above gesture with the first vowel long and hard - AAAAAAA -

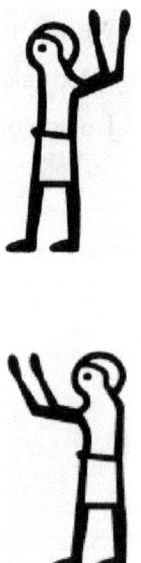

Now starwise, ie turn <u>anticlockwise</u> or widdershins stopping at direction North. Most antique systems move in the directions of the stars.

Again make the gesture "Horus Fighting" and vibrate the second vowel EEEEEEE, using the mnemonic gEt as above.

Then turn to the West

Make the "Horus Fighting" gesture and vibrate ÊÊÊÊÊÊÊ as in GAme

Turn to the South

Make the "Horus Fighting" gesture and vibrate IIIIIII as in fEEd

Return to face the East

Now bend over and reach down to the Earth vibrating OOOOOOO as in HOt

The second body magick posture is similar to one known as the Typhon or Trident in the Golden Dawn system. Combined with the Horus Fighting posture, it is very like a popular sequence of yogic postures known as Sun Salutation.

One begins from a loose forward bend, knees flexed and not locked, touching the earth. It does have a tendency to induce gentle shaking, especially in the lower legs. This is useful. Shaking helps focus the mind.

Gradually unfold, come up and place your hands on your heart and vibrate YYYYYY as in NEw

Finally stretching up to the heavens vibrate Ô Ô Ô Ô Ô Ô Ô as in HÔme.

To finish I suggest a final welcoming of the principal Gods invoked by the rite. It's an odd fact that when one uses simple combinations of vowels, one is spontaneously speaking the ancient Egyptian magical language (More of this later). Make the invoking sign of the pentagram in the air in front of you and vibrate this sequence of vowels:

Aa, Eye, EE, Ou, Uh[83] – Nephthys

Continue thus:

Aa, Eye, EE, Ou, Uh Horus
Aa, Eye, EE, Ou, Uh Isis
Aa, Eye, EE, Ou, Uh Set
Aa, Eye, EE, Ou, Uh Geb
Aa, Eye, EE, Ou, Uh Nuit
Aa, Eye, EE, Ou, Uh Hidden God

Repeat first part that begins "Guardians of the House etc."

Return to the North

After that preliminary rite – settle down – prepare for a short vision quest or visualisation – sit down in a posture suitable for meditation – this is your *asana* – it does not need to be uncomfortable to be effective. In the later Hindu tradition one is recommended to use a posture that is easy and comfortable.[84] The important thing is that your back is upright and neither tense nor slumped, perhaps *poised* is the right term.

When I first learnt this technique I was told to close my eyes and think about the room or place – recalling how it looked to the front – behind – to the sides. With my imagination I visualised a curtain in the east. As I "looked" (my eyes still closed) the curtain had an image on it – an equal armed cross – white on dark ground. This was then augmented with four *elemental* colours taken from the "King" scale from the sphere of Malkuth (the Kingdom) – the realm of earth hence the earthy or

---

83. Ay EAO - in Middle Egyptian this could mean "Oh Hail" - as it is a suitable piece of "magical voice" at the beginning of a line.
84. *Yoga Sutras of Patanjali* - 2.46 "asana is steady, stable and comfortable" – the *Bhagavad Gita* has more detail at 6:13.

natural colours citrine, olive, russet and black.[85] Whilst the above exercise is still valid what follows is more *khemetically* focused version.

The Door

Begins in a similar way to above but the image on the cloth is different. It is the "false door" mentioned earlier (see frontispiece illustration). It has proved a useful piece of magical technology. Indeed it is worth taking some time to make one of these as a canvas backdrop. I move mine around but it could hang behind what I'd call the offering table. Its portable nature means it can also be folded away when not in use. I will explain the meaning of the term "offering table" later.

This particular version of the false door is painted in matt white on a deep black background. This combination of black and white has a particular effect on consciousness. This use of contrasting colours, whether mono or polychrome is one of the important insights, perhaps even "secrets" of the Golden Dawn and is directly related to the colour theories of the ancient Egyptians.

The earliest form of the Egyptian tomb was a simple burial pit. The earliest brick built *mastabas* (from Arabic meaning "bench") augmented this pit with chambers for offerings and grave goods but then also surrounded it with symbolic doors. Later structures extend the theme but in essence there are two spaces, the chamber with burial shaft for the body. This chamber is sealed after the funeral and is then approached via a chapel, often open to the elements, but obviously designed to facilitate the visitation of living family members. The surviving relatives and friends visit the tomb to re-supply, to clean and to *continue* their relationship with their departed. This is ancestor worship - and as such is probably one of the oldest forms of religious activity.

---

85. See *The Qabbalah of Aleister Crowley including 777*.

Figure 4.6. Studio Photograph of the False Door Niche, MFA 21.961, Showing the Incorrect Reconstruction of the Left Outer Jamb (Containing the 𓂂 sign). Courtesy of the Museum of Fine Arts, Boston

"The Giza Mastaba Niche and Full Frontal Figure of Redi-Nes in Museum of Fine Arts, Boston" – Peter der Manuellian (1994) in *For His Ka: Essays in Memory of Klaus Baer,* 1994). There is a very early example of Queen Neithhotep of 1st dynasty, and found at Nagada by Jacques de Morgan.

Illustrated is another very early example from the Old Kingdom cemetary of the Giza pyramid field, probably 6th dynasty circa 2300BCE. My modern redrawn version is based on these ancient Egyptian examples. The connection between these spaces, one for the living, the other for the dead continues via the symbolic door; for this reason it is known by archaeologists as the "false" or "*Ka*" door. The term "false door" is misleading - it is not really false, it is merely impassable for the living.

The Egyptians divided a person into several spiritual componants or *souls*. The *Ka* is one of these parts, is a spirit, and was able to pass through these doors with ease. Communication can be initiated by either party to the door. When the dead initiate the connection this can be a problem and the living need to beware! [86]

More on that "false" door

Despite a door's commonplace nature it is well worth taking some time to re-acquaint yourself with its symbolism. In some senses when all else crumbles to dust, the doorway is often the last thing to disappear. The temples of Egypt are nowadays a shadow of their former selves, a glorious remnant. We moderns are the successors to the mysterious adepts who in the third century of our era (c268CE) prophesised Egypt's vertiginous fall but also its eventual resurgence.

> "...Egypt is an image of heaven or, to be more precise, that everything governed and moved in heaven came down to Egypt, and was transferred there? If truth were told, our land is the temple of the whole world...Oh Egypt, of your reverent

---

86. Emily Teeter (2011) *Religion and ritual in ancient Egypt*, CUP : 48 "contact could be initiated by either side ...The messages from the living were usually practical rather than philosophical. Less controlled, and hence more dangerous, were the messages initiated by the dead."

deeds only stories will survive and they will be incredible to your children! Only words cut in stone will survive to tell your faithful works, and . . . strangers will dwell [here]. . . no one will look up to heaven. The reverent will be thought mad, the irreverent wise, the lunative will be thought brave and the scoundrel will be taken for a decent person. When all this has come to pass . . . then the master and father, the God whose power is primary, governor of the first God, will look on this conduct and these willful crimes, and in an act of will he will take his stand against the vices . . . he will restore the world in its beauty of old so that the world itself will again seem deserving of worship and wonder . . . this will be the geniture of the world, the reformation of all good things and a restitution, most holy and most reverent, of nature itself." [87]

Existentially we stand outside the still ruined temple, literally on the threshold, thus the image of the door is entirely appropriate. It is certainly no coincidence that many books of the European Occult Renaissance had on the frontispiece the image of a door, the portal to the secrets in the book. The history of Pagans and books are intertwined. The book as we know it is very much a creation of the ancient Pagan world. Even the familiar shape of the book conceals the Pythagorian "Golden Mean". One of the most famous examples of a Renaissance Hermetic book is John Dee's Elizabethan masterpiece, the *Monas Hieroglyphica*.

---

87. *The Asclepius* verses 24-27, translation by B P Copenhaver *The Greek Hermetica* CUP 1992 p 81-2

I doubt I have exhausted the ramifications of this image. Everyone who sees it finds in it new connotations. For example some see the Hebrew "Cheth", the twin pillars and lintel upon which the ancient Hebrews daubed magical signs in lamb's blood to prevent the angel of death entering.

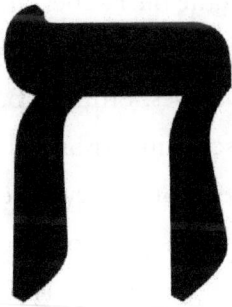

Others see something resembling the trilithon of ancient British megalithic architecture:

Take another look at the image of the false door that appears on the frontispiece. It would be a good idea to make your own copy at a good size and place this where it can be glimpsed during ritual. I have one on the wall opposite my bed. It is often the last thing I see before I fall asleep. This complies with the advice found in the books of Dion Fortune that the adept should "sleep" within the astral temple. This is an important magical instruction especially for those working within the Khemetic tradition where dreams and the dreamscape are the primary theatre of magick. A great many Khemetic ritual techniques are completed in dreams: hence if one invokes a God they are invariably expected to respond via a dream. This is an important technique on which there will be more to say a little later.

But for the moment the rite has begun with the basic opening liturgy and the initiate lingers before a representation of the false door that is the portal to greater mysteries. From its beginnings in early tombs and *mastabas* the door was soon incorporated into the design of temples. The first temples were temporary structures. One of the earliest known is from circa 4000BCE in the abandoned settlement of Hierakonpolis, which means "Citadel of the Hawk." The Egyptian name *Nekhen* links this with the followers of the God Horus and the conflicts that supposedly led at the very beginning of Egyptian formal history, to unification or hegemony of one local tribe over another.

Above is a provisional reconstruction of this proto-shrine deduced from the post holes and foundations. The structure appears temporary and at a push could well have been relocated. It recalls an earlier, more nomadic lifestyle when shrines were portable. Its shape is said to be modelled on the body of a large animal – probably a bull but other *preformal* structures also recall the body of a wolf. It seems likely that early treatment of the deceased involved what's come to be known as 'sky-burial' i.e. exposure to the elements and the teeth of wild animals such as wolves.

These temples share some of the symbology of a tomb. Inside there were two nested rooms, an outer *peristyle* and an inner holy of holies. This structure is pretty much the same as the arrangement of the temple as discussed earlier in connection with the medieval *Book of Abramelin*.

A palisade surrounded the entire shrine forming the *temenos* or sacred enclosure. The temenos of the temple of Medinet Habu is intact and still inspires in one a spontaneous sense of awe. Within the temenos stood a large pole from which fluttered a sacred image. The front end of the shrine was supported on four masts, perhaps also surmounted by fetishes, flags or streamers. The motif of four masts or pillars at the front of a shrine was often repeated in subsequent religious buildings, the most obvious being the shrines seen in the enclosure attached to the Pyramid of Djozer at Saqqara. In Egyptian "Kabbalah" the number four signifies completeness (qv). Coincidentally the design of the Islamic *Minbar* could come from same location.

These early buildings can be read as complete models of the ancient cosmos. It is another of those "mind maps" left by our distant ancestors. As soon as they acquired writing they recorded these ancient secrets in books such as the aptly titled 'The Book of the Primeval Old Ones'.[88]

---

88. E A R Reymond (1969) *The Mythological Origin of the Egyptian Temple*, Manchester.

It "tells that in the primeval times the surface of the planet was covered with water. Below the water lay the remains of one or more previous creations. The divine entities were without form but not without power. The ancient sages or *shamans* call out to these beings, using words of power that they had but recently learnt. There are . . .seven sages [there's that number seven again] or shamans and this is another motif that seems to crop up all over the place. This is, in all likelihood, the origin of the myth of Atlantis." [89]

---

89. See Morgan *Tankhem* page 54

The result is the first and most primal temple, built or moved to the new dry land. The divine entities arrange themselves at the four cardinal points as well as above, below and centre, precisely as spoken in the first part of the sevenfold *Heptagram* rite discussed earlier. When you meditate before the first version of the temple all of this knowledge is manifest plus much more to come.

The tented shrine was the first formal entrance to the numinous, and the Underworld. In ancient times the Egyptian architect Imhotep recreated this cosmic model in stone, reifying the mysteries into the structure of the archetypal Egyptian temple. Imhotep was over time viewed as a God because of his expertise. As time went by the details became increasingly obscure and complex. In essence a temple is a mechanism by which we can return to the source, the primary moment of equipoise, ecstacy and eternity.

Sometimes we need the complexities of the temple, sometimes we need something simpler.

Greek vowels and the elements?

If, like me you were brought up in the Western mystery tradition then you may be wondering whether there is any correspondence between these vowels and the four or five magical elements of earth, air, fire, water and spirit? The liturgy at the end of this book, provides a revised version of an opening (*Heptagram*) rite based on a text in the *Theban Magical library*.[90] In this ritual the magician intones (*vibrates*) the seven sacred vowels in the following order:

---

90. PGM XIII verses 823-835

Alpha	– East
Epsilon	– North
Eta	– West
Iota	– South
Omicron	– Below
Upsilon	– Centre
Omega	– Above

Egyptian Gods and Goddesses are commonly arranged into similar patterns. The "Abydos Arrangement" discussed earlier is one such example. Another common ancient arrangement used the four Goddesses Mut-Sekhmet-Bastet-Wadjet.[91] One can therefore deduce correspondences between the vowel sounds and the Gods.

Carmina figurata

As well as chanting vowels, the Egyptian mage wrote them on amulets, often arranging them in patterns to re-emphasise the power of the written word - hence the name "carmina figurata" – *shaped hymns*. There were three principal patterns, each comprising seven tiers. The patterns are triangle or square or diamond, the later also known as a wing (pterugion). Further variations are available according to whether the triangle or pyramid points up or down and also how the seven vowels appear in the tiers.

These squares are called *plinthion:*

---

91. Richard Jasnow & Mark Smith " 'As for Those Who have Called me Evil, Mut will Call them Evil': Orgiastic Cultic Behaviour and its Critics in Ancient Egypt" *Enchoria: Zeitschrift für Demotistik und Koptologie* Band 32 2010/2011 : 25

```
a  a  a  a  a  a  a
e  e  e  e  e  e  e
è  è  è  è  è  è  è
i  i  i  i  i  i  i
o  o  o  o  o  o  o
y  y  y  y  y  y  y
ô  ô  ô  ô  ô  ô  ô
a  e  è  i  o  y  ô
e  è  i  o  y  ô  a
è  i  o  y  ô  a  e
i  o  y  ô  a  e  è
o  y  ô  a  e  è  i
y  ô  a  e  è  i  o
ô  a  e  è  i  o  ô
```

This one is called a wing (*Pterugion*)

```
a  e  è  i  o  y  ô
   e  è  i  o  y  ô  a
      è  i  o  y  ô  a  e
         i  o  y  ô  a  e  è
            o  y  ô  a  e  è  i
               y  ô  a  e  è  i  o
                  ô  a  e  è  i  o  ô
```

The vowels may be multiplied for example tripled for extra emphasis or written in exponential form: [92]

---

92. PGM I 1-42

```
          a
         e e
        è è è
       i i i i
      o o o o o
     y y y y y y
    ô ô ô ô ô ô ô
```

When we use these techniques, either drawing or intoning them as sound *shapes*, we are following in the footsteps of our Egyptian ancestors. And as we are eclectic, so too were they, incorporating new words of power, such as ABRASAX, into the system. Egyptian magick is in no way purist.

"In praise of nonsense" Ephesian letters[93]

From "vowel song" it is an easy step to the distinctive international code of antique magic, the so-called "*Voce Magicae*". Aleister Crowley coined the phrase "barbarous words of invocation". These were also called "Ephesian grammata" or "Ephesian letters". These were additional letters that had power over and above the sounds they represented.[94] Ephesus was at this time a byword for exotic practice and incantation. These strange word and sound patterns are an essential part of any effective invocation. From the improvised, freeform recitation of vowels, some memorable sound patterns naturally emerge.

---

93. "In Praise of Nonsense" quoted in Frankfurter WoM fn 83 Patricia Cox Miller in *Classical Mediterranean spirituality: Egyptian, Greek, Roman* ed by A H Amstrong (NY 1986) 481-505
94. David Frankfurter (1998) *Religion in Roman Egypt* Princeton page 195

Luscious syllables

These sound pattern favour so-called "luscious syllables". This is the Orphic, musical side of magick. A perennial favourite in the magical literature of the centuries after the death of Cleopatra is:

ABLANATHANALBA

Which was usually invoked for beneficient results, and often occuring in conjunction with:

SESENGENBARPHARANGES.

or

AKRAMMACHAMARA

The meaning is unexplained but some say it contains Hebrew.[95] Another common "luscious" invocation was "DAMNAMENEUS" – which wouldn't be out of place in the pages of a Harry Potter novel!

The sound here is more important than any meaning. Although when written on amulets, the Egyptian doctrine of hieroglyphs is again revealed, for this sound pattern then gets a visual shape such as those used in the vowels eg: here it is as a "wing". In this magick both aspects, sound and image, constantly interchange one with another. The sound pattern becomes a visual thing – the visual becomes sound. This is *synesthesia*.

---

95. Betz (1986) page 331

ABLANATHANALBA
BLANATHANALBA
LANATHANALBA
ANATHANALBA
NATHANALBA
ATHANALBA
THANALBA
HANALBA
ANALBA
NALBA
ALBA
LBA
BA
A

Now this magical or artificial language takes on a life of its own - or maybe the life was there all the time but we had forgotten how to see it. This happened to the Egyptian magicians - who started using this artificial language as an "alphabetic demotic" – preserving but also unintentionally hiding ancient Egyptian God names and epithets.[96]

Our modern perspective is not so different to that of the clients of the ancient mages whose spells were often done for their benefit, even if they did not really understand what was going on. The priests performed direct rituals and acted vicariously on behalf of their clients. Socrates wrote in his dialogue *Charmides*[97] that "without the spoken formula the leaf [spell] has no power". But they also devised many visual

---

96. Dielemann (2005 : 73)
97. 155E

and other techniques with "concrete" efficacy; for example the famous "drinking and eating spells" described elsewhere. Amulets may also function as spoken utterances of a God.

There is an interesting contemporary use of this technique in Nick Farrell's book *Making Talismans*. To rid oneself of a boil, write the word thus:

BOIL

BOI

BO

B

"Twilight language"

Magicians of all times have felt the need for secrecy. In late antiquity codes and euphemisms were used to disguise the socially unacceptable componants of a working. In some spells, for example those to send "evil sleep", the coded sections tells how the spell repeated seven times will kill the intended victim. One possible counter-measure is to block dreams entirely and this is one of the known side-effects of the narcotic blue lily potion discussed elsewhere and widely used by ancient Egyptian specialists. Even so, dreamless sleep is difficult to guarantee!

Use of private languages is also partly about preserving professional mystique. The Egyptians did this via an institution known as the "House of Life", a restricted archive of manuscripts attached to every temple. Secrecy also persisted beyond life, with some texts only known from copies deposited in tombs. There were also books inscribed on the walls of sealed rooms in temples such as Sety I at Abydos. These are ancient Egyptian *Books of the Afterlife* never discussed in other Egyptian records.[45]

Egyptian hieroglyphics is such a complex language it was easy to veil precise meanings by omitting a grammatical element. For example the determinative, a little picture that tells you the context of a word and without which the word has several often conflicting meanings. This is known as *enigmatic writing*. Another twilight language is called *acrophany*, where a particular sound is expressed by means of another common word, of which only the first consonant or syllable has phonetic relevance.[98] A classic example is "Never Eat Shredded Wheat", not that that you shouldn't, just happens to be a handy way to remember the cardinal directions: North, South, East, West. We also call this mnemonics and it is a common part of magick.

Back in the day, the magician was supposed to know the basics, the things already discussed but also special formulae such as the MASKELL – MASKELLO. This obscure phrase is really just the first two words of a much longer spell containing crucial words of power.[99]

"Sigils" – the new hieroglyphs

From the uneasy, arranged marriage of the two magical cultures was forged a new alternative to the hieroglyphs, incorporating elements of the Greek and Egyptian language. These are the so-called "charaktêres". The charaktêres are freeform signs (Latin 'sigils') used as an alternative to hieroglyphs at a time when knowledge of them was becoming lost or attenuated due to official Greek indifference. These signs were still in use on 17th century magical gems and remain effective tools.

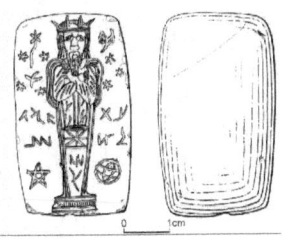

---

98. E Hornung (1999) *The Ancient Egyptian Books of the Afterlife*, Cornell
99. Dielemann (2005 : 78)

Thus the well-known neo-Pagan rite, the Bornless or Headless ritual, made famous by the Order of the Golden Dawn and after that by Aleister Crowley, uses an ancient charaktêre.[45]

The above transcription may differ from some published versions but is taken directly from the standard reference edition of the text.[100] Sometimes a spell has just one sigil or charaktêre, sometimes whole groups are given, suggesting they represented complex words and sentences.

Another name for this ritual is the "Ritual of Jeu the Hieroglyphist" or "painter of Hieroglyphs". This is a very significant name, perhaps related to *Jesus* or *Jahweh*. He or she may have been a famous practitioner of his time, and even if they didn't actually write this spell, they provided a powerful "brand". Amongst Egyptian books re-discovered in our time are the so-called Nag Hammadi "gospels". This cache included several Hermetic texts such as *The Books of Jeu*. Amongst the diagrams is a remarkable survival of Egyptian Hieroglyphic – the famous Ankh symbol morphed into the Gnostic/Christian Khi-Rho.[101]

---

100. K Preisendanz (1928-41) *Papyri Graecae Magica*, Teubner.

101. *The Books of Jeu and the untitled text in the Bruce codex* text ed. by Carl Schmidt; translated [from the Coptic] Leiden : Brill 1978

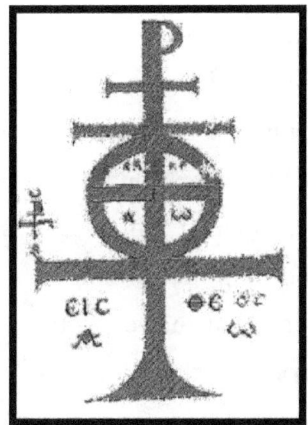

Seven charaktêres for "deliverance"

The total number of charactêres is very large. The first draft of this book made an arbitrary choice of the first seven as they appeared in the Theban magical library. However, I subsequently discovered that my idea was very similar to the "seven seals" of medieval Islamic magick, which is semitic magick ultimately derived from Cuneiform and Mesopotamian sources. Most of us know that during the European "Dark Ages" medieval Islam preserved a great deal of ancient learning. Many magical ideas actually come down to us via this route. The great Islamic sorcerer Al Buni believed the seven seals to be a blend of Hebrew, Islamic and Christian symbolism. Thus the first two seals were, so he says, from the *Koran*, seals 3 & 4 are from the *New Testament* and the final three are from the *Torah*.

To my eye they look older than any of those sources, indeed very much like ancient Egyptian *heiratic* script and some support for this conclusion comes from independent Islamic scholar Lloyd D Graham.[102]

---

102. "The Seven Seals of Judeo-Islamic Magic, possible origins of the symbols" published in www.academic.edu.com

For magicians unfamiliar with Islamic sorcery one's first encounter with the seven seals would probably be via the final book of the *New Testament* (chapters 5-9). This is a magical, apocalyptic text written in the reign of Roman Emperor Domitian (1st century CE) by a mystic who identifies himself as John, an exile on the Greek island of Patmos. Elaine Pagels, the esteemed scholar of Gnosticism says this is a political text, a cryptic attack on the despotic Roman hegemony. This fact is not to deny the presence of ancient magick in the text. The text is very well-known but here are some of the relevant verses:

> *5.1:* And I saw in the right hand of him that sat on the throne a book written within and on the backside, sealed with seven seals.

Unlike other magical texts the seven seals are not shown in any extant manuscript thus far found. However one does encounter what must be equivalent seals almost as soon as one looks at any magical "grimoire" or papyrus of the late classical period. Hence PGM I 262-347 says that to invoke the Sun God Apollo "take a seven-leafed sprig of laurel and hold it in your right hand / as you summon the heavenly Gods and chthonic daimons. Write on the sprig of laurel the seven charactêres for deliverance."

The spell in question actually then shows eight charaktêres, which makes me think the phrase "seven charaktêres of deliverance" is either a stock or generic phrase or, as happens in later examples, the first, and perhaps most important seal is repeated.

The seven seals are

(a)   7 6 5 4 3 2 1   Islamic
:

1st Seal: The Pentagram

"6.1: And I saw when the Lamb opened one of the seals, and I heard, as it were the noise of thunder, one of the four beasts saying, Come and see.

6.2: And I saw, and behold a white horse: and he that sat on him had a bow; and a crown was given unto him: and he went forth conquering, and to conquer."

The series is to be read right to left. The first of these is the pentagram. In modern magick the inverted pentagram is usually thought of as "satanic". Both kinds are known from medieval magick. Lloyd Graham examined 58 examples and found that the downward pointing variation occured in 15 of these; which suggests the downward pointing is rarer and perhaps always did have a different meaning.[103]

The sequence of seven in ancient religion is perhaps related to a primary constellation of the seven most powerful Gods and their seven powerful adversaries. The actual stellar counterpart would be the

---

103. Lloyd Graham, personal communication 2012 "Interesting question about the orientation of the pentagram. I've now looked at 58 representations of the Seven Seals and found the upwards orientation (i.e. single point at top) in 43 cases, downwards pointing (i.e. two points at top) in just 15 cases. So it seems that there is a strong bias against the "horns" orientation even in old inscriptions from Islamic lands. So perhaps the modern Western distinction between the two orientations has ancient roots."

constellation of the Pleiades for most of Mesopotamia; Ursa Major for Egypt.

This pentagram symbol is very old, it occurs for instance on pottery as an ancient predynastic maker's or owner's mark. For certain technical reasons is seems likely that the asterisk-like symbol shown below is an alternative version of the pentagram. As a word it is pronounced "An" in ancient Sumerian and means sky or heaven. It was used to introduce the name of a God. Probably it is equivalent to Greek vowel Alpha.

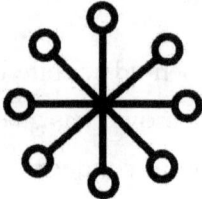

Egyptian hieroglyphic, words to do with stars, time etc are determined by a five pointed star.[104] I'd remind you that a pentagram can be formed by joining the arms of a five pointed star.

The asterisk form of this sigil is what finds its way into the medieval grimoires such as the *Key of Solomon*, where it is part of the design on the handle of a magical knife or *Athame* – and this turns up again in the Gardnerian *Book of Shadows*.

---

104. See Lloyd Graham op cit., See also Cambell-Bonner Database for two examples of pentagrams and asterisk star on talismanic gems.

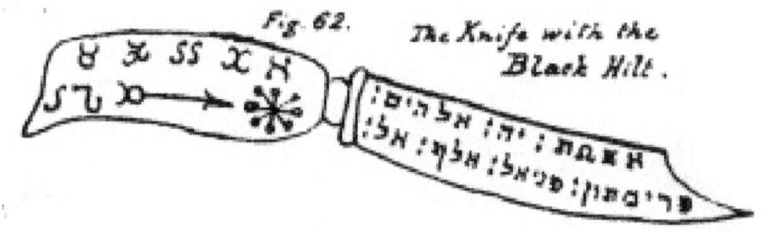

Fig. 62. The Knife with the Black Hilt.

The point to remember is that the pentagram and its variant the asterisk is a very old hieroglyph. Its precise grammatical meaning may be lost but knowledge of its magical power endures. Perhaps it was always emotive, coming straight from the unconscious. The pentagram is said to be related to the fifth letter of the Arabic alphabet isolated *Ha* sound (*He* in Hebrew). Al Buni says this and second seal originate in the *Koran*.

2nd Seal

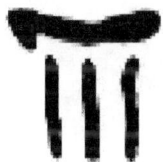

"*6.3:* And when he had opened the second seal, I heard the second beast say, Come and see. *4:* And there went out another horse that was red: and power was given to him that sat thereon to take peace from the earth, and that they should kill one another: and there was given unto him a great sword."

There is less to say about the second sigil. Ancient Arabic sorcerers saw the first letter of their alphabet (Alif), repeated three times. Al Buni says it is Koranic.

3rd Seal

"*6.5:* And when he had opened the third seal, I heard the third beast say, Come and see. And I beheld, and lo a black horse; and he that sat on him had a pair of balances in his hand."

If you rotate the third seal (*mem*) 90 degrees is does resemble a balance. It also looks like the Arabic letter mem (mim), perhaps "M" for Mohammed, although others cite a Biblical origin. Al Buni says it comes from the *New Testament* (Evangelists).

4th Seal

"*6.7:* And when he had opened the fourth seal, I heard the voice of the fourth beast say, Come and see.

8: And I looked, and behold a pale horse: and his name that sat on him was Death, and Hell followed with him. And power was given unto them over the fourth part of the earth, to kill with sword, and with hunger, and with death, and with the beasts of the earth."

Some see a ladder in this seal, on which the blessed may ascend to heaven. It is also a box-grid of nine squares or chambers well known in Kabbalah. The central square is could also be the marking out of the fourth part of the earth that perishes under the hoofs of the fourth horseman! Al Buni says from the glyph is from *New Testament* (Evangelists).

5th Seal

"6.9: And when he had opened the fifth seal, I saw under the altar the souls of them that were slain for the word of God, and for the testimony which they held: *10:* And they cried with a loud voice, saying, How long, O Lord, holy and true, dost thou not judge and avenge our blood on them that dwell on the earth?

11: And white robes were given unto every one of them; and it was said unto them, that they should rest yet for a little season, until their fellow servants also and their brethren, that should be killed as they were, should be fulfilled."

This sign occurs in amulets and is interpreted by some scholars as the Semitic letter *het* which is similar to the following Egyptian hieroglyph:[105]

The four strokes like four alifs could also be a reference to Tetragrammaton, the fourfold name of God. Four is also the number of Jupiter. Al Buni says its origins are in the *Torah*.

6th Seal

"*6.12:* And I beheld when he had opened the sixth seal, and, lo, there was a great earthquake; and the Sun became black as sackcloth of hair, and the Moon became as blood; *13:* And the stars of heaven fell unto the Earth, even as a fig tree casteth her untimely figs, when she is shaken of a mighty wind. *14:* And the heaven departed as a scroll when it is rolled together; and every mountain and island were moved out of their places."

---

105. N14 in the standard hieroglyphic sign list.

Al Buni says this sign also originates from the *Torah*. Other authorities see in this sign a hand gesture or even a phallus.

The 7th Seal

"*8.1:* And when he had opened the seventh seal, there was silence in heaven about the space of half an hour.

2: And I saw the seven angels which stood before God; and to them were given seven trumpets."

The Biblical text continues with the appearance of the seven angels with trumpets that sound to herald general death and destruction. It may also represent Arabic *waw* – which is the main conjunction in Arabic and when prefixed to some nouns gives them greater significance as in "I swear by". The seal might also represent the sound of those trumpets. Rotated 90° clockwise and it is an eye, benign, evil or eye of destruction! Destruction in Pagan thought is good and bad. Like the opening of the eye of Shiva, which sweeps away illusion along with much else, clearing the ground for something new in the world or within one's psyche.

Outside of a Christian Fundamentalist context, the *Book of Revelation* is an extraordinary example of a class of magical/apocalyptic texts of the late classical world. It is high magick, dealing with the ultimate *Gnostic* revelation. If my working hypothesis about these seals raises concerns about revealing too much dangerous knowledge, let me reasure you that something more is required for that. Despite all this drama, the later use of the seven seals is not invariable apocalyptic. They are used in different ways on charms with a wide range of intents. They are still widely used in the construction of magical squares as an alternative to the seven Greek vowels for example this power 7x7 and 8x8 amulets against misfortune (the first seal repeated at the end):

Usage

So in summary, I've presented the seven most prominent charaktêres or seals from amongst hundred of others. The entire body of charaktêres are in effect the freeform magical language that developed in late classical Egypt. They are new, spontaneous hieroglyphs used in the magick of the time. You may find that these seven are the only that one really needs.

The ring of power

I was asked to work magick to bring someone prosperity and success in their chosen career. For this I used material from two linked manuscripts from the Graeco-Egyptian magical library.[106] I was grateful for this opportunity as my own magical ring was a gift from another magician and didn't really require any additional work. I was provided with a rapid lesson in the magical power of such objects when I almost lost it. Those of you who have become attached to a wedding or engagement

---

106. Betz (1986 : 336) PGM IX . 10, XXXVI 342

ring will know precisely how that feels. It's surprising how much emotion one invests in a ring. Maybe there is a warning there.

The author of the spell in the magical library wrote in the tongue of his or her Greek masters. Even so he often added a note to remind himself of the Egyptian original. The second spell is an alternative to the first and uses some but not all of its recipes. The actual lines of the ritual can be found in the rites for the sun in chapter 7.

This little ring is for success and favour and victory. "It", the opening lines of the spell tell us, "makes men famous and great and admired and rich as can be, or it makes possible friendships with suchlike men. The circlet is always yours [to use] justly and successfully for all purposes. It contains a first rate name."

Having consecrated [the ring], wear it when you are pure. "Pure" in this context is probably another reference to priestly i.e., magical activity. A "wab" or pure is a grade of (part-time) priests. Thus the instruction is to wear the ring when doing the work of Egyptian Gods (Theurgy).

Such a ring, so the spell tells us, will enable you to, "get whatever you want from anybody. Besides it calms the anger of master and kings. Wearing it, whatever you say to anyone, you will be believed, and you will be pleasing to everybody. Anybody can open doors and break chains and rocks, if he touches them with the stone, that is, the gem and says the name written below. It also works for exorcising hostile demons. Just give it [to one to wear, and the daimon will immediately flee.]"

Some of this is hype, but all in all it is a useful and common enough artefact for a magick worker. The contemporary magician can and indeed unconsciously already has learnt much from these rituals. The ritual begins with a list of ingredients and then progresses to the ritual proper. The preparation for the rite starts with acquisition of a suitable ring, ideally one with a semi-precious gem. If you buy one with an existing inscription such as a permutation of the seven seals, it will still need to be "opened" or consecrated.

A sky blue Jasper; or green Heliotrope is ideal for this spell. According to Pliny's *Natural History*, heliotrope is a green chalcedony with small spots of red jasper. The "classic" bloodstone is green jasper with red inclusions of iron oxide (red jasper). The name "heliotrope" comes from the Greek *Helios* meaning Sun and *trepein* meaning "to turn", an ancient notion about the manner in which the mineral reflects light. Both stones are amongst several we might recognize as having solar qualities or *correspondences*.

The example used in the spell was engraved with the "Ouroboros" serpent – a serpent swallowing its own tail. This symbol is widely used on talismanic gems and is found on Egyptian monuments such as in the Tomb of Tutankhamun.

The "ouroboros" frames or encircles another image. These must have been magnificent and expensive objects. We also see here another way of "casting a circle". One of those snakes encircles the crescent Moon, with stars at either horn beside the name Helios. The Moon here is in the service of the Sun, being in the bright or "solar" part of the lunar month.[107]

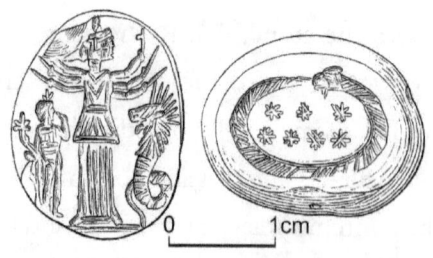

---

107. Cambell-Bonner Magical Gem Database, EA 56360A, 17th century gem shows Christ-Osiris with Greek words and charaktêres. See also Kirsten Dzwiza http://www.charakteres.com

This ancient example from the British Museum shows the Ouroborus with the seven stars. The reverse shows Harpokrates, Hekate, & Chnoubis.

In another ring the Ouroboros encircles the scarab beetle Kephra. This and the other ring designs are connected with the *young* Sun; the Sun at its freshest and most vigorous moment. In the Egyptian lunar calendar the Moon is similarly fresh when its first crescent appears on the second day of the month. For the Egyptians, the Sun, like the Moon, had a triple form. Khephra, the scarab beetle represents the youthful, rising Sun. Khephra means "to become". Ra as a falcon is the Sun God in his *prime*. And Tum, the Ram represents the *ageing* Sun, in his twilight years. And all three phases are mentioned in the ritual for "opening" or "initiating" the ring.

The reverse side of the gem stone was also used to bear various names in hieroglyphics and other languages but always with a clear solar connection. Examples include Helios, ABRASAX and IAO SABAOTH. ABRASAX or ABRAXAS by numerology using its Greek spelling totals 365, and thus corresponds to the solar year as mentioned in several other spells.[108] So you get the message – the solar imagery is reinforced, over and over again.

---

108. Crowley's well known solar ritual "Liber Resh" follows its own internal logic. Its cardinal schema is based on four Gods listed on the XXVIth dynasty stele of Ankh f n Khonsu, found at Qurna, Luxor, the so-called "the Stele of Revealing" viz Ra, Tum, Kephri and Hathor. See the translation he commissioned from two fellow occultists and Egyptologists Alan Gardiner & Battiscombe-Gunn. see Aleister Crowley (1988) *The Holy Books of Thelema*, NY p 253.

Timings for solar rites:

The ring can be consecrated at dawn facing the rising Sun. In the book *Supernatural Assault in Ancient Egypt* there is a discussion of the importance of dawn (the *Duat*) as a key twilight in Egyptian magick. The cult of the Sun, and the continuation of its course is one of the two major concerns of Egyptian religion, surviving into the *Corpus Hermetica*. The other being the protection of the mysteries of Abydos – the cult centre of the God Osiris.

I used a slightly different although equally authentic set of solar times. I did it three times each day at approximately the third, sixth and ninth hour of the Egyptian clock. These times have long be standardized to 9am, 12noon and 3pm. The threefold execution re-enforces the division of the Sun into three phases as dawn, midday and sunset. The rite was repeated for fourteen days beginning when the Moon begins its third quarter.

The ritual occurs during the moon's fall or dark trimester. This period is often associated with Horus. It is also what we might call the moon's absence, or "seizure" and therefore sun's strength. "Solar" and "lunar" rites are almost always mutually exclusive. Rites to the Sun being more often done on the "dark nights". Malign rites tend to cluster in the full Moon or period of "white nights" and this also corresponds with ritual information I provided for the correspondence between the Egyptian God Seth and the full Moon and Horus, his antithesis, corresponding with the new Moon.

It is recommended that the month be one in which the Moon is rising in Taurus, Virgo, Scorpio or Aquarius. When performing the consecration one is simultaneously to hold the ring (or object to be consecrated) in the smoke of the burnt offering. In my garden there is currently a small shrine over the tomb of my pet cat Aleister, who is now an "Akh" or otherworld helper. The shrine has a small brick altar on which I burn candles and incense to him and also the spirit of other household pets who have passed over, including Shoni the lurcher. I place the ring in a small chamber covered with a skylight and place the burning frankincense and cake of light in this chamber. I can leave the ring *in situ* for the entire period of the consecration without fear that some passing beast will carry it away.

The original consecration required similar equipment; a pit in a holy place open to the sky or a clean, sanctified tomb orientated to the east. An altar or platform of wood of fruit trees was built over this upon which a white goose, three roosters and three pigeons were sacrificed and burnt to cinders. Cover these offerings with all sorts of incense, although elsewhere it says avoid frankincense. Libate the cinders with wine, honey, milk and saffron and hold the stone over the smoke for the invocation.

We can surmise that all of these ingredients have solar qualities. In modern practice animal sacrifice is mostly avoided and since the time of early 19th century magus Francis Barrett, appropriate incense has been thought sufficient. Or, if you follow the nostrums of *Liber AL* "The best blood is of the Moon monthly" and the burning of a infused "cake of light" is widely considered to be more effective than animal sacrifice.

You need some appropriate words - the papyri give some very long examples that combine Hebrew, Greek and Egyptian elements. Using current research here's a restored version in the "original" Egyptian idiom. This invocation is rather long but one soon gets used to it. Almost every line implies a philosophical attitude and in order for the spell to work you have to have satisfied yourself that you understand and agree with this implicit theology. So even if you never use this spell – reading it, especially as part of a meditational practice is an important spiritual exercise. I'll first set out the whole invocation and follow this with a discussion of what it means to me.

I've shortened this somewhat as I suspect that over time parts that were once instructions have become incorporated into the words of power. The vibe is an address to the Sun, both visible and symbolic, as the pivot of the whole celestial hierarchy.

The text of the spell is included in chapter seven below as part of the ritual material for the Sun.

Hermeticism, and the inner meaning of magick spells

The following spell has a complex structure that is characteristic of "grimoires" of this time in Roman Egypt and elsewhere. These principles have universal applicability. The spell has five parts:

1. An address to the triple Sun
2. Assumption of the God form
3. Hymn to the All Lord (Demiurge)
4. Hexametrical Hymn to the All Lord
5. Invocation of the deity.

The theoretical counterpart of this magick is a set of short dialogues (Libellos) known as the *Corpus Hermeticum*. The *Corpus Hermeticum* belongs to a Pagan world that felt itself under threat from the rise of a new, fanatical religion that came to be known as Christianity. Under this onslaught, classical Pagans developed a new sense of their own identity as Pagans, and ralleyed behind a manifesto known as Hermeticism. Hermeticism combined the best elements of Greek, Babylonian and above all Egyptian magical religion. Hermeticism is part of a *fightback* and resistance to the rising tide of fundamentalism. Fundamentalism and fanaticism are exclusive religious views of the kind "we are right and everyone else is wrong". Unlike Paganism, the Christians were militant and viewed anyone who did not sign up for their army of God as a civilian, literally a "Pagan".

The *Corpus Hermeticum* represents a crash course in the main tenets of the Pagan religious view. It is the ancient equivalent of a magical correspondence course. In it we read that the candidate enters a fellowship of *like-minded* individuals, of both sexes, who share a common aim. Initiates of *all* levels of attainment gather *together* to learn of the Hermetic way from experienced adepts.

The ultimate aim of Hermeticism is to raise oneself up through a series of steps to a final state of "gnosis" in which one becomes like a God. The Hermetic magicians shared a common view, plan or to use a technical term, a cosmology. This divine plan was a hierarchical vision of creation as divided into a series of steps ascending from the base to the top of the pyramid or symbolic mountain. Creation implied a creator who stands above a divine hierarchy and from whom its various parts emanate.

Egyptologists call this system the Heliopolitan theology. Heliopolis is the Greek name for the ancient city of "Iunu", just outside modern Cairo. It was centre of the all important Solar cult.

The Heliopolitan theology is one of the most famous aspects of the Egyptian magical religion. It describes a holy family of Gods – Ra, Geb, Nuit, Shu, Tefnut, Isis, Osiris, Seth & Nephthys. It is the family relationship between these Gods that is so revealing of Egyptian theology.

The founder of the family, known as the All-Lord or All-Father, is the God Ra. Sometime round 1350BCE during the Kingship of Ramesses II, Egypt experienced some big religious changes. Amongst them was the rise to prominence of a God known simply as *Amun*. Amun means 'hidden one' thus we can surmise that this God signifies some sort of *hidden* or mysterious power. Amun may originally have also been some sort of "lord of winds" – understood as the bodily breath but also the four winds, which are sometimes personified as four primary couples:

Amun – Amaunet;
Nun – Naunet;
Kek – Kauket;
Huh – Hauket.[109]

Amun is therefore quite a complex cosmic deity whose cult eventually fused with that of the Sun God Ra. Thus the *All-Lord* or *All-Father* is also known as Amun-Ra. Although in Egyptian religion as in later Hermeticism this All-Lord is bisexual meaning male *and* female.

This system is well-known because it has survived in many inscriptions. Ra or Amun-Ra is translated into the Greek system as *Helios* – the sungod. In the *Corpus Hermeticum* and related practical texts, the ultimate Creator and source of the cosmos is often referred to as Helios. The Creator is assisted in the task of emanating the cosmos by other divine forces, most notably Thoth. The ideas of the *Corpus Hermeticum*, written in Greek, are entirely compatible with the Egyptian magical religion!

This Egyptian theological scheme can be arranged into a hierarchical tree, reminiscent of many later mystical arrangements such as the Golden Dawn "Tree of Life".[110]

The whole schema looks thus

Amun-Ra (Solar Crown)
Shu (Wind)   +   Tefnut (Fire)
Geb (Earth)   +   Nuit (Sky)
Isis + Osiris;   Set(h) + Nephthys

---

109. This is the "Ogdoad" – the theology of Hermopolis, cult centre of Thoth etc).
110. Hebrew: *Etz haChayim*; Greek: *Tetratis*

These God names have their Greek equivalents. In the Ring Spell transcribed above I gave them in their original Egyptian form based on a Greek text which actually renders them:

AmunRa	=	Helios
Shu	=	"Sender of Winds" (See also *Decans*)
Tefnut	=	Aphrodite
Geb	=	Kronus
Nuit	=	Mother of the Gods
Osiris	=	Osiris
Isis	=	Isis
Seth	=	Typhon
Nephthys	=	Esenephus (A phonetic writting of Nephthys)

The spell mentions a secret *unspeakable* name and this is also in keeping with a literal reading of Amun meaning "mysterious". So the theology of the spell is quintessentially Egyptian. This is also the basic theology of Hermeticism.

The opening dialogues or "libellos" of the *Corpus Hermeticum* introduce the idea that our universe was created, and the Creator God is both male *and* female. This mysterious God stands at the beginning of a series of divine emanations of which we and our earthly plane, are the final and lowest level. It was once thought that Hermetic texts were essentially works of the Greek mind with Egyptian local colour. Actually they are "Pagan" texts in the truest sense, combining the best of Egyptian, Babylonian and Greek magical religion. Indeed later magick is also a synthesis or pan-religious phenomenon – incorporating elements from Judaism, Christianity and Islam.

The "Pagan" or "Hermetic" way has changed little since it was codified in Roman Egypt. Magick is still widely seen as a path to spiritual liberation. Magick is the "path of return" to the source. The magician rises, ascends or transcends through ever finer layers of existence. Magical spells are more often than not aids to this process of ascent. In the classical world this was called "theurgy" – literally the "work of God". This approach is very old and is certainly part of the older Egyptian magical religion. One can see this in for example the ancient Egyptian *Book of Gates* which is all about this mystical journey that ends when the magician flings open the doors of heaven or gates of earth (*The Book of Gates*)

In the ancient world, Egyptian priests were reknowned for their wisdom. The above shows there was real substance to this view. In fact when it came to special knowledge of the divine names, high priests were a class apart. If you look at the fifth part of the spell, the Gods are hailed and welcomed according to the Egyptian, Jewish and other ways. The "High Priests" of Egypt get an additional mention in their own right!

Assumption of the God form

The second part of the ring spell is all about the "assumption of the God form", something still widely used in modern magick. The interaction between these priests, and I'd say adepts of the Egyptian magical religion is very intimate. The *Corpus Hermeticum* adopts a similar point of view, the magician boldly stating: "*I am* etc etc." This progression from "I *summon* you, x" through various stages until the magician states: "I *am* x" – implies that one moves from duality to identification/assimilation with God. The devotee merges his or her consciousness with the Divine. There is no reason to think all Egyptian cults, even that of Seth, understand it as so.

It is also noteworthy that the spell implies that the divine body and physical nature are counterparts – to use the familiar terms of the

Hermetica and other classical texts – they are connected as microcosm/macrocosm – "as above, so below".

Invocation & Devotion

Another crucially important thing that emerges from these rituals, especially with the invocation and hymn to the Sun-God, is the devotional side of magick. This gives the lie to all those commentators who suggest that magick is a purely technocratic pursuit.

The spell discussed above also provides us with an important example of the "vowel" magick described earlier. The magician recites a litany of 15 Godnames. The 15 recitations of the formulae may be *lunar* in intent – one for each day of the lunar half month. Each name is prefaced with the call "EI IEOU" – vocalised as "Ay IAOU". Is this pure vowel song - probably? Although some recent research suggests that in Egyptian this had an actual meaning - 'Oh Hail' (*ꜥI i3w*).

This ancient ritual to first consecrate and then use a magical ring of power is based upon Egyptian religious ideas and techniques. In fact the original title of the spell, written in Demotic, likens it to the very old Egyptian litany of "opening the mouth". This ceremony formed part of the mummification process but was also applied to the animation of cult objects such as statues, buildings and in this instance a magical ring. A long time ago I learnt that wearing a special ring or talisman is a good way to keep one's magical quest in mind during the hussle and bustle of mundane life.

Colour symbolism

The primary colours are:

Red Ochre	=	Fire / Blood
Yellow Ochre	=	Eternity / Gold
Copper Blue	=	Sky & Waters

Malachite Green	=	Living things
Carbon Black	=	Night, death and Osirian otherworld
Chalk White	=	Purity

To state the obvious, ancient Egypt was a very visual culture. Symbols abound and what we moderns call symbolism is still an important way of interpreting the underlying meaning of many things. Although not obvious from presentation in books, every hieroglyph, is coloured in a natural or logical way, ie red for the Sun and yellow for the Moon; the same darker tones used for men, and women respectively. Parts of the body are red, vegetation is green although some have a symbolic colour – hence bread is blue and metal sometimes red rather than black. Hair is black or blue. The Goddess Nephthys is blue, as often is the Ankh rather than the yellow one might expect for fabric. So colour correspondences are mutable, mostly for stylistic reason but also perhaps because of some principles we no longer fully understand. Thus the "knot of Isis" should be fabric yellow but is often shown as red or its *contrary* colour – green. Precious and semi-precious stones were utilised more for the colour opportunities they presented rather than other intrinsic qualities.

Number

1   Oneness – individuality & permanence. But often unstable as monads have an inherent capacity to create.

2   Duality & Unity. The God "Heruifi" in the *Book of Gates* has two heads, one of Horus and one of Set, which perhaps implies an underlying unity behind the duality. "Eternity" has two aspects – male (neheh) and female (djet).

3   Plurality – witness the ubiquitous hieroglyph of three strokes used to represent great number. See also the rare triple headed image of "Ash" which may represent plurality or the cyclical

nature of a thing. Egyptian liturgy is often repeated three times.

4   Totality and completeness - see for example the fourfold Djed pillar and also the four baboons often shown on the base of obelisks etc. Heaven is also envisioned as a four-sided canopy (see for example the heaven hieroglyph) but viewed from one edge or side so that one only sees the supporting poles nearest – hence two by extension here represents four.

5   Other numbers meaning is derived from principal four:

6   2 x 3

7   4 + 3 i.e. plurality and completeness 42 judges = 6 x 7

8   2 x 4 i.e. totality doubled

9   3 x 3 i.e. plurality trebled viz: a great number

10 Space & time. Ten days in a week but also a ten-day period or decan is a basic unit of measurement in astronomical charts.

12   The Egyptians were the first to divide the day into 12 parts or hours, although length of these hours would vary according to time of year.

The Egyptian "alphabet", "kabbalah" number, meanings

"What Ptah has created and Thoth has written down"

The God Ptah as patron of artists etc, crafted the hieroglyphic signs, as the shapes and names of everything. Thoth's role is to make the script that embodies the sounds of what was already there.

Because the world is so complex Ptah had to make more than 800 signs in order to fully describe everything. But underlying this is a basic structure of just 24 *phonemes* or alphabetic signs with which we can vocalise the name of all things in our world.

As time went by the number of phonemes expanded. Egyptian, like many ancient languages did not express vowels in the written script. This does not mean there were no vowels merely that their written form was kept as a scribal secret. The vowels can be considered as the hidden heart or "soul" of the language.

In the period when Egyptians were ruled by Greeks, the people spoke a less formal, vernacular form of Egyptian for which the Greeks coined the term "Demotic" meaning "popular". Egyptian Demotic was written in 28 signs. It is as well to remind yourself that the Greeks considered the lunar month to have approximately 28 days, as did many of the cultures that came after the Egyptian such as the Arab.

The Romans took over Egypt from the Greeks. This last period coincides with the final stage of the native language when it is becomes Coptic. The underlying language doesn't change but it is written in a mix of Greek and Demotic characters. The motivation for this change is probably the desire by Coptic Christians to dispense entirely with the "Pagan" hieroglyphs, whilst at the same time expanding the total number of characters to 30. Again remind yourself that the Egyptians considered the lunar month to have 30 days.

In order to understand and use Egyptian magick from this time, there is no need to fully understand the Egyptian language. Indeed the system now transcended any particular language and became international and universal. Nevertheless it is necessary to be aware of some of the basic building blocks derived from the original alphabet.

As I mentioned, there is a rough equivalence between the characters of the alphabet and the days of the lunar month. With the rise of Arab sorcery this relationship between the (Arabic) alphabet and the lunar days was maintained. It is from this stream of thought that a great deal of modern magick draws its inspiration and techniques. Aleph is the first letter in all these languages – Egyptian, Greek, Hebrew or Arabic. Aleph corresponds with or is the alphabet's *New Moon*. For me this is new and incomplete knowledge. But some things are certain. The following table shows the entire list of available Egyptian phonemes and a hypothetical correspondence to the lunar cycle: [111]

---

111. Twenty-five Greek characters and six retained Egyptian Demotic.

Lunar Day	Sign	Transliteration	Sound	Image	Numerology	Hieroglyph
1	ꜣ	Aleph		Vulture	1	
2	I	Yodh		Flowering reed	2	
3	y	y		Two reed flowers	3	
4	ꜥ	'ain		forearm	4	
5	w			quail chick	5	
6	b			foot	6	
7	p			stool	7	
8	f			horned viper	8	
9	m			owl	9	
10	n			water	10	
11	r			mouth	100	
12	h			Reed shelter	200	
13	ḥ		emphatic h	wick of twisted flax	300	
14	ḫ		ch as in loch	placenta	400	
15	ẖ		ch as in German	animal's belly with teats	500	
16	s			bolt	600	
17	š			pool	700	
18	ḳ		qoph	hill slope	800	
19	k		kaph	basket with handle	900	
20	g		hard g	stand for jar	1000	
21	t			loaf	2000	
22	ṯ		tj	tow rope	3000	
23	d			hand	4000	
24	ḏ		dj	snake	5000	
25		Epsilon			6000	
26		Eta			7000	
27		Iota			8000	
28		Omicron			9000	
29		Upsilon			10000	
30		Omega			100000	

Take 24 Characters of Middle Egyptian and add six Greek vowels to the end. (Coptic added six extra

4. The Temple or Imaginarium

What else is a temple but a representation, in material, of the cosmology of the people who built it? The temple represents the archaeology of gnosis, the sequence of a journey through the temple represents the initiatory journey to the 'holy mountain'.[112] It can be an imaginarium or House of all Possibilities, a theatre in which to locate one's magick. The Temple of Seti I is one of the finest such designs in the whole of ancient Egypt. There is a stele, found at Abydos, that refers to a place called the 'Stairway to the Gods' which may be an as yet undiscovered natural phenomenon. Alternatively, given its step like structure, the stairway could be the Temple of Seti I. It is full of magical knowledge if you know how to decode it. In the time I have been studying this temple, numerous important pieces of information and synchronicities have befallen me. Anyway, this is one suggested model for an imaginal temple.

In many cases I am going to reproduce the words of Omm Sety ('The mother of Sety') not an ancient Egyptian but a woman of our own times, born in 1904, died in 1981.

The following extracts are taken from *Omm Sety's Abydos* courtesy of Benben Publications, Society for the Study of Egyptian Antiquities.

112.1 E S Edwards *The Pyramids of Egypt* (Pelican 1947/1970)

'Autobiography: 'A Fall that Led to Abydos'

I was born in London, England in 1904, and was christened Dorothy Louise Eady. My father was then a Master Taylor, but later switched over to the cinema industry. Neither he nor my mother had any interest in Egypt, ancient or modern.

When I was three years old, I fell down a long flight of stairs and was knocked unconscious. The doctor was called; he examined me thoroughly and pronounced me dead. About an hour later he returned with my death certificate and a nurse to 'lay out the body', but to his astonishment, the 'body' was completely conscious, playing about, and showing no signs of anything amiss! Soon after this accident I began to dream of a huge and lovely building (which I later found out was actually the Temple of Sety I at Abydos). On waking, I would cry bitterly and beg to be allowed to go home. This longing to 'go home' became a joke in the family, and I was assured that I was at home, but I was equally sure I was not.

When I was four years old I was taken to the British Museum in London as part of a family party. Mother said I paid no attention to anything until we reached the Egyptian Galleries. Then I went simply crazy, running about and kissing the feet of all the statues that I could reach. When the family were ready to leave, Mother said I clung to a glass case containing a mummy and screamed, 'Leave me here, these are my people'. She was so surprised that she never forgot the incident.

When I was six years old I saw a picture of the Temple of Sety I at Abydos, in a magazine. I recognized it at once as the place I had always dreamed about, but was puzzled because the photo showed it to be somewhat ruined. I showed the picture to my father, told him it was my home, and that I wanted to return there. Of course, he told me not to talk nonsense. He told me that it was an old temple in a country called Egypt, and that I had never been there in my life.

When I started to go to school, I was bored to tears unless there was a lesson in which there was any reference to Egypt. So I got the bright idea of skipping school and going to the British Museum instead. Old Sir Ernest Budge, who was then Keeper of the Egyptian Collections, saw me nearly every day mooning around the Egyptian Galleries, asked me why I did not go to school. I replied that the school did not teach me what I wanted to know; I wanted to learn hieroglyphs. So he offered to teach me, and did so.

Then came World War I, and because of the air-raids over London, the British Museum was closed. I was sent to my Granny's farm in Sussex. There I regularly rode a large white horse (which I named Mut-hotep, after one of the favourite horses of Ramesses II) to the nearest town, Eastbourne, to borrow books on Egypt from the Public Library. So it went on, through the remainder of my childhood, through adolescence – always reading and studying ancient Egypt.

When I was 27 years old I went to work for a small organization run by some Egyptians whose aim was to publish a kind of public relations magazine, explaining the Egyptians to the English reader. While there, I met a young Egyptian who was on a short visit to London to study English educational methods. We exchanged addresses and for a year corresponded regularly. Finally, he wrote and asked me to marry him, enclosing a group photo of his family, decent upper middle-class people. I accepted but my parents refused. However, as I was over age, they could not stop me. Of course, I do not wonder that they refused. They were then living in Plymouth, Devon and had not met my future husband.

So in 1933 I set off for 'home'. When I landed at Port Said, I knelt down, kissed the ground, and swore that I would never leave Egypt – a vow which I have willingly kept. I was warmly welcomed by my new family and I settled down to *try* to be a good housewife. My poor anxious parents came out to visit us and when they met my husband they were charmed by him. In fact, Mother said that he was much too good for me. He, poor fellow, got the same idea, and after two years he got fed up with my haphazard housekeeping, really awful cooking, and passion for ancient Egypt. He decided to divorce me and marry his cousin, a nice girl who was a good cook and did *not* like antiquities. In the meanwhile I had produced our little son, whom I insisted on naming Sety, after my beloved Pharaoh. That is why the people here call me 'Omm Sety', meaning 'Mother of Sety'. Among the peasants, it is considered very impolite to call a married woman by her real name and so they refer to her as the mother of whoever is her eldest child.

After my divorce, I went to work for the Egyptian Department of Antiquities, first with Prof. Selim Hassan, who was excavating some tombs in the necropolis surrounding the Pyramids of Giza. It was a wonderful and rewarding experience, and I count myself favoured for having worked for such a brilliant and kindly man.

After Prof. Selim Hassan retired, I worked for Dr. Ahmed Fakhry at Dahshur, and again I was lucky in finding a wise and considerate boss. But in spite of the interesting work and kind treatment, my heart was set on Abydos. Since for many years my aim had been to work, live, die and be buried in Abydos, I had, of course, already been there on pilgrimage to the ancient Holy City. After Dr. Fakhry finished his work at Dahshur, he offered me the choice of a well-paid, comfortable job in the Records Office in Cairo, or a not well-paid and somewhat physically hard job in Abydos. Needless to say, I chose the latter! So in 1956 the first part of my dream came true.

The Temple of Sety I was then undergoing restoration and I was given over 2000 inscribed fragments of stone to catalogue, fit together and translate the inscriptions. The job took 2½ years.

I bought a small house on the edge of the cultivated land near the

Temple. In 1969 I reached the official retiring age of 65 years, so the Antiquities Dept, gave me a small pension and 'turned the old mare out to pasture.' I have a tomb prepared in my garden, in the ancient style and am now waiting for the second half of my wish to come true – to die and be buried here.

In the meantime, I am enjoying life, I have some very good friends in the village, seven cats, and a polite cobra who comes and goes as the fancy moves him. I consider myself to be a very lucky woman, and give heartfelt thanks to the ancient gods who heard my prayers and brought me home. Omm Sety, Abydos, May 1979

Abydos, The Holy City

Introduction

Since long past ages, and in all parts of the world, there have existed sacred cities or places, to which devotees of various religions have made pilgrimages - Mecca, Jerusalem, Benares and Rome, to mention just a few of them. However, the oldest of such holy places of which we have concrete evidence is Abydos in Upper Egypt. From scenes and inscriptions dating back to the age of the Pyramid builders (about 2700BC), we know that all worshippers of the god Osiris were expected to make a pilgrimage to Abydos to visit the most sacred tomb of their god, who had been worshipped there since even earlier times.

The ancient name of this Holy City was Ab-du, which means 'The Desired Mountain'. And Abydos is a Greek corruption of this name; its modern Arabic name is Arabet Abydos. Until recently the modern name was Arabet el Madfouna, which means 'The Buried Arabia'. Abydos was originally the necropolis of the nearby town of Thinis, the capital of Upper Egypt and the kings of the first and second dynasties had their mud-brick tombs there.

In very primitive times Egypt was divided into several petty kingdoms, each with its own ruler and its own local god. In the course of time these small kingdoms became amalgamated into two large kingdoms, Upper and Lower Egypt. In about 3200BC Mena-Narmer, King of Upper Egypt, made war on his northern rival, conquered him, and united the two halves of the country into one whole. Thus he became the founder of what Egyptologists call the First Dynasty.

For political reasons, Mena decided to build a new capital city at the apex of the Delta, a city later to become famous under the name of Memphis (a little to the south of Cairo).

For the same reason, Mena and his successors built two tombs for themselves, one at Abydos and another at Sakkara, the necropolis is Memphis, the latter probably being cenotaphs.

In those far-off days, Abydos was only a small hamlet housing the priests attached to the royal funerary cults, and to the service of a local god called Khenti-Amentiu. With the rise and spread of the cult of Osiris, and the institution of the pilgrimage, Abydos prospered and eventually became a large and important city. Its downfall came with the enforced abolition of the ancient religion in about 565AD; and today Abydos consist of three small villages; Beni Mansour on the north, Arabet Abydos (which is the most important) and Ghabat, on the south.'

The *Sem* priests wore leopard skin tunics during rituals. They are habitually shown grasping the lower paw of the pelt. It strikes me that this is another instance where magical practice tends to hark back to earlier, more primeval days. These same priests are also shown with a particular hair-knot, which is to say they are still technically in the child stage of life ie. Like the Brahmacharin status of Hindu priests. Unlike the Hindu priests, there is also a possible element of taboo breaking in the wearing of animal skins in the temple. The leopard's spots are said to be one of the marks of Seth, branded as a criminal for his murder of Osiris.

What follows is a fairly orthodox account of the Osiris myth that nevertheless succeeds in exposing some of the ancient seasonal cycle. The ritual year will be discussed in a later chapter. This account is, of course, that of one particular sectarian point of view, that of the Osirians.

The God Osiris

You may wonder why so much attention is about to be given to Osiris? However, whatever way you look at it, Osiris is an important part of the topocosm and always will be. It is also my working hypothesis that by deconstructing the primary centre of the Osiris myth, that the true nature of Seth and his journey will also be revealed.

'As Abydos is so closely linked with the cult of the god Osiris, It is better, before going any further, to mention what is now known about that god. The standard version of his story, as it was during the New Kingdom, was that Osiris, his two brothers Seth and Horus the Elder, and his sisters Isis and Nepthys were all children of Nuit, Goddess of the Sky, and Geb, God of the Earth. Osiris married Isis and Seth married Nephthys.'

[The Egyptians believed that when] 'Osiris became King of Egypt, the Egyptians were a totally uncivilized people. They lived in temporary settlements along the edge of the desert, dressed in the skins of wild beasts, and lived by hunting and herding wild cattle. They also indulged in human sacrifice and cannibalism.

Osiris taught his subjects the arts of agriculture and irrigation.

He showed them how to build houses of sun-dried brick and erect temples of the same material so that they came to live together in harmony in settled communities. Osiris gave them laws and education and even the skill of writing, using the hieroglyphic script invented by his friend, the wise god, Thoth.'

Sun-dried bricks remained the standard material for all domestic architecture in Egypt until the 19th century and is still used in all the villages. It was also used in parts of the temple, perhaps for convenience but maybe also for symbolic reasons connected with the past. Thoth, let me remind you, is the son of Seth and bears a striking resemblance to his father.

'The goddess Isis helped her husband in every possible way. She persuaded the people to cultivate flax and taught the women how to spin thread and weave cloth so that they could wear clean garments of linen instead of animal skins.

Both Osiris and Isis were dearly loved by their subjects. But their evil (sic) brother Seth hated Osiris and was bitterly jealous of his popularity with the people. Seth finally managed to pick a quarrel with Osiris, murdered him, and cut his body into fourteen pieces which he scattered all over Egypt.' [The symbolism of the numbers fourteen and indeed fifteen are important elements in the lunar mysteries of this cult.]

'As soon as she heard of this tragedy, Isis set out to search for the fragments of her husband's body, embalmed them with the help of the god Anubis, and buried them in the spot in which they were found. Another tradition says that Anubis and Isis assembled the embalmed fragments and buried them at Abydos. In the oldest versions of the story, which are found in the Pyramid texts, and date from the fifth

Dynasty, it is merely stated that Seth murdered Osiris at Abydos and left his body lying on the banks of the canal. It was found by Isis and Nephthys, embalmed by Anubis and buried at Abydos.'

It is interesting that a Jackal god, more renowned for eating corpses than embalming should be synthesized in the cult. The earliest ancient tombs were even shaped like Anubis's body with the corpse lying in his belly. Could it be, that the early hunter-gatherers practiced sky burial, leaving the corpses in special enclosures in the desert for that sole purpose? The remains of this massive enclosures can still be seen a few mile from Abydos. According to this version of the story, the head of Osiris was buried at Abydos. The heart was buried on the Island of Philae, near Aswan. The phallus was thrown into the Nile and was swallowed by a fish. For this reason the eating of fish was forbidden to the priests. A similar taboo exists in India and in Tantrism the taboo is reversed and the eating of fish is one of the five powerful enjoyments or Makaras. Note that the murder of Osiris actually takes place at Abydos, perhaps on the banks of old channel of the Nile that runs in front of the Temple of Seti I but is now dry. The official standard of the city of Abydos represents the head of Osiris on a stake

> 'At the time of his murder, Osiris and Isis had no children but by mystical means, Osiris achieved a physical resurrection for one night and slept with Isis. By this means she conceived her son, Horus, who was later to avenge his father's death.
>
> Seth seized the throne of Egypt and ruled as a despotic tyrant. Isis fled away to the north where she hid herself in the vast marshes of the Delta to await the birth of her son, Horus. She was joined by her sister Nephthys who, horrified by the crimes of Seth, left him forever.
>
> When Horus had grown to manhood, he challenged the right of

his evil uncle to the throne and after many legal battles, actual wars and trials of strength, eventually overcame him, avenged the murder of Osiris and regained the throne of Egypt. Horus ruled Egypt in the same high traditions as his father Osiris and became the type of the perfect Pharaoh. In fact, until the end of the Pharaonic period, all the rulers used the name of Horus as one of their official titles.

Some scholars think that the cult of Osiris originated in the Delta and that he was identified with a god named Andjty who was worshipped at Busiris (now Abusir el Malek). But it seems more likely that the opposite is true, because Osiris has always been represented as wearing the white crown of Upper Egypt and never the Red Crown of the North. There are others who believe that the story of Osiris contains a kernel of truth, and that he was an actual historical character, but when he actually lived cannot, up to now, be proved. In the writer's opinion, there is a possibility that Osiris and Narmer-Mena are the same person. For one thing, the people of Egypt before the first dynasty were a primitive people, but with the founding of that dynasty by Narmer-Mena, the Egyptian civilization sprung full-blown, yet purely Egyptian in character; it was not a foreign importation. Tradition says that Narmer-Mena was killed by a hippopotamus; Osiris was murdered by Seth, who sometimes took the form of a hippopotamus, as shown in the reliefs at Edfu Temple. Narmer-Mena was succeeded by his son, Hor-sha. The later had two tombs, one at Abydos and another that seems to have been a cenotaph, at Sakkara. In this, Prof. Walter Emery found an alabaster vase, inscribed 'Hor-sha the son of Isis', the only example of a pharaoh bearing this title. The name 'Hor-sha' means 'Horus the warrior'. So as the person later to be worshipped as the god Horus was indeed the son of Isis and was also a warrior, one cannot help wondering; it seems to be more than a mere coincidence. Furthermore, an ivory label found in the tomb of Hor-sha at Abydos shows him performing a ceremony in front of Narmer-Mena, who is clad in the traditional costume of Osiris!'

'Omm Sety's theory, was rejected by most Egyptologists, although the process by which historical characters were in later times regarded as ancient deities is fairly well documented in ancient Egypt and indeed elsewhere. There is another theory that the ancient methods of killing the moribund pharaoh (Heb-Seb), was by the use of a wild hippopotamus. The Heb-Sed festival fell on the thirtieth Jubilee year of the King. He had to run a race and if he failed he was killed and replaced. Some believe this is the origin of the motif of ritual kingship and indeed because of the time period the whole notion of the 'Saturn return'. This rite was replaced by symbolic race. Omm Sety had a vision in which the old King was killed in the Osireion, which has a water channel and connection to the Nile, perhaps for this purpose. In other words, Narmer-Mena may have been reenacting a much older custom. It is in the belly of Seth that the deceased 'king' is taken to the underworld, as was later depicted on the walls of the restored Osireion. This is another important metaphor from the ancient Near-East.'

'Mankind is indebted to Osiris for a decent, orderly way of life, a firm promise of resurrection and everlasting life, and a creed that made man responsible for his behaviour. For tradition says that because of his goodness on earth, the Great God (whom the Egyptians called 'Lord of All') appointed him to be king and Judge in the Otherworld. Each person after death had to enter the great Judgment Hall where, in the presence of Osiris, his heart, symbolizing his conscience, was weighed in a balance against an ostrich plume, emblem of absolute truth and justice. At the same time, the deceased must be able to deny committing 42 sins, and if his denial is false, his heart will speak up and contradict him. Whatever the outcome of the judgment, it was Osiris who meted out the reward or punishment. If the deceased was innocent, Osiris would grant him a place in his kingdom, Amenti (which means 'The West'), a replica of the earthly Egypt he loved so well. If the deceased was guilty, he was banished to a place closely resembling the Christian idea of Hell. There was no mercy, no death-bed repentance in the cult of Osiris; but the god in his wisdom, and remembering his own life on earth, took account of the reasons that led the deceased into sin and decreed a light or heavy punishment accordingly.'

This whole scenario lends itself to several different contemporary interpretations, including a shamanic ordeal to be encountered in this life, not necessarily post-mortem. The above account also shows that the ancient Egyptians were closer to the Hindu idea of Karma than they were to Christian one of sin. Of course the Tantrik ideal is to avoid Karma. If you have committed a supposed sin, it is not possible to change that state of affairs. It is, however, possible to alter how you *feel* about that event. The essence of the ordeal in the Judgment Hall of Osiris seems about how clear is your conscience, not whether you have done this or that 'bad' act. Part of the function of Seth's journey is deconditioning, so that you feel fully reconciled to those acts that are part of your humanity. Other ancient versions of the myth omit the 'negative confession' altogether.

'So Abydos has the honour of being the birthplace of this cult that later spread all over Egypt, and in Roman times was carried all over Europe, even reaching the misty isle of Britain, the existence of which the Egyptians had never dreamed.

A Brief History of Abydos

As the Egyptians did not have a fixed dating system, it is, with few exceptions, difficult to assign an exact date to a period or event. They dated events, monuments, etc., to the year of the reign of each king. Thus, we know the length of each reign only by its last dated monument; in other words its minimum length.

Approximately 4000BC Abydos was a small hamlet inhabited by priests who served the royal tombs of the Thinite kings of the first and second dynasty, and the small temple of the local god, Khenti-Amentiu, whose name means 'President of the Westerners', the 'Westerners' being a synonym for the dead. The modest temple of this god was built of sun-dried bricks and consisted of only three chapels and a small courtyard. With the deification of Osiris as ruler and judge of the Dead, he also was called 'President of the Westerners' and it was not long before the earlier god was fully absorbed and identified with him.

Abydos in the Old Kingdom
(About 2723BC – 2475BC.)

With the rise of the cult of Osiris, Abydos began to grow in size and fame. The old temple of Khenti-Amentiu had been enlarged, with stone masonry; its site was in the great enclosure, now known as Kom el Sultan (The Sultan's Mound). Here Prof. Flinders Petrie found what is still the only portrait that we have of King Khufu (Cheops), the builder of the Great Pyramid. It is a small statuette of ivory, only about three inches high, but so forcefully carved that the minute face fully expresses the iron will and determination of the man who reared a veritable mountain of accurately aligned and fitted masonry. The mysterious building, now known as the Osireion, probably dates to the Fourth Dynasty.

By the time of the Fifth Dynasty, Abydos had become so holy that

King Nefer-ir-kar-ra passed a royal decree forbidding any priest or lay workers attached to the temples and necropolis to be removed from their posts, and put to work in any other place. Any governor or high official who would infringe this law should have all his personal property confiscated and the offender himself consigned to the temple workhouse, to be employed in hard, forced labour. This decree, engraved on stone, was found by Prof. Petrie while he was excavating in Kom el Sultan.

Abydos in the Sixth Dynasty

By the time of the Sixth Dynasty, Abydos had become one of the most important cult centres in Egypt. Long since the goal of an obligatory pilgrimage, it is now also a favoured place of burial for private persons, the chief centre for the worship of Osiris, and the reputed site of his burial.

Pepy II, who came to the throne at the age of seven, and ruled for ninety years, took a great interest in Abydos. He rebuilt the ancient temple on a larger and grander scale. He also made a monumental gate of limestone in its temenos wall [that which delineates a sacred enclosure], and this is still standing.

Abydos during the First Intermediate period

Following the death of the aged King Pepy II, there was a complete break-up of the central government and a period of anarchy, now called the First Intermediate Period. No doubt Abydos, as the rest of the country, suffered during this time. General poverty as well as insecurity of travel would have reduced the number of pilgrims, yet, while no great monuments were now being built, several good tombs from the period are known.

It is towards the end of the First Intermediate Period that we get the first recorded example of the 'Curse of the Pharaohs'; King Khati of the Tenth Dynasty, who was one of the many petty rulers who had divided Egypt up among themselves, became ambitious. Apparently he had overcome most of his rivals and annexed their 'Kingdoms', and then turned his attention to the powerful prince of the Theban House, whose territory extended a little to the north of Abydos. A fierce battle took place in Abydos, during which some of the tombs were damaged. Following this, King Khati suffered some misfortune, and in a document addressed to his son, King Merikara II, he attributes his troubles to the desecration of the tombs, and says: 'Egypt fights in the cemetery, smashing the tombs. Thus did I myself, and the same happened as was done to one who transgresses against the way of the god. The town of Thinis, which was the southern boundary, I captured it like a waterflood. Be long-suffering in ruling that country, act wisely, having regard to the future.'

Abydos during the Middle Kingdom

Egypt gradually emerged from her period of chaos and eventually a powerful ruler from Thebes, Amenemhat I, seized control of the entire country and founded the XIIth Dynasty (2013-1785BC), one of the most glorious periods of Egyptian history.

By now the importance of Abydos was fully and finally established. The ancient temple at Kom el Sultan, cradle of the cult of Osiris, was enlarged and embellished and a new necropolis of private tombs and cenotaphs sprang up in its vicinity. The Temple of Osiris was entirely renewed by Amenemhat II (1849–1801 BC) and was surrounded by an immense temenos wall of mud brick. Influential persons were permitted to erect memorial stele or statues within this sacred enclosure.

From this period also we know for certain that the famous 'Mystery Play' of Osiris was being performed at Abydos. This, the oldest drama yet known, was performed during the annual pilgrimage. It consisted of seven episodes in the life, death and resurrection of Osiris, each episode taking place on a separate day. The king, or his deputy, played the part of the god Horus and other deities were played by the priest and priestesses of Osiris. The women playing the parts of Isis and Nephthys were traditionally supposed to be virgins, but as most of the priestesses were married, this may have presented a problem. Curiously enough, the part of Osiris was never played by a living man; he was impersonated by a life sized, jointed wooden statue. This reluctance to portray a divine personage by a human actor has persisted until modern times.'

With very little modification the ritual drama described by Omm Sety could be compared with the eight sabbaths of contemporary witchcraft, which may owe their existence to the work of Egyptologist Margaret Murray in collaboration with Gerald Gardner. According to folklorist Theodor Gaster, they may also be the origin of 'Punch and Judy' and the Mummer's play. Omm Sety now goes on to describe was known anciently as Pega the Gap, supposedly the route through which the souls of the dead made their way to Amenti, the Kingdom of Osiris, and through which they would return to re-visit Abydos on the occasion of the Feast of Osiris.

'At this time also, the sacred tomb of Osiris, the goal of the pilgrimage, was said to be at the western edge of the plain, near the gap in the mountains. In reality this was the mud-brick mastaba of King Djer of the 1st Dynasty. It appears that the archaic writing of this king's name was confused with Khenti-Amentiu, which was now one of the epithets of Osiris. It was to this tomb that all the pilgrims came, bearing offering of food and drink in earthenware or alabaster vessels. In the course of time, a veritable mountain of offering pots covered the whole area surrounding the tomb, and remains to this day. It is now known as Omm el Gaab, which means 'Mother of Potsherds'. It is still possible to find small, complete cups, and the modern local children believe that these are made by 'afreet' (ghosts) on a Wednesday, baked on a Thursday and may be found on a Friday morning. But after noon on Friday, no more will be found until the following week!

But there were secular as well as religious reasons why Abydos flourished during the XIIth Dynasty. Then, as until quite recently, the main route to the oases of Kharga and Dahleh in the western desert, lay close to Abydos, and government officials travelling this route on state business usually took the opportunity of making their pilgrimage to the holy city, and erecting a monument there to commemorate the event. The kings also were now making cenotaphs for themselves in Abydos. Senusert III (1887–1849 BC) built a splendid tomb and mortuary chapel at the southern end of the necropolis. This was clearly a cenotaph, as he was actually buried in a large brick pyramid at Dahshur, south of Sakkara. Two monuments from this cenotaph suffered rather undignified fates in modern times. One is a naos in crystalline limestone in which is seated a life-sized statue of the king. The local people dragged it to the edge of the desert, laid it on its back, and filled it with water for use as a cattle drinking trough! Perhaps not so inappropriate for a worshipper of the Apis bull. However, the Egyptian Department of Antiquities stepped in and rescued poor King Senusert from his ignominious fate! Cleaned and set upright, he now graces the second court of the Temple of Seti I.

The other monument is the lower half of what was once a very fine seated statue of King Senusert. The upper part, from the waist, is missing but the lower half and the throne on which he is seated is intact. Somehow or other, his majesty has gained a reputation for solving problems of infertility, and it is not uncommon sight to see wouldbe mothers seated on the royal lap. Curiously enough, it often works! Which shows how ancient a tradition of folk reverence can be.

Abydos during the second intermediate period

The Kings of the XIIIth Dynasty were a far different type from the wise and powerful rulers of the previous royal house. King Neferhotep was a well-meaning soul, and he decided to have a new statue of Osiris made for the old temple at Kom el Sultan. In order to be sure that the statue was correctly fashioned according to the ancient tradition, he went personally to the library of the great temple of Heliopolis, where there was a papyrus roll setting forth precise specifications for the construction of the various divine statues. He also personally supervised the fashioning of the statue.

It was not long before internal political disputes and struggles began to take place and taking advantage of Egypt's weakness, a hoard of Asiatic nomads invaded the country and made themselves masters of the delta and middle Egypt. They were called the Hyksos and their rule was a disaster for the country. Their domination lasted for about 150 years, and during that time the monuments were destroyed, the tombs plundered and the people persecuted. Eventually one of the princes of the old royal house of Thebes gathered enough supporters to raise an open rebellion against the Hyksos, and after many fierce battles finally defeated then, drove them out of Egypt into western Asia.

However, Hyksos domination never extended so far south as Abydos, which had quietly continued on its own peaceful way. Certainly no great monument had been built there during this period, and far fewer pilgrims were able to come and pay homage to their beloved god, Osiris. Nevertheless his cult continued to flourish, and people were still building their modest tombs and cenotaphs in the sacred necropolis.

Ahmes I (1580-1557BC) the heroic king who had finally driven the Hyksos out of Egypt, had made for himself a fine rock-cut tomb at

Abydos. In order to hide the whereabouts of this tomb, and to protect it against possible plundering, he had all the rock cut from its excavation carted to the edge of the desert, piled into a great heap, and cased with limestone, to form a false pyramid. In this, he played a good joke on posterity, for ancient tomb-robbers and modern archaeologists have spent many fruitless weeks of hard work tunneling through, under and around this 'pyramid' in a frantic search for the non-existent 'burial chamber filled with treasure'. Ahmes also added to the old temple of Osiris at Kom el Sultan and so popular was he in Abydos, that he was deified and his statue was regarded as an oracle.

Abydos during the New Kingdom

Amenhotep I (1557–1547 BC) the founder of the glorious XVIIIth dynasty, built monuments in Abydos in honour of his father, the heroic Ahmes I, and his dearly loved grandmother, Queen Teti-sheri. Amenhotep embarked on a project of making millions of mud-bricks for use in the rebuilding and restoring cities devastated by the Hyksos. In this work, it is known that he was employing thousands of Semitic workmen, which suggests that he might have been the pharaoh of the Bible. Many of Amenhotep's successors, the great warrior kings of the XVIIIth dynasty, embellished Abydos, and the massive walls, red granite doorways and thresholds of Thothmes III ('Egypt's Napoleon') may still be seen at Kom el Sultan.

But Abydos received its crowning glory at the beginning of the XIXth Dynasty (1312BC) when Seti I built his wonderful temple of Osiris, a masterpiece of Egyptian art and architecture that annually draws admiring visitors for all parts of the world. Seti also built here a temple on behalf of his father Ramesses I, another temple dedicated to the ancient kings of Egypt, and a small place for his own use which he called 'Heart's Ease in Abydos'. He also restored many of the monuments of his predecessors. Seti's famous son, Ramesses II, also built a temple here in honour of Osiris.

In the XXth dynasty, Ramesses III (1198-1167BC) gave some rich endowments to Abydos. The great Harris Papyrus mentions some of his gifts which included a temple of stone (so far undiscovered) equipped with priests and lay-workers to the number of 844, offering vessels of gold and silver, a new sacred barge of Osiris made of cedar wood, and a statue of himself.

Ramesses IV built a small temple for Osiris a little to the north of that of Ramesses II. Fragments from it have come to light, bearing rather flat and lifeless reliefs. Ramesses IV seems to have been a somewhat overbearing, even impious fellow, and a liar into the bargain. On an inscribed stele which he erected in Abydos, he not only claims to have made more benefactions than he had done in reality, but also he adopted a high-handed, almost bullying tone towards Osiris, demanding rewards for all that he had done. He says to the god: 'You shall give me health, a long life and a prolonged reign, sight to my eyes, hearing to my ears, and pleasure to my heart daily. You shall give me to eat until I am full, and give me to drink until I am drunk, and let my descendants rule as kings in this land for ever and ever. You shall double for me the long reign of Ramesses II, for I have done more for you in my four years of reign than he did in his 67 years'. What a nerve.

Abydos during the Saitic period

The XXIst dynasty was founded by Heri-Hor, High priest of Amon-ra, who seized power from the weakling Ramesses XII and thus began the disastrous rule of the priest-kings (1090–945BC). These well-meaning blunderers ruled Upper Egypt, with their capital at Thebes, while a family of Libyan origin governed the Delta. A son of one of these latter had a splendid burial at Abydos which still remained the coveted place of burial. But division is weakness and once more Egypt fell prey to foreign intervention.

The XXVIth dynasty (663–525 BC) brought a new period of prosperity and settled government to Egypt, which was again united under the rule of a powerful house. Their capital was at Sais in the Delta, hence the dynasty is usually known as the Saitic Period. At this time there was a tendency to look back to the great 'good old days' of the past and in religion, art and daily life there was a conscious attempt to revive the old styles, traditions and institutions.

Needless to say, this period brought a new prosperity to Abydos. King Ahmes II (the Amasis of Herodotus) (569–525BC) carried out some work there apparently having been prompted by his personal physician, a confirmed lover of the Holy City. The doctor, who rejoiced in the name of Pef-nef-di-Neit, had been on a pilgrimage to Abydos and found things not at all to his liking, Apparently the Governor of Abydos at that time was one of those who believed 'feathering one's own nest'. He had neglected the temples and the fields of the sacred estates. On top of that, he had taken away the free ferry-boat that used to ply between Abydos and the Nile, and took for himself the 'duty' paid on all goods entering the Nile Valley from the oases of the western desert, the 'customs office' being situated in Abydos. All these short-comings Pef-nef-di-Neit reported to King Ahmes, who gave him an order on the treasury (an ancient 'blank cheque') and sent him off to Abydos to put matters right. He performed his task to everyone's satisfaction, except the Governor's! The latter was dismissed from office and all his property confiscated. The funds from the stolen customs duty was now used to build tombs for the poor of Abydos, and the free ferry was again put to its proper use. In recognition of his service, he was permitted the honour of erecting a statue of himself in the court of the temple of Osiris. This statue, which is inscribed with the story of the doctor's exploits, is now in the Louvre in Paris.

During the Saitic Period the cults of the sacred animals began to gain prominence and, at Abydos, there was a large and important canine cemetery. At the Old IInd dynasty enclosure (the original purpose of which is not certain) mummified ibis-birds sacred to the god Thoth, were buried in earthenware jars. The modern name for this enclosure is Shunet el Zebib which means 'the storehouse of raisins'. But this is surely a corruption of the ancient name of Shuna pa Hib, meaning 'the storehouse of the Ibis'.

Abydos during the Graeco-Roman period

The sacred reputation of Abydos was maintained all through the Greco-Roman period (332BC until the Vth century AD). Strabo and other classical writers visited it and recorded its wonders. The beautiful temple of Seti I had gained a reputation for healing, and sick people were allowed to sleep in one of its courts in order that a dream might reveal a remedy for their illnesses. Many returned, cured, to write or scratch on the walls expressions of gratitude for their recovery.'

Prostitution was well known in the Holy City. Omm Sety tells us that in addition to these graffiti, which were written in Egyptian, there are others in Greek, Phoenician and Aramaic. Sacred sexuality and so-called sacred prostitution is discussed in a later chapter.

'Sad to say not all these scribblers turned their thoughts to sacred matters. One fellow mentions nothing about his recovery from sickness, but left a detailed and glowing account of the anatomical perfections of one of the 'ladies' of Abydos. She must have been a well-known character, because someone else came and wrote underneath the first inscription saying, 'I agree with you, she is everything you say - but to my mind, she is too short.' Human nature does not change much.

Incidentally, the custom of sick persons going to sleep in the sacred places has not yet died out. There are several tombs of Moslem holy men in the neighbourhood of Abydos where sufferers go to pass the night in the hope of a cure, and very often, not in vain.

It was in Roman times that an oracle of the little dwarf god, Bes, appeared in Abydos and became very famous. It was finally prohibited by a Coptic saint named Moses, in the VIth century AD

With the final downfall of the ancient religion, Abydos became for a while a Christian stronghold and several churches and monastic buildings were erected there, often of stones taken from ancient monuments. One of these churches, dedicated to Saint Damiana and Saint Moses, was built in another 2nd dynasty enclosure, a little to the north of Shunet el Zebib. It is still in regular use by the Coptic community in Abydos.

Since the day when a Christian emperor of Rome ordered the burning of the Egyptian temples, the murder of the priests and the pillaging of the sacred treasuries, Egypt has undergone two changes of national religion. The modern inhabitants of Abydos, simple peasants, know nothing of the ancient religion, yet they and their neighbours for miles around, still come to the temple of Seti and the other monuments, imploring help in their problems from powers whose names they do not know. Abydos has not quite lost its sacred reputation, which it has held for almost 6000years, can any other religious centre in the world rival this claim?

The Temple of Seti I

Having given a very brief outline of the rise and decline of the city of Abydos, it is time to consider its most important monuments. Of these, the most famous, beautiful and best-preserved is the Temple of Seti I. It stands on the eastern edge of the desert, and dominates the village of Arabet Abydos. The entire building was completed during the reign of

Seti I (1313–1292 BC), as well as all the beautiful bas-relief sculpture. Unfortunately, the decoration of the building was incomplete at the time of the King's death, and so the reliefs on the exterior, and in the first hypostyle hall were carried out by Seti's son and successor, Ramesses II. He filled up all the blank walls with scenes showing himself adoring the gods, and also left long inscriptions on the façade of the temple reminding us what a good boy he was to complete his father's monument!

King Seti I

Before describing the temple, let us have a glimpse of the career of the man responsible for this masterpiece, King Seti I.

The XVIIIth Dynasty, which had begun so gloriously, seemed doomed to end in disaster. Akhenaton, the heretic king, lost the great Egyptian Empire through sheer neglect and his weak and incompetent successors worsened the situation. Fortunately for Egypt, General Horemheb, an upright and far-seeing officer in the army, seized the throne from the corrupt old King Ay, and proclaimed himself King of Upper and Lower Egypt.

Instead of trying the now hopeless task of regaining the Egyptian Empire, Horemheb set to work to set the internal affairs of the country in order. He cleansed the corrupt government, introduced land reforms, and drew up laws for the protection of the falahin. Apparently Horemheb was childless, as he nominated as his successor his friend and brother officer, Ramesses, who had also been acting as his vizier. When Horemheb died in 1315BC, this man ascended the throne as Ramesses I and founded the XIXth dynasty.

Ramesses I, who came of an old established military family living in the eastern Delta, had a son named Seti, also an officer, who before his father's accession had been Commander of the Eastern Frontier garrison in a place now called Kantarah. But on reaching the kingship,

Ramesses I recalled Seti to Thebes, to act as his vizier. But Ramesses was now an elderly man and after a brief reign of two years, he died and was succeeded by Seti. The latter proved to be one of the finest rulers that Egypt has ever known. He completed Horemheb's internal reforms, restored peace and security to the Middle East, built many beautiful monuments, as well as restoring older ones that were falling into decay. He was also a kindly, humane man, thoughtful of the welfare of his meanest subjects. On one occasion, he heard that the conditions of life in a gold mine in the eastern desert were so bad that the workmen (convicts sentenced to hard labour) were dying like flies. Instead of sending an official to investigate the complaint, Seti insisted on going himself. Apparently the situation was very bad, and the men had insufficient supplies of fresh water and food. Seti remedied the situation by having a well dug and vegetable gardens planted. He then made a decree ordering that every man working in the mine should have a daily ration of ten loaves of bread, five bundles of fresh vegetables and two large slices of meat; also *new* clothes twice a month. One hardly expects a king in those far-off times to trouble himself over the welfare of some convicted criminals; one would rather expect the reaction to be, 'They die, so what? Plenty more where they came from.' No wonder some ancient texts say of him, 'you spread yourself in protection over the common people. The youth of the nations, you know their needs, and you supply them.'

A DESCRIPTION OF THE TEMPLE

The temple, enclosed by a vast temenos wall of mud-bricks, occupies a site that slopes from west to east. This meant that it had to be artificially leveled into four steps, rising up from the east, before ever a stone could have been put in place. According to an inscription, Seti was commanded by an oracle to build the temple in this unpromising site.

The main fabric of the building is fine limestone from a quarry in the neighbourhood, with roofing-slabs, architraves, columns and doorways, all parts under great stress, of Nubian sandstone. The plan, instead of being the traditional rectangle, resembles the Roman letter L in reverse. The space between the eastern and southeastern part of the temenos wall and the short 'arm' of the L was occupied by a royal reception hall and twenty magazines. These were all built and paved with mud-brick, but had limestone columns, doorways and window grills.

Immediately to the east of the temple was a quay, built of sandstone, on the banks of the old Nif-wer channel, which once connected Abydos with the Nile.

Then comes a level space, (originally paved), from which a fine stairway leads up to a terrace. This stairway, as most of those in the temple, consists of two sets of steps with sloping treads, and having a ramp between them. It has now been restored on the foundation of the original. The terrace, the front of which was decorated with war-like scenes relating to Ramesses II, supported the massive, but now ruined First Pylon.'

The design of the temple, with its gently slopping stairways and ramps perhaps facilitating long 'snake-like' processions on festival days.

The First Court

'A great doorway in the centre of the pylon (only opened on special occasions) gives access to the First Court, the walls of which were decorated by Ramesses II with scenes of his battles and triumphs. Unfortunately most are badly damaged, but on the south wall, there still remains a large scene of Ramesses returning after a victory, bringing a number of prisoners-of-war. His pet lion runs beside his chariot. On the north wall is a very natural representation of Ramesses about to mount his chariot; he places one foot on the floor of the car grasps

EGYPTIAN MAGICK — THE TEMPLE ᛝ 199

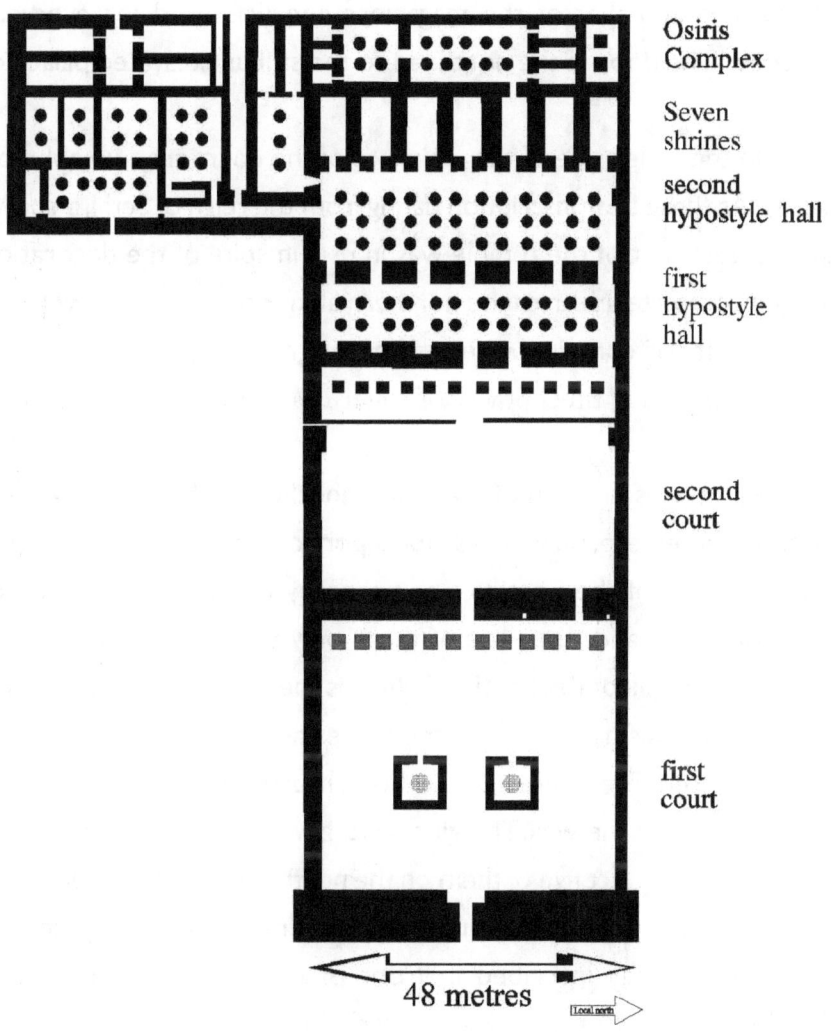

the front rail with both hands, and is about to spring up into the vehicle. In each of the southern and northern walls of the court is a small doorway. The south one opens from a passage between the wall of the temple and that of the magazines and was used for everyday purposes. The door in the north led to the still unexcavated palace of Seti.

On the other side of the main axis of the court are two ablution basins. As these bear inscription dating from the reign of Seti I, it shows that at least part of the temple was in use, in spite of the decoration being incomplete. Near to the northern ablution basin, is the well that fed them. It still contains water and never grows dry.'

The purifying ritual power of water is a feature of most religions ever since.

'At the western end of the court, another double stairway leads up to a low terrace, on which stood a portico fronting a pylon shaped wall. The roof of the portico was borne by twelve square pillars of limestone and sandstone, but of these only the lower parts remain. On the west wall of the portico (which is the eastern face of the false pylon) Ramesses has recorded the names and figures of some of his many children, The figures of the boys, mostly damaged, are on the southern half of the wall. The girls, who have fared better, are on the northern side, in fact five of them on the north wall are almost perfectly preserved, and very pretty and elegantly dressed girls they are. All have their names inscribed in front of them. The middle one is Tenpitnefert, which means 'Happy Year'. Presumably she was born on New Year's Day! The last one is Merit-neter, 'God loves-her'. Some ancient Egyptian personal names have a somewhat puritan flavour!

The Second Court

On the days when the great central doorway was closed, access to the second court was through a small door in the northern end of the false pylon. The wall scenes in this court have quite a different theme. On the east wall are shown some more of the royal children, but on the north and south walls, Ramesses is shown offering to the different gods. In other words, while in the first court he brags about his battles and victories, here he is 'behaving himself', and being nearer to the temple, shows his religious devotion to the gods.

At the west end of the northern wall is a curious alteration. The last two religious scenes have been partly erased and in their place is a gigantic figure of Ramesses. It was never finished, but seems intended to represent him binding a captive enemy. Near by is a large stele, built in one with the wall of the court. On it is a long inscription recounting all the benefactions that Ramesses made of the gods of Abydos. A similar stela exists opposite, on the south wall, near it, is an ancient well.'

It is my hypothesis that the changes to the design of the temple, made by Ramesses, represented the beginning of a movement away from Seti's own philosophy. Given what Ramesses put in this place, (and the kind of rituals that occurred in this part of the second court) it seems likely to me that the erased images were relating in some way to the cult of Seth *and* Horus. These are not the only iconographic changes made by Ramesses and his family. I believe that it was at this time that stone masons were instructed to carefully incise the Seth-animal from the cartouche of Seti. The Seth-animal functions, as a syllabic sign in the script, thus the name of Seti-mer-en-ptah, would be spelt with the Seth animal as the first character. The erasers only missed three examples of the syllable, all in the sanctuary of Amon Ra. You can see an example of their work on a statue of Seti now in the British Museum.

The Second Portico
'At the western end of the second court, a flight of steps, divided as

usual by a ramp, ascends to the second portico and the façade of the temple. The roof of the portico (now restored) rests upon twelve rectangular limestone pillars on sandstone bases. They stand six to the north and six to the south of the main entrance to the temple. Each face of every pillar is adorned with a representation, mostly showing Ramesses being embraced by a god or goddess, as well as some depicting the now dead and deified Seti I. On the sides of the pillars flanking the main entrance, we see Ramesses about to enter the temple, On the northern side of the entrance he appears as King of Lower Egypt and wears the Red Crown, while on the southern side he is in his role as King of Upper Egypt and wears the White Crown. In both scenes he wears handsome toe-thong sandals, the front of which turns up in a graceful point. The fact that he is wearing sandals shows that he is supposed to be still outside the temple, as once inside the holy place of the gods he must go bare-footed.

The western faces of some of the pillars, which were protected by the roof of the portico, still retain much of their original colouring.

On the northern wall of the portico are two large scenes. That to the east, which is outside the roofed part, shows Ramesses symbolically clubbing a bunch of Egypt's Asiatic enemies, who kneel in terror before him. The god Amon-Ra helpfully offers him the curved war-axe. This ceremonial sacrifice of enemies had long ago perhaps been an actual fact, but there is evidence that since at least as early as the XVIIIth Dynasty it was merely symbolic. The prisoners were led in front of the temple, made to kneel and the King lightly tapped them with his mace, and let them go. The poor wretches must have had a few bad moments if they did not understand the nature of the ceremony!

The second scene is under the roof of the portico, and so has retained much of its colouring. It shows Ramesses (still outside) wearing his sandals. He is reciting the offering formula in front of Osiris, an act which will magically provide an inexhaustible supply of food and drink for the god. The same formula was also recited for the dead, and for the same purpose.

At the northern end of the west wall of the portico, which is also a facade of the temple, is a small doorway for everyday use. Next is a very large coloured scene. The gods Horus, and the ram-headed Khnum, take Ramesses by his hands and lead him to the Temple of Ra-Horakhty at Heliopolis. Here he stands before the sacred Tree of Life, and the god writes his name upon the leaves. For every leaf so inscribed the King will rule for one year. As Ramesses reigned sixty-seven years, Ptah had plenty of writing to do.

There is a belief among Moslems in Egypt that in Paradise there is a tree called 'Tree of Destiny', which bears as many leaves as there are people in the world. Each leaf bears the name of each person living, but in the middle of the Arabic month of Shaaban (which is followed by the fasting month of Ramadan), the tree shakes, and the leaves bearing the names of those persons destined to die in the coming year fall down. It has long been the custom for children to gather in groups at sunset on the evening of the fateful day, and go round the streets singing: 'O Lord of the Tree of Destiny, make our leaves strong and green upon its branches. For we, O Lord, are Your little children.'

The vaulted chapel of Amon-ra

The eastern half of the chapel of Amon-ra is rather badly marred by smoke blackening, as well as by wanton damage to the figures, as this chapel was also coloured during King Seti's lifetime. In the first scene of note on the northern wall, Seti, wearing the costume of a ritual priest come to wash the statue of Amon-ra. The god, dignified and stately has his flesh coloured blue, as is usual in his representations. Egyptian religious tradition said that men were created from the tears of the god. The name 'Amon' means 'hidden' or 'mysterious', and the ancient hymns to Amon refer to him as:

'Thou art the One,
Maker of all things that are;
the only One, maker of what has been.
For whose eyes men came forth
at whose word the gods came into being.'
It was also said that no one knew his form.

In the following scene, the god represented is the ithyphallic Min, giver of fertility to man, beasts and crops, but he is referred to as Amon-Ra in the accompanying inscription.

On the upper part of the western end of the southern wall is a beautiful scene showing King Seti burning incense in front of the sacred boat of Amon-Ra. The latter is a truly splendid vessel, its prow and stern adorned with great golden rams' heads, the ram being the sacred animal of Amon-ra. Behind the great boat are two smaller ones belonging to Khonsu, the son of Amon-Ra, and Mut, the wife of Amon-ra. Each boat has a figurehead representing the deity to which it is dedicated.

Immediately below this scene, Seti presents vases of perfume to Amon-Ra. It is interesting to see that the accompanying inscription recording the speech to be uttered during this rite, is taken word for word from the Pyramid texts, written nearly two thousand years earlier.

extracts from Omm Sety ends

The 'three' forms of Ra

Storytelling can be a useful way of exploring the imaginal world. The presence of an audience, adds the necessary element of dialectic that can be so conducive to magical intuition. It was whilst preparing a story for a session that I came upon the following passage, which is so relevant to the shrine of Amon-Ra.

It comes from Margaret Pinch's *Magic in Ancient Egypt* (BM 1994 p. 30-1). It is extracted from the *Turin Magical Papyrus*, which has a long section on charms to cure snake venom.

The same manuscript has a similar story concerning Horus and Seth whereby Seth is compelled to reveal his true name, and therefore nature. It is also an important point of contact between the Egyptian and Tantrik traditions. The power to deal with deadly snake venom is one of the celebrated abiltities of Ayurvedic physicians, a brand of medicine with much in common with Tantrism. See my *Tantra Sadhana* for details about the caste of Matanga sorceresses, whose skills were used by the Buddha to counteract serpent infestation. It is perhaps significant, that the hieroglyph that in the Egyptian language is used to connote 'goddess' is the striking cobra. It may be a coincidence but the same image is worn by Shiva as an earring.

In my rendering of the Egyptian story I have taken the liberty of interpolating an episode from the mythology of Parvati, Lady of the Mountains in the tantrik tradition. She also constructs a magical child from the sweat of her body.

> 'Isis was a wise woman who was familiar with millions of gods and spirits. There was nothing in heaven and earth that she did not know, except the secret name of the sun god Ra. Isis decided to find out the name of the highest of the gods. Ra had become old. His limbs trembled and he sometimes dribbled.'

And when Ra dribbled it would often fall to the earth. And Isis, the magician, took the saliva of Ra and hid it in a safe place. Then she began to dance, gently at first, but soon, as the mood of exaltation took hold of her, her movements became more frenetic and soon she was dancing round and round in wild abandon. Her feet beat the earth to keep time. And still she danced, and when she was exhausted, and could dance no more, she stood still, her whole body quivering and shaking with lust and earth energy. Now her whole body was hot to the touch and her skin glistened with her own sweet smelling perfume of sweat. And Isis took her own sweat and put it with the saliva of Ra. And Isis mixed it all with some clay. And out of this clay She made a snake and animated it with her magick. Isis hid the snake near the path taken by Ra each day.'

Ra left his palace to walk through the land. The magick snake bit the highest of the gods and then disappeared. Ra cried out. The gods who were with him asked what had happened. Ra could not answer. He trembled as the venom penetrated his body as the Nile irrigates the land. He was blinded by the poison. Ra could not identify what had poisoned him, so he ordered the deities who were the most skilled at magick to attend him. Isis diagnosed that Ra had been bitten and claimed that she needed to know his name in order to cure him.

Ra told her that he was the god who had created heaven and earth and that it was he who made the Nile rise. Darkness fell when he closed his eyes and it became light when he opened them again. His names were Kephri in the morning, Ra at midday and Atum in the evening. The venom continued to circulate and Isis said that Ra's true name was not contained in what he had told her. The fiery pain became unbearable, so Ra allowed knowledge of his name to pass from his body to hers. Then Isis the great magician, conjured the venom out of Ra.

This is still a secret and is not revealed in manuscripts. Perhaps this is why some invocations say:

'In the name, and in the name and in the secret name of'

Simple way of using this model

Use it in your magick. If it helps then take on the form of Seti, who is in this instance the representative of any human operator in the temple. I have pictures of Seti, carvings and indeed of his mummified body, one of the finest surviving and still a beautiful thing.

Seti took his name from the god Seth, who was worshipped in Seti's native province. He did not alter this when he moved to the holy city of Abydos. Seth is sometimes seen as the evil opposer, but try to think of him (or her) as a human being. Many of his supposed crimes, as we shall see, are actually very human indeed.

It can help to construct an imaginal journey to the temple. You come to the temple via the river Nile, the floods are over and navigation is possible. A the boat brings to the oasis of Abydos via a very ancient channel called Nif-Wer. The ferry stops at a special jetty and you, along with other pilgrims alight.

The sacred enclosure of the temple is delineated by a high wall made of mud bricks. This is the temenos of the entire sacred enclosure. Move through the temenos and towards the eastern front of the temple proper, the stone built pylons forming a massive ornamental gateway in the Egyptian temple style. The wooden doors of the temple are shut. This is not the normal way to enter the temple, these are ceremonial doors, and are only used on special festival occasions, when the images of the gods inside are brought out through them and paraded on special boats. There are several other entrances into the temple, depending upon your status and experience. But before moving on, take a good look at the face of the pylons. They are decorated with two full size reliefs, representing two apparently opposing principles that the temple aims to reconcile. You may also see the colossal sculptures of gods, representing similar principles, perhaps male and female, spirit and matter, dark and light. If you can see the top of the pylons, you will see seven flags, the hieroglyphic symbol of the gods or *Neters*.

Now move on. Your way in is via a small door in the northern wall of the temple, near its corner with the eastern pylon front. There may well be an 'official' stationed here to ensure the correct etiquette is observed, shoes are removed etc. You may also buy special offerings for your devotion, usually bread and a small clay pot of beer.

Once inside, you see two square ablution basins in the centre of a perfectly square courtyard, open to the sky. Wash yourself, removing any unnecessary associations of your journey. Look around you. Depending upon time of day and season, different part of the relief on the walls will be clearly visible. But in general the images are of Ramesses II and his various achievements in the outer world. For the ancient Egyptians, warfare, imperial expansion and defence of secure borders were pinnacles of earthly achievement. Accept this, try to see the essence that lays behind it, and give it your own meaning, what the equivalent might be. Pause for a while and explore this.

When you are ready, move towards the western wall and the second pylon; from the hot overhead sun (if it is daytime) to the shade of a portico. As you do so, your steps are slow as you climb a gentle sloping stairway to the next level about five feet higher than the last. Others are here, perhaps passing some of the fruits of the temple – divination, sacred objects and food, blessed by contact with the holy of holies. Move on beyond this, through the central doorway into the second courtyard. (Some are allowed to sleep in the courtyards, and elsewhere as an aid to dream incubation).

This is similar to the first court, but more refined. You have moved further towards the west and away from the grosser, but still important elements of the spiritual life. There are different images to be seen representing physical achievement but closer to home than those described earlier. They concern such things as the joys and responsibility of family in all its aspects; the outer observances of festivals and religion; the mysteries of water and of the ecology of the river Nile. Pause for a while here and observe the difference in the imagery as the light shifts and changes. Further to the west is another portico. Once again you must climb a small staircase or ramp rising about five feet under the portico. Now you are just outside the temple proper. Only someone pursuing their true will can pass beyond this point. Notice before going any further, the symmetry of some of the images, again remind yourself of opposites that need to be reconciled. Here are images of Horus and Seth, shown in a unified form.

Now move through the central doorway into the dark interior of the temple. You are confused. Everything is dark and you are in a labyrinth or forest of papyrus pillars. Strange noises, sights, smells and sounds assail you. Sometime a shaft of light and oil lamps illuminate a particular image, try to remember this and record its meaning later. For this experiment, stick, as far as possible to the central pathway through the pillars. In front of you are in fact seven vaulted, cave like shrines of equal prominence. Seven is a special number in this system, very special indeed. Your first task is to remind yourself of the origins and thus you keep to the central colonnade, that leads you inexorable and through gentle rising steps to the vaulted shrine of Amun. As you approach the height of the room decreases with every step. Just outside the shrine are two phallic and colossal statues of Min. You must pass between them, acknowledging each day the sexual nature of your being. Before you is the vaulted, womb-like shrine of Amun. The door is locked. An iron bolt, known as the finger of Seth, is held in place by a clay seal. If you think you have the understanding, then break this seal perhaps with the words:

'The finger of Seth is withdrawn from the eye of Horus and it is well. The cord is undone from Amon, the sickness is unloosed from the god.'

Now the doors may be opened and you can look inside. Try to remember your first impressions. The actual form of Amon is unknown, thus his name means *mysterious*. All the historical imagery such as Baphomet, The Goat of Mendes, are metaphors for the creative vortex. Sometimes the image is blue to represent more of the mystery. The image is about your own size and will be facing you from an ornamental wooden box. Beyond this image you can see other strange things. There is a diaphanous veil or screen and beyond this the hint of a secret door.

You may wish to make an offering, saying:

'I offer what is in my hands'.

If you have nothing in your hands, then offer your hands, laying them on the god, meaning that you will later do some work on the god's behalf. If you don't feel ready for this, then leave your offering in a niche, that you will find outside the shrine, in the wall between this shrine and the next one. You might consider performing the orthodox function of the priest, then do to the god, what he/she would like. Primarily this means to clean and tidy the shrine, to change the god's clothing and decoration and to leave some food and drink, taking away the offerings of previous times (this will be given to pilgrims in the temple courtyards).

When you have done, sweep the floor as you retreat, obliterating your footprints and then close the door, replacing the seal with one of your own that you can remember. When you are ready, either explore a little further as is your will or return the way you came. Mentally repeating the process in reverse.

I suggest that this point of contact with the creative Amun is the basic practice that should be done before moving onto other deeper mysteries. End the ritual as taught, and do some vibration of god names to make sure you are fully *earthed* and everything is finished.

Directional Orientation

Ask yourself what is the largest flow of energy in your immediate vicinity? The ancient Egyptians had a clear answer to this, the river Nile. According to Margaret Murray, this accounts for the precise compass orientation of the pyramids of Giza, as the Nile flows precisely north-south at that point. There is an interesting principle here that can be applied in any locale. At Abydos the direction of the Nile indicates what is called *local* north, (it differs from magnetic north by several degrees.) The whole temple is orientated to local north.

Meanings

The whole exercise is really about building inner landscapes as a theatre for your magick. The courts could be connected with the following mysteries: The mysteries of material success, which was represented by Ramesses I (Seti's son) as his military victories. Bear in mind that the Egyptians recognised no radical distinction between religious and military purposes. The mysteries of earthly love including family and friendship. The mysteries of water and especially the sacred river as the nurturing source of all life. These were depicted as androgynous river gods, one for each of the *nomes,* as they termed the adminstrative provinces of Ancient Egypt. The mysteries of magical religion in its exoteric form, i.e. as official religion and its relationship to the ruler and the ordinary people.

5. Initiation
The Classical Mystery Cult

A detailed account of the workings of the later mystery cults dedicated to Isis is recorded in Apuleius' Latin novel *The Golden Ass*. This story concerns Lucius who sets out on a quest to learn the secrets of magick but also to find sexual love. He is tricked and cursed, being metamorphosed into an Ass. The story is all about initiation and rebirth. The Ass in this period is very much viewed as an avatar of the god Seth, and therefore the enemy of Isis. The story is in turns hilarious, bawdy, tragic but then liberating. As mentioned above, when the goddess does appear it is as a saviour: hence in the "hymn" she says "I am here taking pity on your ills; I am here to give aid and solace".[113] The transformed Lucius becomes an initiate of the Iseum in whose vicinity he has been rescued. The novel's final chapter recounts in some detail the workings of the mystery cult into which he is inducted. Most expert commentators see this element of spiritual regeneration as the innovation made by Greek and Romans to an otherwise Egyptian tradition. Indeed traditional Egyptian temples may well have been modified or supplemented to accommodate this new cult activity.

Often overlooked, *The Golden Ass* could be classed as text of the

---

113. Gwyn-Griffiths *The Isis Book* (1975 : 77)

Hermetic tradition. Other aspects of the mystery cult do have a clear Egyptian background, the most obvious being that it is Isis, who is the goddess into whose cult Lucius is initiated. The rhythm pattern used in the Greek texts is even said to replicate the shaking of the sistrum viz U – – UUUUUUU where U is a short syllable and – long).[114]

Whilst Lucius is still in his lowly animal body he overhears the allegory of Cupid and Psyche, which is another tale of metamorphoses that Gwyn-Griffiths feels could well have originated in the Egyptian world. It is also a story that resonates with the Indian culture especially what we might call the *tantrik* tradition. It is a tale of Psyche's sexual awakening through her connection with Cupid, then their separation and continued yearning, itself a sentiment that can engender a transformation of consciousness.

Psyche embarks on a quest to find Cupid and this erotic feeling is a prelude to their union with god but also the achievement by both of immortality through commitment to sexual love. These are all important aspects of Hindu esoteric lore.

Meanwhile for Lucius, his liberation is about to occur in Cenchreae, a place that in the ancient Greek world functioned as the harbour of Corinth. Here he experiences an epiphany, Isis appears to him in a dream, and she tells him to seek the annual procession at the beginning of the shipping season on the 5th of March. This is a form of the goddess adumbrated in very ancient Egypt, where Isis as patroness of boats, the sea and of navigation. Hence her name Isis *Pelagia*, "mistress of the sea", a popular form of the goddess at the time evidenced by the large numbers of Alexandrian coins which bear her image. She is shown holding the situla, the breast shaped libation pot and the sistrum.

Ultimately this role in connection with navigation is one she took

---

114. Gwyn-Griffiths, *The Isis Book* (1975 : 348)

over from Hathor, whose head regularly adorned the prow of the sacred boat of Sokar, an ancient Underworld god and precursor of Osiris.

In *The Golden Ass* the liberation of Lucius from his asinine disguise occurs at the blessing of a special boat in honour of the goddess. Here, at the head of this procession a priest holds a bouquet of roses, emblematic of Isis. Lucius is to eat those roses and this act will miraculously return him to human shape.

The magick of *The Golden Ass* is another feature that connects it to the Egyptian world-view. Hence here and in another work of Apuleius, *the Apology*, two kinds of magick are mentioned but with only an arbitrary distinction based on whether their instigator is Typhon ie Seth or Isis. The purpose in either instance would often be morally ambiguous. This is similar to the distinction made in early Christianity, where all pagan magick is "bad" by definition whilst Christian magick is "good".

In the story many important instructions and revelations come to the characters in dreams. Once again this view of the dream time as the theatre of magick is one with a long history best instantiated in the Egyptian tradition where the idea is first articulated.

Mystery Cults

The goddess Isis promises to end the cursed existence of Lucius who has been turned into an Ass. The mechanics of his transformation, the eating of the roses, had been transmitted to him via the same dream discussed above. Given the despised status of the Ass in ancient and indeed modern society, one must wonder how the creature will bring this off given the routine cruelty meted out to these lowly beasts of burden. Luckily Mithras the priest has been instructed via his dreams to let it happen. In another dream Lucius communes with the goddess who tells him his fate is to be initiated into her mystery cult. In "Pagan mystery cults ... the initiate is given a share in the fortunes of his or her

Forchner G (1988) Die Münzen der Römischen Kaiser in Alexandrien, Frankfurt
www.coinproject.com

deity, and by means of ritual dying and rising, attains salvation".[1] In this the initiate is identified with Osiris, the husband of Isis. Her command to Lucius is that he should "enrol your name in this holy service, whose solemn oath you were asked to take not long ago, and vow yourself from this moment to the ministry of our religion. Accept of your own free will the yoke of service."

His religious vow is likened to a military oath, a feature of other mystery cults of the time. Interestingly one of the possible meanings of "Pagan" as used by early Christians is "civilian" ie one who has not enrolled in the army of the Jesus.

Initiation

The first initiation of Lucius follows several older Egyptian patterns. First he prepares with a ten day fast or dietary restriction. Egyptian weeks were also divided into ten days. His initiation begins on the evening of the final day, a symbolic death during the hours of the night. He begins with a ritual purification or lustration. These rites were staged in a special underground crypt beneath the Iseum. Here there is also some kind of arrangement for the pre-initiation baptism and lustration. In Egyptian temples there were sacred lakes for the same purpose.

With the *uninitiated* "far removed", the candidate assumes the posture of Osiris, not in a coffin but on a special ritual bed, perhaps modelled on that used to re-assemble Osiris after his dismemberment by Seth. The culmination occurs nominally in the sixth hour of the night with a vision of the sun-god in the Underworld. This is also the moment in Egyptian religion when the sun god was remade anew each day.

We can assume that the candidate was in a deep hypnotic sleep; according to Plutarch this was induced by burning special incense he calls *Kyphi*. It could also be induced by the administration of a mild narcotic such as the Egyptian Blue Lily (*nymphaea caerulea*) known to influence dreams and widely used in Egyptian and indeed later Hindu esoteric rites. All of this is entirely in accord with the schema set out in ancient Egyptian books of the afterlife such as *The Book of Gates*. At dawn the candidate is reborn with the sun.

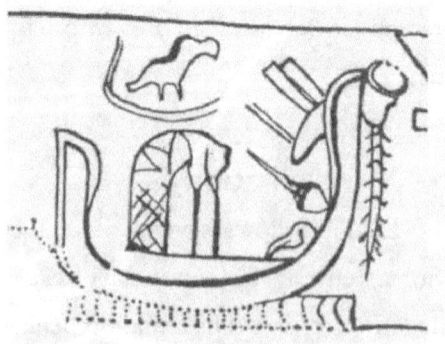

Sokar barque

Egyptian temples of all periods often do contain special crypts but this is much more obviously so in those temples built during the late period under the patronage of the Greek and after them the Romans. At Thebes in Upper Egypt one finds a collection of local temples that have been so adapted. At Karnak, an entire suite of rooms, the so-called Opet, was attached to the temple of Khonsu, complete with several crypts. A few miles further south is the temple of Isis at Deir el Shelwit which also has a crypt. There is another ruined temple in the Valley of the Queens, a small temple possibly dedicated to Thoth in Habu village, nowadays known as Qasr el-Aguz (lit. the castle of the old lady) and a large temple of Hathor close to the pharaonic worker's village of Deir el Medina. There was even one lost local shrine connected with Seth, although thus far only a few small relics of this have been found. All of these are part of a late classical mystery cult and are suggestive of a ritual sequence of rites connecting all these shrines. The best preserved of these at Karnak had its own dedicated entrance gate cut through the Temenos wall, facilitating activities set apart from those of the main temple campus.

Initiation visualized

As an exercise in "experimental archaeology" here is an imaginative reconstruction of the candidate's journey culminating with initiation into the mystery cult. The setting are the already mentioned complex of small temples in ancient Thebes in Upper Egypt. Your first initiation will be into the cult of Isis. For some weeks you have been living in special accommodation in the small Roman town that surrounds the temples of Isis at Deir el Shelwit. You exercise by walking to the nearby cultivated fields and beside the irrigation canals and lakes.

West of the town, beyond the fields, begins the desert where people only venture to bury their dead in the mountain necropolis. The desert is the domain of dangerous animals, wild dogs and wolves who howl in the night. Although there are well trodden paths across the desert, your mentor advises you to beware of some of the creatures who have no inhibition against attacking a person when they are alone or defenceless. Beyond the low desert, mountainous cliffs rise up to form the Libyan plateau.

You cast your mind back over the period leading up to your initiation. As the fateful day approaches the rhythm has changed. You now spend the best part of your time reading sacred books in the temple, sometimes discussing an obscure point with a mentor known as Hierogrammatos. He is a scribe in the service of the temple, a priest who interprets sacred texts for you and guides you through the process of initiation. Mostly you meditate in the quiet rooms set aside for this within the temple proper. You make a point of only eating simple food, which invariably means vegetarian, nothing to over stimulate the senses. You have also cut down on wine, preferring to drink pure water sometimes prepared with a calming cordial made by boiling hibiscus herb and allowing it to cool to a delicious sustaining drink. Everything is designed to calm the senses and to avoid nourishing negative thoughts. Some say these thoughts are like daemons that should not be fed.

Your mentor has already recommended that you pay special attention to *The Book of Gates*. You know it almost by heart and find it comforting. You feel it will be your guide in the transition to the new life that awaits you.

You mull over the events of what will soon be your old life. You think about the chain of causes that has led you to this moment and about the new life to come. It is a period of incubation, almost as if you will give birth to a new you, it reminds you of how the philosopher Socrates spoke of himself as the *midwife* of knowledge. The Egyptian way of reckoning things says there are ten days in every week. They also say that ten months is the period of time a mother incubates a baby in her womb.[115] In your meditation each day of the ten corresponds to one of those ten months; so as each day progresses, you become ever more mature and ready for rebirth.

Other things your mentor told you, that once seemed obscure and required much thought, now begin to make sense. He asked you to make a decision about the emblems to be present at your place of sleeping on the last night. He made you think about the design of the beds in the temple sleeping chambers. They all have four legs, but these are carved to resemble those of particular animals. The head-boards have been individually carved with one of three animals. You surmise that it is one of these animals that will carry you over to the otherside during your night journey. Those animals are the fearsome hippo, the cow with the sun suspended between its horns, and the leopard. All three are rich in symbolism. It dawns on you that your mentor is asking you to consider the nature of each of those beasts as it relates to your transformation. In what sense are you like a hippo, cow or leopard? The hippo does not eat meat but is extremely fearsome, especially when protecting its territory or young, the cow is a symbol of Isis herself, powerful but also nurturing. The leopard is a carnivore whose form represents pure, naked power.

The fateful evening arrives, the eve of the New Moon. You bathe in the temple baptistry, a brick lined sacred lake east of the temple. You change into a simple full length robe of natural, undyed cloth. Your mentor leads you to the special chamber in which is a comfortable couch in the form of your chosen animal. On it is a mattress of folded linen. There is a small table, upon which there are two small terracotta jugs;

---

115. Egyptians began the count from 1 rather than 0, hence 10 rather than 9 months.

one filled with water, the other contains a mysterious substance which your mentor tells you to drink, promising that it will be pleasant and help you through the night. This done, you settle down on the couch. Your mentor reads the familiar lines that open *The Book of Gates* (My rendering of the full text in next chapter but other versions are available for adapting and use. I'd also recommend other underworld books such as a detailed version of the *Amduat* available from Mandrake.

As your mentor reads, you drift into the world of sleep and *dreams*:

"You who came into being from Re,
from his Glorious Eye.
Granted to you is a hidden seat in the Desert.
Come together all those created by the Gods.
The God has taken your measure in the Necropolis.
As he does for all those living on this Earth;
created as it is, from his right eye, the Sun.
The desert is bright,
I give it light,
With what is in me.
Souls of the West, those who would destroy humanity,
my glorious Eye is on you.
I have ordered the destruction,
destruction of the enemies of Ra;
of the enemies of those upon the Earth,
where the chosen ones are.
Breath be given to you, among whom I am
Let there be rays for you,
dweller in the region of offerings.
To you is restored the diadem in the desert.
To you is restored the diadem in the necropolis.
The Gods shall say:

Painted reliefs in the Opet depict special mythological scenes. One of the most enigmatic in all, Osiris been visited by a night bird complete with phallus.

Special entrance connecting the Opet to the Khonsu temple (left) at Kharnak

"Your presence is commanded by the great God,
He who lifts up his arms and moves his legs; as shall you,
Come to us, you who share his essence; and say
Hail to the One in His disk,
Great God with numerous forms."

The Egyptians divided the period between sundown and sunrise into twelve equal parts called hours. Although you sleep through this whole time, you are roused at the beginning of each hour by the sound of a priest reading the appropriate section from *The Book of Gates*. Each of its twelve chapters corresponds to each of the hours. You are momentarily excited by those words before again lapsing into sleep. Your dreams keep pace with the lines as you rest, half heard and half remembered. In those hours you dream of entities and your soul's journey from dusk to dawn. In the silence it is as if you are watching a drama at the theatre or observing the progress of a night pageant. Sometimes you are one of the actors in the drama:

"*1st Gate*
At the first gate, a large serpent stands
His name guardian of the desert is upon the door.
He opens for Ra, and those upon the Earth,
Full with the chosen ones of the Gods.
Your mind as a God speaks,
from the prow of the sun-boat
Saying to the wise serpent: Guardian of the Desert"

You hear lines concerning the star goddess and you recall how you've been taught that she is also a form of the goddess Isis, your patron. In the morning you rise, reborn:

"On the sun boat of the morning, lifted by the Abyss
Abysmal waters surging up, from the faraway world.

Kephra the sacred scarab,
As new sun born through the eastern mountains
Isis and Nephthys bearing him up,
to the waiting Goddess of the sky.
Who stands above this earthly sphere,
out of the old and into the new,
You are lifted into her arms,
Mother of the Gods, Nwt."[116]

You wake refreshed and renewed. Details of your visions during the night journey are for you. One ancient initiate commented on the whole experience thus:

"I approached the boundary of death and tread on Proserpine's threshold, I was carried through all the elements after which I returned. At midnight I saw the sun flashing with bright effulgence, I approached close to the gods above and below and worshipped them face to face". [117]

In *The Golden Ass*, the ancient hero Lucius does not remain in the temple but resumes his normal life. He moves to Rome where he takes up residence in the Iseum Campensis and after a further gestation period of nine months is offered a second initiation on the winter solstice. A third initiation swiftly follows. In all Lucius is initiated as priest of Isis, then priest of Osiris, then of Isis & Osiris together.

---

116. Based on Alexandre Piankoff (1974) *Egyptian religious texts and representations*, 6 vols, Bollingen 1974. The complete rendition is published in Rodgers & Maskell, *Contemporary Western Book Of The Dead*, 2012 : 168sq

117. Gwyn-Griffiths, *The Isis Book (Apuleius of Madauros, Metamorphoses, Bk XI)*, 1975 : 52

6. Books of the Nightworld (duat)

The *Corpus Hermeticum* are a collection of texts written in the twilight years of Egyptian pharaonic culture. The Renaissance classical scholar Meric Casaubon dismissed the idea that they were the work of an ancient priest or demi God called Thoth. He correctly recognized their provenance as late Roman Egypt. Far from debunking, this vital time adds greatly to their meaning and significance. They are the last testament of Egypt, writing whilst it was increasingly caught in the triple net of Christianity, the Roman Empire and Islam. Many Egyptologists now view the "theurgy" of *The Corpus Hermeticum* as the final legacy of Egyptian religion.

So to end I wanted to reintroduce some of the older, mythological books of the Egyptian magical-religion. This is the font from which the authors of the *Corpus Hermeticum* drank. Popular studies on Egypt have made famous *The Book of the Dead* or *Book of Coming Forth by Day.* Less well known but perhaps more significant are a series of Underworld books such as *The Book of Gates* and *The Book of Caverns.* The sequence of Egyptian religious literature begins with the Pyramid texts, closely followed by the *Coffin Texts. The Book of Coming Forth by Day* is a compilation derived from these earlier books. Next in sequence of composition are the *Underworld Books.* Their secret location in royal tombs implies they were intended for the eyes of the initiated.

The *Book of the Dead* is not really a book in our understanding of the term. It is not a continual narrative, it's a compendium, in papyrus form, comprising linked spells offering practical help to the deceased. There are spells for provisioning (feeding) and protecting the dead as he or she makes their ascent from the grave to the heavenly realm. Early sections addressed the wish for family re-union in the afterlife. The deceased begins their journey at dawn and reached heaven in several distinct steps (see Spells 144-147). One of these steps is the compulsory appearance and judgement before Osiris.

The Underworld Books present an *occult* counterpart to the above. These are coherent, illustrated books, charting mysteries such as the fate of the "Sun at Midnight". The Egyptologist Erik Hornung describes them as religious phenomenon founded in the resurgent New Kingdom circa 1600BCE. Compositions such as *The Book of Caverns*, *The Book of Gates* and the *Book of What is in the Netherworld* share a new religious sensibility.

Copies of these books are painted on the famous tombs of various New Kingdom Pharaohs. Fine examples are found on the tomb of Sety I in the Valley of the Kings. And the entire *Book of Gates* is carved onto his wonderful, alabaster sarcophagus currently displayed in the John Soanes Museum, London. Another example, *The Book of Caverns*, is carved on the walls of his "mortuary temple" at Abydos. These locations lead one to deduce that they were protected from profane eyes. Jan Assmann says "they are codifications of cosmological knowledge that belonged to the solar cult and constituted the basis of its successful practice." [118]

All these books chart the nightly journey of the Sun from death at sunset to birth at Sunrise. The Sun's journey is also the odyssey of the soul. The Egyptian word for soul (Ba) is identical with the word for Ram - the iconic image of the Sun-God. The Sun-God is thus our guide and role model, through various times and situations in our life on the journey from Death to Life and Life to Death.

Reading these books become a little easier when one takes account of ancient literary conventions. For example the "discourse" is arranged

---

118. Assmann (2001 : 64)

in "registers", most commonly three, to represent the sacred river Nile between its two banks. The central register, as your might expect, is central. The activity on either bank is interesting but peripheral.

The beginning, middle and end of the journey are priviledged moments. At midnight the sun faces a difficult ordeal. He is reunited with his "corpse" which perhaps represents the memory of his/her previous self. Assisted by the God Seth he must overcome the serpent Apophis, "demon of non-being". The famous God Osiris may make an appearance but is always passive and never speaks.

The *Book of Caverns* envisions this journey as the traversing of six spaces or caverns of the underworld. The *Book of Gates* charts the same journey as it progresses in time through the 12 "hours" of the night. The *Book of What is in the Netherworld* maps it in terms of movement of the constellations. It is the same journey with different maps.

The average Egyptian found many of these ideas challenging and difficult to comprehend. Special edited versions were produced for the perplexed or struggling. A whole class of mythological papyri is almost entirely pictorial with text kept to a bare minimum. The heart of the matter can be reduced to a handful of mythological scenes.

Here is one famous episode from one of those pictorial versions:[119]

One can focus on it as preparation for the inevitable journey. I suggest each of us would benefit from the drawing up of a personalized version of that scroll. This could encapsulate traditional elements together with personal insights from research but also dreams, memories and reflections that are sure to assail you when you undertake this task. The selection of Egyptian liturgy below includes my own rendition of the *Book of Gates*.

---

119. Alexandre Piankoff (1974) *Egyptian religious texts and representations*, Vol 4, Mythological papyri (Papyrus Her-Uben B) Bollingen

THE BOOK OF GATES
A PROSE ARRANGEMENT

I suggest this could be read during the 12 hours of the night or the night watch. The journey through the mountains of the East and West is something achievable in life and indeed at death. If the latter then these lines could be used during the long night before the burial or cremation and over the coffin of the deceased or perhaps addressed to a death mask or photograph (the modern equivalent).

You who came into being from Re, from his Glorious Eye.
Granted to you is a hidden seat in the Desert.

Come together all those created by the Gods.
The God has taken your measure in the Necropolis.

As he does for all those living on this Earth;
created as it is, from his right eye, the Sun.
The desert is bright,
I give it light,
With what is in me.

Souls of the West, those who would destroy humanity,
my glorious Eye is on you.

I have ordered the destruction, destruction of the enemies of Ra;
of the enemies of those upon the Earth, where the chosen ones are.

Breath be given to you, among whom I am
Let there be rays for you, dweller in the *region of offerings*.

To you is restored the diadem in the desert.
To you is restored the diadem in the necropolis.

The Gods shall say:
"Your presence is commanded by the great God,
He who lifts up his arms and moves his legs; as shall you,
Come to us, you who share his essence; and say
Hail to the One in His disk, Great God with numerous forms."

1st Gate

At the first gate, a large serpent stands
His name *guardian of the desert* is upon the door.
He opens for Ra, and those upon the Earth,
Full with the chosen ones of the Gods.
Your mind as a God speaks, from the prow of the sun-boat
Saying to the wise serpent: *Guardian of the Desert*,
"Open the Netherworld for Ra,
Open the door for the *One of the Horizon*.
The Hidden Chamber is in darkness,
Waiting for him to create his forms anew."

You and the God sail through,
On the winding waterway,
The great door closes after you,
which makes the dead souls wail.

2nd Gate

Sentiments drift, an hour already, floating in the Hidden Chamber,
You are at the second gate of the night,
guarded by the wise serpent,
the one called *The encircler*.

"Open the gate", call the Gods,
"For the One of the Horizon, has arrived; throw open the door,
For those who are in heaven, Hail, come, let them pass
travelling in the west."

"Open the door", my mind says:
"Open the door for Ra,

throw open the door for the One of the Horizon,
where he lightens the complete darkness,
and makes the Hidden Chambers bright."
You and the God sail through
On the winding waterway,
The great door closes after you,
which makes the dead souls wail.

3rd Gate

The great serpent of time unravels, the hours before,
the hours to come,
The trembling centre of the Earth, where earthquakes live.

A hungry ghost, slipping deeper, deeper in the primal waters,
An ocean of souls, a sea of story,
folding and unfolding before & after.

Mistress of food is the name on the gate, she opens the earth,
guarded by the spitting cobras, those who light for Ra, the sun God.

The Gods say, "You have opened the earth,
You have opened the door, O Heavenly One,
Ra uncovers those who are in darkness,
Hail, Sun God, come to us"
Mind says to Serpent, *Stinging One*, who sits upon the gate,
"Open for Ra,
throw open the Netherworld for the *One of the Horizon*,
While he lightens the complete darkness,
and makes the Hidden Chamber bright."

You and the God sail through,
On the winding waterway,
The great door closes after you,
which makes the dead souls wail.

4th Gate

Jackals circle and prowl, on a gate called *She who acts*,
Warmed by the wise serpent, *Flame Face* guards the door.
The company of heaven say: "Let us open for Ra,
Throw open our gate for *Horus of the Horizon*.
Hail Ra, Come to us, Great God, Lord of Hidden things"

Your mind as a God speaks, from the prow of the sun God's-boat,
"Open the door, open for the *One of the Horizon*,
Let him lighten the complete darkness,
and make the Hidden Chamber bright."

You and the God sail through,
On the winding waterway,
The great door closes after you,
which makes the dead souls wail.

5th Gate

Twelve Gods stand on the outer wall, *Mistress of Duration*'s gate,
In the Judgement Hall of Osiris, Gods and Goddesses call out.

"Come to us. He at the Head of the Horizon,
Great God, Light of the Earth,
May thou open the Holy Gates,
throw wide the two mysterious Doors."

In the crenulated Hall, nine steps lead to a throne,
where a sovereign weighs, your whole life in his hands.
On every step a God, Behold your life in the balance,
Through all its phases, Rising, culminating and decline.

A confusion of images, Four antelope heads look down,
Anubis broods, monkeys sailing, pigs fly by.
Shepherded by a baboon, wielding a crooked staff,
Steady your heart to say:
"Never did I do any bad thing against the people!"

You and the God sail through,
On the winding waterway,
The great door closes after you,
which makes the dead souls wail.

6th Gate

You fair, united, through a gate called *seat of her lord*,
Guarded by a Serpent, *He whose eye roves about*.

Mind says: "Open the door for Ra,
throw open thy door for the *One of the Horizon*,
He lightens the complete darkness,
and makes the Hidden Chamber bright."

You and the God sail through,
On the winding waterway,
The great door closes after you,
which makes the dead souls wail.

7th Gate

At the seventh gate things come together,
brightness at the end of the tunnel.
All downstream to *The Brilliant One*,
guarded by *Closed eyes* serpent.
He is blind and cannot see you,
Or anything you lack.
Mind says;
"Open the Netherworld for Re,
throw open thy door for the One of the Horizon,
he lightens the complete darkness,
and makes the Hidden Chamber Bright."

You and the God sail through,
On the winding waterway,
The great door closes after you,
which makes the dead souls wail.

8th Gate

The eighth gate is *Glowing*, the guardians you embrace
Your heart with emotion overflows, you remember *Flame Face*,
The wise serpent is familiar,
His warmth feels so good.
Open the door for Ra,
throw open the door for the One of the Horizon,
he lightens the complete darkness,
and makes the Hidden chamber bright.

You and the God sail through,
On the winding waterway,

The great door closes after you,
Which makes the dead souls wail.

9th Gate

The ninth door is called, the *Gate of Honour*,
Guarded by the Serpent: *Horn of the Earth*.

The outgrowing of the earth, the joy of rising up,
Encompassing, supporting, the life force coming back,
Mind says: "Open the door for Re,
throw open thy door for the One of the Horizon,
He lightens the complete darkness,
and makes the Hidden chamber bright."

You and the God sail through,
On the winding waterway,
The great door closes after you,
Which makes the dead souls wail.

10th Gate

At the tenth gate, you see more on the lintel,
The company of heaven, changed to twenty four cobras,
But you fear them not, the upper guardian with his knife of flint,
you know his name *executioner*, impostor you are not.

You have passed the lower regions, know the names of all,
The Uniter is the wise serpent, things are coming together.

Minds says:
"Open the Netherworld of Ra, throw open thy door.

He lightens the complete darkness,
and makes the Hidden Chamber bright."

You and the God sail through,
On the winding waterway,
The great door closes after you,
which makes the dead souls wail.

11th Gate

The eleventh gate is clearer still, its name *Mysterious of Approaches*,
Guarded by the Serpent, *The One in his discharge*.

On the lintel two sceptres rest, capped by the heads,
Of father and son, Horus and Osiris.

Each wears the red crown, of the south the sceptres say:
"Peace thou whose forms are numerous,
Peace thou whose forms are numerous."

The old body is gone, cut away from you by the knives
of the cutting one, what remains is the crowned head.

Your soul is in heaven,
your body in the earth,
greatness has been ordained,
by your very own self.

Mind says: "Open the Netherworld of Ra, throw open thy door,
He lightens the complete darkness,
he gives light to the *Chamber of Purity* (wabet)."

You and the God sail through,
On the winding waterway,
The great door closes after you,
which makes the dead souls wail.

12th Gate
After your long night, the final gate is here,
She whose power is holy, two pillars with human heads.
They face each on each, Atum the setting sun,
Kephra rising, coming, the beginning with the end.

Through twin doors of the horizon, it is the dawn,
When holy serpents fly and two cobras rest.

Isis & her sister Nephthys, those who light for Ra,
going after this God, into the mysterious Door of the West.

Mind says to a serpent at the door, the *One of the Morning*,
You who open for Ra. "Open the gate,
throw open the door, for the One of the Horizon,
for he comes out of the mysterious region,
to rest upon the body of Nuit."

Minds says to the *Encircler*, You upon the door:
"Open the gate for Ra, open for *The One of the Horizon*,
for he comes out of the mysterious region,
to move over the body of Nuit."

You and the God sail through
On the winding waterway

The great door closes one last time
which makes the dead souls wail.
Come out into the light, and contemplate death and birth,
The eternal sun, towed by eight Gods of earth.

On the sun boat of the morning, lifted by the Abyss
Abysmal waters surging up, from the faraway world.
Kephra the sacred scarab,
As new sun born through the eastern mountains
Isis and Nephthys bearing him up,
to the waiting Goddess of the sky.

Who stands above earthly sphere,
out of the old and into the new,
You are lifted into her arms,
Mother of the Gods, Nuit.[120]

---

120. Alexandre Piankoff (1974) *Egyptian religious texts and representations*, 6 vols, Bollingen : 154

7 The Ritual Year

Lunar rites

The celebration of a ritual year is one of the most useful components of a magician's life and work. The very oldest Egyptian ritual calendar was lunar. The evidence for this is very complex and in the words of Professor Leo Depuydt, "does not exactly jump out at you!" This ancient lunar calendar continued a veiled existence alongside the dominant solar or civil year. In it we see a very ancient pantheon of gods, including Nuit, Min, & Hathor, one for each month of the lunar year. No doubt there were local variations, hence my own preference for Set in the first month. If this doesn't suit then I recommend making your own substitution, perhaps replacing Set with his offspring Thoth. Thoth presided over the "intercalary" month. As explained below, "intercalary" months were needed every three years to keep the lunar in synch with solar year. This then would be a year with a double helping of Thoth!

I have provided for them a unique collection of liturgy, ritual and prayers as may have been offered in the homes, sanctuaries and temples of the original Egypt.

Many of these feasts of Ancient Egypt were celebrated on the phases of the moon – principally when it was new or full. So whatever is your chosen favorite god or goddess, if you make your offerings or rituals on either of these days, you will be reviving the oldest and I'd say most authentic form of the ancient Egyptian magical religion.

So for example, rites for the god Horus, would fall in the moon's dark nights around the new moon; whereas those of his dark twin Seth occur on the full moon, the 'white nights' and especially the sixteenth day of the lunar month.

Inscriptions on Old Kingdom tombs (*mastabas*) tell us that the Egyptians observed ritual feasts at other phases of the moon.[121] Details on these celebrations are sketchy, but included the day of the moon's first visibility (*tep 3bed*). The heliacal rising of Sirius (*wep renpet* or *peret sepedet*) whose first appearance just before dawn heralded the season of Nile inundation was once used to calibrate the lunar calendar.

---

121. Parker (1950 : 34)

Rituals for thirteen lunar months

Table 1: Gods of Lunar Year				
Month	Neter	Name	Hieroglyphs	
(Jul)	Thoth	Thoth	$dhwty$	
1 (Jul-Aug)	Seth	Tekhy	thy	Akhet (inundation)
2 (Aug - Sep)	Min	Phaophi	$p\ n\ jpt$	
3 (Sep - Oct)	Hathor	Athyr	$Hwt\text{-}hr$	
4 (Oct-Nov)	Sokar	Choiak	$k3\ hr\ k3$	
5 (Nov - Dec)	Neith	Tyby	$t3\ ^cbt$	Peret (planting)
6 (Dec - Jan)	Nuit	Mechir	$mhyr$	
7 (Jan-Feb)	Anubis	Pharmenoth	$p\ n\ jmn\ htp$	
8 (Feb - Mar)	Renenutet	Pharmuthi	$p\ n\ rnwtt$	
9 (Mar - Apr)	Khonsu	Pachons	$Hnśw$	Shemu (harvest)
10 (Apr - May)	Horus	Payni	$Hnt\text{-}hty$	
11 (May - Jun)	Ipet	Epiphi	^cIpt	
12 (Jun - Jul)	Ra Horakhti	Mesore	$mswt\ r^c$	

Table 1: Months of the Lunar-Sothic Calendar

Standard "Tankhem" Opening

1. Hekas, Hekas, Este Babaloi

"Love and do what you will"
Face North and try to see the constellation
Ursa Major. Draw down its power

Now turn to the East and say:
"Guardians of the House of Life at Ombos
Before me In the East: Nephthys
Behind me in the West Isis
On my right hand in the South is Set
And on my left hand, in the North Horus
For above me shines the body of Nuit
And below me extends the ground of Geb
And in my centre abideth the 'Great Hidden God' "
Make the "Horus Fighting" gesture.

[Breath in and in one perfect movement, form both hands into fists and raise them up and to the left of your head, stretch your right hand and arm in front of you and bring the left hand and arm to join it. As you finish the intonation, bring both hands back to the centre of your body]

Vibrate the first vowel long and hard - AAAAAAA -

Now turn to the North
Make the gesture "Horus Fighting" and vibrate the second vowel EEEEEEE, using the mnemonic gEt as above.

Then turn to the West
Make the "Horus Fighting" gesture and vibrate ÊÊÊÊÊÊÊ as in GAme

Turn to the South
Make the "Horus Fighting" gesture and vibrate IIIIIII as in fEEd

Return to face the East

Now bend over and reach out to the Earth
vibrating OOOOOOO as in HOt

Then gradually unfolding, come up and place your hands on your heart and vibrate YYYYYY as in NEw

Finally stretching up to the heavens vibrate Ô Ô Ô Ô Ô Ô Ô as in HÔme.

Now make the sign of the (invoking) pentagramme in the air in front of you and vibrate
Aa, Eye, EE, Ou, Uh (Ay EAO - Oh Hail) Nephthys
Aa, Eye, EE, Ou, Uh (Ay EAO - Oh Hail) Horus
Aa, Eye, EE, Ou, Uh (Ay EAO - Oh Hail) Isis
Aa, Eye, EE, Ou, Uh (Ay EAO - Oh Hail) Set
Aa, Eye, EE, Ou, Uh (Ay EAO - Oh Hail) Geb
Aa, Eye, EE, Ou, Uh (Ay EAO - Oh Hail) Nuit
Aa, Eye, EE, Ou, Uh (Ay EAO - Oh Hail) Hidden God

Repeat first part that begins "Guardians of the House etc."

Return to the North

Timings for ritual

Ancient Egyptian liturgy was mostly done thrice daily at approximately the third, sixth and ninth hour of the Egyptian clock. These times are sometimes standardised to 9am, 12midday and 3pm. The threefold execution reflects the traditional division of the sun into three phases as dawn, midday and sunset. (These times pass into Christian liturgy as *Terce*, *Sixt* and *None*.) But some rituals lent themselves to a night-time, or midnight execution, and yet others predawn twilight, the so-called duat, is essential.

You might find it useful to have a copy of my *Demonic Calendar of Ancient Egypt* which has a more precise ephemeris for the lunar months.

Sutekh of Hibis Oasis. Persian period image showing Sutekh or Seth subduing the "evil" serpent Apophis. This image thought by many scholars to be the prototype for St George and the Dragon.

1st Month – Tekhy (July-August)
Set

New Year's day was day one of the new lunar year (*tepy renpet*). This is an extra special new moon feast. The name of this month is Tekhy, which means literally 'the cup' hence a feast of drunkenness or intoxication. Alcohol was a big part of this, but also, the cup has additional associations with a psychoactive infusion made from the Blue Lily – as discussed in my book *Supernatural Assault in Ancient Egypt*. Although in later times this feast of drunkenness was associated with the goddess Hathor, it also seems to be very appropriate for the god Set whose existence is otherwise almost completely suppressed in later festival calendars.

In my book *The Bull of Ombos*, I discuss the controversial issue of whether Set could be the god sometimes referred to as 'The Elder Magician', i.e. as the first emanation of his father the Sun god Ra. Since writing, I have found further confirmation that 'The Elder Magician' has a defensive function guarding Ra from the Apophis. The Elder Magician is Set.

Full Moon

As good a month as any to celebrate the ancient god Set. For many years I used the Bornless or Headless one ritual based on "The Stele of Jeu the Hieroglyphist" from the PGM. I did this principally because of scholarly opinion and contemporary tradition that associates Seth as part of the hybrid or ambiguous entity invoked in the rite. I find this still a valid approach and indeed an important ritual. It has a complex hybrid of entities which we might consider as typhonian aspects of

---

(If an alternative is preferred use Thoth)

Osiris. There are indeed key magical secrets encoded in the Bornless rite. However, I've recently added the following more thoroughly Sethian spell from the same library of an ancient magician. Use it in whole or part as appropriate:

An ancient Sethian rite

2. PGM IV 154-285 - *Nephotes (Nefer Hotep ie Khonsu) to Psammetichos*

First comes a frame story also known by scholars of this material as a *Historiola* (qv). Work with this long complex ritual is in an early stage - but I found that just reading the prologue is enough to set the process in motion, with gnosis intruding into dreams, with help of some special, discrete techniques, which I won't elaborate too much here.

Prologue Nephotes (Nefer Hotep ie Khonsu) to Psammetichos, immortal king of Egypt. Greetings. Since the great god has appointed you immortal king and nature has made you the best wise man, I too, with a desire to show you the industry in me, have sent you this magical procedure which, with complete ease, produces a holy power. And after you have tested it, you too will be amazed at the miraculous nature of this magical operation. You will observe through bowl divination on whatever day or night you want, in whatever place you want, beholding the god in the water and hearing a voice from the god which speaks in verses in answers to whatever you want. You will attain both the ruler of the universe and whatever you command, and he will speak on other matters which you ask about.

You will succeed by inquiring in this way: First, attach yourself to Helios in this manner: At whatever sunrise you want (provided it is the third day of the month), go up to the highest part of the house and spread a pure linen garment on the floor. Do this with a mystagogue.

But as for you, crown yourself with dark ivy while the sun is in mid-heaven, at the fifth hour, and while looking upward lie down naked on the linen and order your eyes to be completely covered with a black band. And wrap yourself like a corpse, close your eyes and, keeping your direction toward the sun begin these words.

Prayer:

"O mighty Typhon, ruler of the realm
Above and master, god of gods, O lord
ABERAMEN [ThÔOU]* (formula),
O dark's disturber, thunder's bringer, whirlwind,
Night-flasher, breather-forth of hot and cold,
Shaker of rocks, wall trembler, boiler of
The waves, disturber of the sea's great depth,
IÔ / ERBÊT AU TAUI MÊNI,
I'm He who searched with you the whole world and
Found great Osiris, whom I brought you chained.
I'm he who joined you in war with the gods
I'm he who closed heaven's double gates and put to sleep the
serpent which must not be seen,
Who stopped the seas, the streams, the river currents
Were'er you rule this realm. And as your soldier
I have been conquered by the gods, I have
Been thrown face down because of empty wrath.
Raise up your friend, I beg you, I implore:
Thrown me not on the ground, O lord of gods,
AEMINA EBARÔThER REThÔRABE ANIMEA*
O grant me power, I beg, and give to me
This favor, so that, whensoe'r I tell
One of the gods to come, he is seen coming

Swiftly to me in answer to my chants,

NAINE BASANAPTATOU EAPTOU MÊNÔPhAESMÊ PAPTOU MÊNÔPh AESIMÊ TRAUAPTI PEUChRÊ TRAUARA PTOUMÊPh MOURAI ANChOUChAPhAPTA MOURSA ARAMEI IAÔ AThThARAUI MÊNOKER BORO PTOUMÊTh AT TAUI MÊNI ChARChARA PTOUMAU LALAPSA TRAUI TRAUEPSE MAMÔ PhORTOUChA AEÊIO IOY OÊÔA EAI AEÊI ÔI IAÔ AÊI AI IAÔ."

After you have said this three times, there will be this sign of divine encounter, but you, armed by having this magical soul, be not alarmed. For a sea falcon flies down and strikes you on the body with its wings, signifying this: that you should arise. But as for you, rise up and clothe yourself with white garments and burn on an earthen censer uncut incense in grains while saying this:

"I have been attached to your holy form.
I have been given power by your holy name.
I have acquired your emanation of the goods,
Lord, god of gods, master, daimon.
ANThThOUIN ThOUThOUI TAUANTI LAÔ APTATÔ."

Having done this, return as lord of a godlike nature which is accomplished through this divine encounter.

Inquiry of bowl divination and necromancy. Whenever you want to inquire about matters, take a bronze vessel, either a bowl or a saucer, whatever kind you wish. Pour water: rainwater if you are calling upon heavenly gods, seawater if gods of the earth, river water if Osiris or Sarapis, spring water if the dead. Holding the vessel on your knees, pour out green olive oil, bend over the vessel and speak the prescribed spell. And address whatever god you want ask about whatever you wish, and he will reply to you and tell you about anything. And if he has spoken dismiss him with the spell of dismissal, and you have used this spell will be amazed.

The spell spoken over the vessel is:

"AMOUN AUANTAU LAIMOUTAU RIPTOU MANTAUI IMANTOU LANTOU LAPTOUMI ANChÔMACh ARAPTOUMI, hither to me, O NN god; appear to me this very hour and do not frighten my eyes. Hither to me, O NN god, be attentive to me because he wishes and commands this

AChChÔR AChChÔR AChAChACh PTOUMI ChAChChÔ ChARAChÔCh ChAPTOUMÊ ChÔRAChARAChÔCh APTOUMI MÊChÔChAPTOU ChARAChPTOU ChAChChÔ ChARAChÔ PTENAChÔChEU" (a hundred letters)."

But you are not unaware, mighty king and leader of magicians, that this is the chief name of Typhon, at whom the ground, the depths of the sea, Hades, heaven, the sun, the moon, the visible chorus of stars, the whole universe all tremble, the name which, when it is uttered, forcibly brings gods and daimons to it. This is the name that consists of 100 letters. Finally, when you have called, whomever you called will appear, god or dead man, and he will give an answer about anything you ask. And when you have learned to your satisfaction, dismiss the god merely with the powerful name of the hundred letters as you say, "Depart, master, for the great god, NN, wishes and commands this of you." Speak the name, and he will depart. Let this spell, mighty king, be transmitted to you alone, guarded by you unshared.

There is also the protective charm itself which you wear while performing, even while standing: onto a silver leaf inscribe this name of 100 letters with a bronze stylus, and wear it strung on a thong from the hide of an ass.

Divine encounter of the divine procedure:

Toward the rising sun say:

"I call you who did first control gods' wrath,
You who hold royal scepter o'er the heavens,
You who are midpoint of the stars above,
You, master Typhon, you I call who are
the dreaded sovereign over the firmament.
You who are fearful, awesome, threatening,
You who're obscure and irresistible and hater of the wicked,
you I call,
Typhon, in hours unlawful and unmeasured,
You who've walked on unquenched, clear-crackling fire,
You who are over snows, below dark ice,
You who hold sovereignty over the Moirai,
I invoked you in prayer, I call, almighty one,
that you perform for me whatever I ask
of you, and that you nod assent at once
to me and grant that what I ask be mine

(add the usual) because I adjure you GAR ThAIA BAUZAU ThÓRThÓR KAThAUKATh IAThIN NA BORKAKAR BORBA KARBORBOCh MO ZAU OUZÓNZ ÓN YABITH, mighty Typhon, hear me, NN, and perform for me the NN task. For I speak your true names,

IÓ ERBÉTh IÓ PAKERBÉTh IÓ BOLChOSÉTh OEN TYPhON ASBARABÓ BIEAISÉ ME NERÓ MARAMÓ TAUÉR ChThENThÓNIE ALAM BÉTÓR MENKEChRA SAUEIÓR

RÉSEIODÓTA ABRÉSIOA PhÓThÉR ThERThÓNAX NERDÓMEU AMÓRÉS MEEME ÓIÉS SYSChIE ANThÓNIE PhRA;

Listen to me and perform the NN deed."

The Bornless One Ritual

It uses a special "beneficial" sign or *sigil* known as a charaktêre as a focus. These signs are a specialised form of Egyptian Hieroglyph that developed at a time when the language was becoming part of a universal magical language still in use by practitioners. "Jeu the Hieroglyphist" was a famous practitioner of his time; his name crops up in several places including in the magick of Gnostic Christians.

This ritual that has become important for occultists of the Thelemic tradition under the title "The Bornless One Rite" although we now know that "Headless" would be closer to the original sense. The ritual calls upon the services of a daemon known as the "Headless One" whom most Egyptologists say is a form of the god Seth. The "headless demon" is one of the many epithets of Seth and has numerous mythological and stellar meanings. In classical Paganism, there were thirty-six principal daimons, one for every ten day period, that which in astrology is known as a decan. These daemons are therefore the main influences of our personality and fate. One of the purposes of magick is to modify or even remove these conditions, enabling us to follow our own path. Thus "exorcism" can be viewed as a form of initiation.

Personally I find it useful when approaching new and complex ritual material to begin slowly by just sitting somewhere peaceful and reading the rite out. I may do this everyday over the course of a month, gradually working it all out before attempting a full "dramatic" performance, assuming that is the end in mind. I record dreams, memories and reflections in my lunar diary.

Preparation: The original rubric suggests writing a formula on a new sheet of papyrus and wearing this as a headband. The magician faces north during the recitation. An alternative would be to draw with red pigment the special charaktêre on the forehead of those present. This charaktêre looks very much like the head of Set. Some of the words and chants may be unfamiliar thus as suggested elsewhere here is my mnemonic for the seven Greek vowels: FAther GEt GAme to FEEd the HOt NEw hÔme . These can be added in pencil next to each line where necessary.

Start with the *Tankhem* opening then:

"I summon you, Headless One,
Who created earth and heaven,
Who created night and day,
You who created light and darkness;
You are Unas, the beautiful whom none has ever seen;
You are Iabas;
You are Iapos;
You have distinguished the just from the unjust;
You have made female and male;
You have revealed seed and fruits;
You have made men love each other
And hate each other."

"I am Moses your prophet to whom you have transmitted your mysteries celebrated by Israel; you have revealed the moist and the dry and all nourishment; hear me."

"I am the messenger of the beautiful Pharaoh Unas
This is your true name,
which has been transmitted to the prophets of Israel.
Hear me, Hear me,
ARBATHIAÔ REIBET ATHELEBERSÊTH [ARA]
BLATHA ALBEU EBENPHCHI CHITASGOÊ IBAÔTH IAÔ
Listen to me and turn away this daimon"

"I call upon you, awesome and invisible god with an *empty spirit,*
AROGOGO-ROBRAÔ
SEKHMET
MODORIÔ PHALARCHAÔ OOO

Holy Headless One. Deliver us
From the daimon which restrains us,
ROUBRIAÔ MARI ÔDAM BAABNABAÔTH
ASS ADÔNAI APHNIAÔ
ithôlêth abrasas
Aï¿ ½y ;
Mighty Headless One,
Deliver us
From the daimons that restrain.
MARARRAIÔ IOÊL KOTHA ATHORÊBALO ABRAÔTH,

Deliver us:
AÔTH ABRAÔTH BASYM ISAK SABAÔTH IAÔ"

"He is lord of the gods;
He is the lord of the inhabited world;
He is the one whom the winds fear;
He is the one who made all things
By the commands of his voice."

"Lord, King, Master, Helper, save the Soul-*Ba* (Psyche)
ieou pyr
iou pyr
iaôt
iaêô
ioou
ABRASAX SABRIAM
OO YY EY OO YY
ADï ¿ ½ᴀ,

Immediately, immediately
Good messenger of the God
ANLALA LAI GAIA
APA DIACHANNA CHORYN"

Assumption of the God form

"I am the headless daimon with my sight in my feet;
[I am] the mighty one [who possesses] the immortal fire;
I am the truth who hates the fact that unjust deeds
    are done in the world;
I am the one who makes the lightning flash and the thunder roll;
I am the one whose sweat is the heavy rain, which falls upon the
    earth that it might be inseminated;
I am the one whose mouth burns completely;

I am the one who begets and destroys;
I am the Favour of the Aion;
My name is a heart encircled by a serpent;
Come forth and follow."

"Subject to me all daimons,
So that every daimon,
Whether of the heavens
Or the air
Or earthly
Or under the earth
Terrestrial or aquatic,
Might be obedient to me
And every enchantment and scourge
Which is from God."

Closure:

When you want to finish do so by for example repeating the first part of Tankhem opening and then a "license to depart":
"I release any spirits entrapped by this working,
May you go in peace to your lovely abodes.
Farewell Headless One,
Lord of the inhabited world,
Farewell Akephalos,
The son of Nuit
Leader of the company of heaven in their diurnal motion,
Senebty, great Bull of Ombos."

After which pour any remaining offerings such as those of the chalice on earth and clear equipment, extinguish lamps etc .[9]

Notes & Sources

I've used some "poetic licence" with the text which is mainly from PGM V 96-172 translated D E Aune and published Betz, H D (1986). Betz cites Reiling, J "Hermas and Christian Prophesy" NT.S 37 (Leiden Brill 1973) 41-48 as an informant on Pagan technical term "empty spirit" but I didn't find him that revealing on the Pagan usage and was really an apologia for the Christian use of same. This ritual is translated (in German) and discussed in *Abrasax II* Merkelbach & Totti pp 153-70. They also concur that the "headless" god combines elements of several gods, principally Set. I've rendered the god name "Osor-Onnophris" (Egyptian *Wsir Wn-nfr*) as "Unas the Beautiful" rather than "Osiris, the beautiful being". Aleister Crowley, in his celebrated version of the rite also "suppresses" the name *Osiris*, rendering it as "Myself made perfect". My intuition is that Pharaoh *Unas* of the fifth dynasty fits here. He was one of the builders of the great pyramids with their innovative magical texts. There are other interesting coincidences between Unas and this text. It's the only substantive change I've made. I've not followed Crowley versions of the god names, e.g.: he substitutes "Ankh ef n Khonsu" for "Moses"; who at the time of the rite's composition was regarded in Egypt as an important magician.

2nd Month (August-September)
Min

Celebrations of Min's birthday are recorded on Egypt's oldest memorials such as the 1st Dynasty Palermo stone. But his cult is even older reaching back to the prehistoric era when he was a deity of fertility, sexual reproduction and natural phenomenon such as storms. His erection is his most famous attribute – combined as it is with his raised arm and flail some have speculated that this is all part of an aggressive/protective posture?

His main centres were Koptos (Kuft) & Panopolis (Akhmim). His symbols are the Thunderbolt, the White Bull, the Flail and the Phallus. Wallis Budge speculates there was also a lunar component to his cult. Min is also called *ka-mwt-f* "Bull of his mother" a reference to the incestuous impregnation of his mother, an epithet of various gods, including Horus, also Geb who kills his father Shu in order to ravage Tefnut. Before getting too outraged, it's as well to remember this is an agricultural motif and refers to reproductive activity of bulls and cows. Min's archaic shrine was a phallic shaped hut, woven from two significant and emblematic plants – the White Lotus & the (narcotic) Blue Lily (*Nymphaea caerulea*).

The blossoms and foliage of these flowers are to be woven into model phallus or perhaps crown. The traditional hymns are referred to as "Danced", implying they are rhythmic chants.

Danced Hymn for Min who is on his staircase

Hail to you,
Min, Min Ra
Welcome

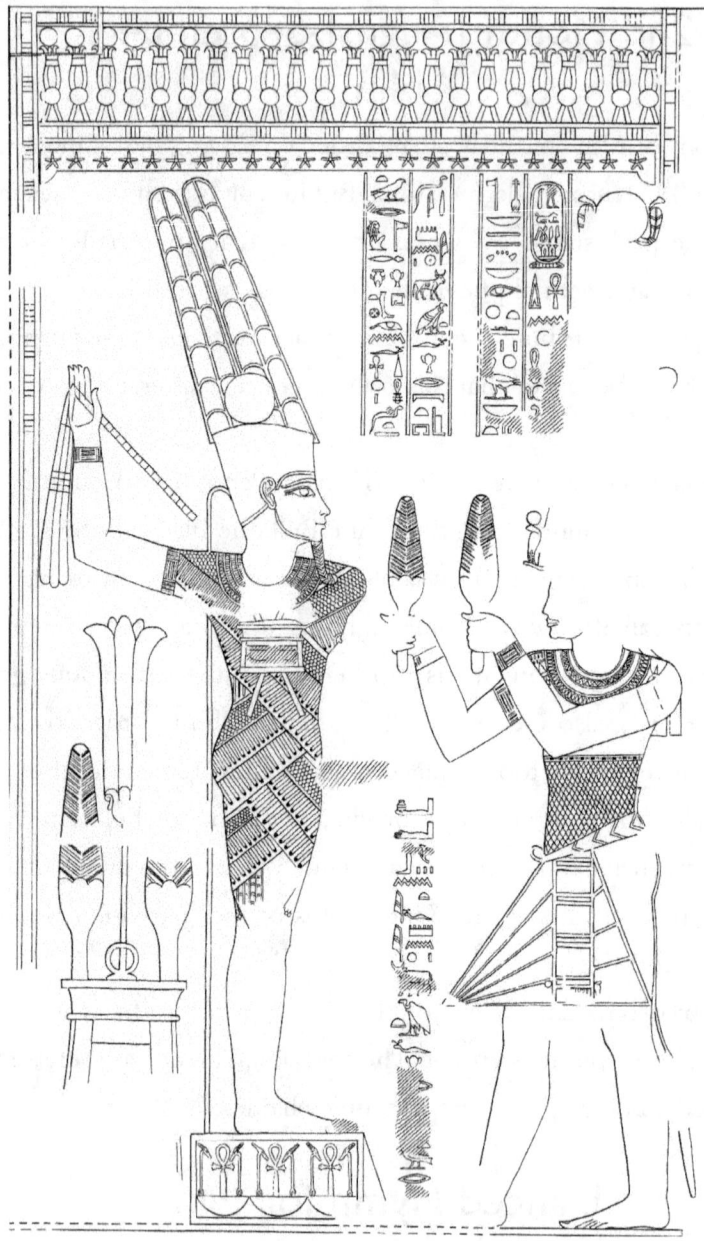

Min from The Temple of Hibis in El Khargeh Oasis (see Winlock, et al 1941-1954). The god's phallus mutilated in late classical period, probably as an act of counter magick. The worshipper is shown offering Min lettuce, his preferred food.

On your staircase

Hail to you
Min, Min Ra
And the crown you wear
on your forehead

Hail to you
Mysterious Min
"Bull of his mother"
Much that you do remains in obscurity

You are unique
To whom praise is given
You have power to give life
To those you love

Powerful to give him to be propitiated
He is unique here
To whom has been conferred the function
of the unknown god

While you go out of the great door
And are standing on your stairway of truth
Speaking with Osiris hour by hour
See, that which you ordain
For protection
Against all bad things
Min justified before your enemies

In the sky and on the earth
By the judges of all the gods
And all the goddesses.

Hymn to Min as the Sickle (Kapesh)

[To be performed whilst offering a sheath of wheat to Min as White Bull)

Prophets of Min
We carry his sceptre and crown
The town of Buto does not push us back
Seizing your white & red crown
The servitors of Horus & Set
Are at peace in Thebes & Coptos
Those of the bee [are at peace]
The Prophets of Min [are at peace]
The Dancers of Min [are at peace]
The people of Gold [are with us/me]
The northern place, of Pe [are with us/me]
The southern place, the Ape of Thoth [are with us/me]
And place of Natron [are with us/me]
The image of Min approaches its resting place

3rd Month (September – October) Hathor (or Isis)

Although the goddess Hathor is known as the bestower of human fertility, there are traces that this quality extents to animals and indeed crops. The myth of "Seth & the Seed goddess" concerns *seed* in all its connotation including semen and the female equivalent. The following dedication is adapted from traditional spells of the time of King Rameses II.

Why this is so
(This part of the spell is to be read out)

Once upon a time
The Seed Goddess Hathor (*t3 mtwt*)
Took a bath on the shore in order to purify herself in the oasis
Seth was out walking and he saw her
He saw her jewel encrusted girdle, he saw her bare ass,
And it turned him on
Then he mounted her as a ram mounts a ewe
He covered her as a bull covers a cow
But for the seed goddess it was all wrong
And she went straight to his head
To the region between his eyebrows where the full moon sits
And he lay down, exhausted on his bed
and was stricken with the seed become poison
Then his other wife Nephthys (Anath),
The victorious goddess
An androgynous woman who acts like a warrior
Who wears a man's kilt
Tied with a woman's sash

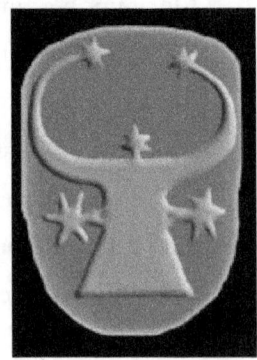

Top: Pectoral ornament, Horus and Set worshipping Bat, an archaic goddess later assimilated to Hathor. Middle Kingdom, 12th Dynasty, probably reign of Senworsret II or III, 1898-1841BC, probably from Dahshur. Electrum with remains of lapis lazuli, carnelian and feldspar inlays. Height 1.5 ins. Myers colections, Eton College. Published in Spurr, Stephen, *Egyptian Art at Eton College* : New York, N.Y. : Metropolitan Museum of Art; Windsor: Eton College, c1999.
Bottom *Left*: Another image of Bat from 1st Dynasty Narmer Palette,
Right: The predynastic "Hathor Palette" showing Bat as celestial cow - Petrie (1953) *Ceremonial Slate Palettes*.

Hathor from Tomb of Sety I, From I Rosellini (1832-44)
Monumenti dell' Egitto e della Nubia, Pisa.

Distressed, went to her father the Sun god Ra
He said "what is the matter with you"
Nephthys, victorious goddess
Androgynous woman who acts like a warrior
Who wears a man's kilt
Tied with a woman's sash
I am near to my evening setting
I know you want me to cure Set of the effects of his
overstrenous coupling with Hathor
The poison of the bad seed out of place
Let Set's stupidity be a lesson for him
Hathor, the seed goddess was destined for the bed
of the sun god above
He will make love to her with his heavenly fire
His will be as hard as steel when he enters her.

Hearing this the divine Isis said:
I am the Nubian woman
I have come down from heaven
I have come to realise the seed in the body
of every mother's son and every mother's daughter
And cause them to return in good health
For as Horus lives
So shall all live:

The lunar blessing:

1. I place Hekayet in my forehead
So no bad thing shall take its stand in there

2. I place Horus Mekhantenirti in my eyes
So no bad thing shall take its stand there

3. I place Khenem-tjaw of Hesret (Breeze-sniffer) in my nose
Beware lest she extinguish the north wind in the presence of the great ones

4. I place Anubis in my lips
So no bad things will take its stand there

5. I place Sefekh-'abui in my tongue
So no bad things will take its stand there

6. I place Buto in my neck

7. I place the voice goddess Meret in my throat
Beware lest her voice be lacking in the presence of Ra

8. I place Nut in my nipples
The lady who bore the gods and gives them suck

9. I place Montu lord of both arms
So no bad thing will take its stand there

10. I place Ra Lord of the vertibrae
So no bad thing will take its stand there

11. I place Set lord of the side
So no bad thing will take its stand there

12. I place the four sons of Horus in my liver, lung, heart and kidneys, spleen, intestines, ribs and flesh
So no bad thing will take its stand there

13. I place Hathor in my flank
So no bad thing will take its stand there

14. I place Horus in my phallus
So no bad thing will take its stand there

15. I place Reshpu in my bone marrow
So no bad thing will take its stand there

16. I place Horus in my thighs
So no bad thing will take its stand there

17. I place Sia (wisdom) in my knees
So no bad thing will take its stand there

18. I place Nefertem in my shin
So no bad thing will take its stand there

19. I place Nebet Debwet, Lady of the soles of my feet
So no bad thing will take its stand there

20. I place Anukis in my toe nails
So no bad thing will take its stand there

21. I place Serket, lady of the bite
So no bad thing will take its stand there

This above is an example of a very important magical technique known from several different traditions, including those of India, an act of self divinization. This important spell can be simplified to just one deity, Hathor, who is installed in each part.

Notes & Sources

Gardiner (1935) *Hieratic Papyri in the British Museum 3rd Series* p 61-65 spell Vs I 4-6, 7; Van Dijk, J (1986) " 'Anath, Seth and the Seed of Ra" in Hospers, J H, *Scripta Sigma Vocis*, Gronigen; Pinch, G (1993) *Votive Offerings to Hathor*, Oxford; Roberts, A (1995) *Hathor Rising, The Serpent Power of Ancient Egypt*, Northgate

4th Month (October – November) Sokar or Osiris

Sokar is a more primitive version of his well known successor Osiris. He is an archaic god of the underworld and the necropolis. He is depicted as a mummiform god with a hawk's head. He is associated with kingship but also agriculture and rituals of water. His rites began as "sabbatic" rather than annual celebrations; inscriptions talk of a festival every six years. These rites involved hoeing or breaking the earth, probably as a symbolic beginning of the winter sowing; also circumambulation around the boundaries of cities, buildings, temples and tombs not unlike the rite known in some parts of Europe as "beating the bounds". Celebrants wore necklaces woven of vegetables - usually onions or garlic. It was also a time to offer vegetables to the dead.

The focus of cult acts was a distinctive ritual boat – that of Maarty (double Maat). For the following rite I draw an image of this boat on the earth in cornflower rather like a Voodoo Veve or Hindu mandala. The participants – "Prophet" (priest) and a congregation representing the seven "Hathors" arrayed around the image.

The priest begins with the following "voice offering".

To Sokar: In his shrine called Shetayet
To Sokar: In the house
To Sokar: In centre of the temple (Hry Ib)
To Sokar: In the necropolis
To Sokar: Upon the distant hills
To Sokar: Presiding one in the tent of the craftsmen
To Sokar: In many places and lands

Image of Sokar from Tomb of Sety I, From I Rosellini (1832-44)
Monumenti dell' Egitto e della Nubia, Pisa.

To Sokar: In the boat of double Maarty

To Sokar: In Egypt

To Sokar: And in foreign lands

To Sokar: In the southern and northern lakes

To Sokar: In heaven, on earth and in all his temples

To Sokar: In all of his places, shrines and tombs

To Sokar: In every place he likes to be

To Sokar: In all his images

To Sokar: We celebrate your festival, eternally

To Sokar: We walk the boundaries and beat the earth.

Litany of Sokar

Hail: Be triumphant O Sovereign

Hail: How sweet is the fragrance that you love

Hail: Behold, I perfume the things you love

Hail: I shall do what you please

Hail: I kiss the earth; I open the way with libation

Hail: Oh favoured one of Abydos

Hail: Fiery of eye, son of a prophet

Hail: I make protection according to what you say

Hail: I love your face when you rest in the god's broad hall within the temple

Hail: Abydos has for name Abydos

Hail: Abydos has for name Abydos

Hail: How pleasant is the fragrance of Abydos

Hail: Abydos is doubly protected

Hail: My God, hearken to this rite

Hail: Pray be joyous and hearken thou to the worship that comes from the mouth of Egypt

Top: A table with the name of Egypt's first pharaoh, Menes. Restored and reproduced in Allan Gardiner (1961) *Egypt of the Pharaohs*, OUP.
Bottom: detail from the same table showing the Boat of Sokar.

Hail: As for a servant who follows his lord,
Bastet shall not have power over them
Hail: Please drive away our enemies
Hail: Please come and instruct the young
Hail: Put the fear of you into the chaotic
Hail: Be thou seated and come thou, O weary hearted one
Hail: The son of a prophet it is who recites this ritual
Hail: Enduring of name in Djedu
Hail: Secret fragrance of Djedu
Hail: May you live forever
Hail: Your festivals shall be everlasting
Hail: The Lord of Djedu has come
Hail: He has smitten our enemies
Hail: For the good god beloved of Sokar
Hail: He may grant very many returns to us

The rubrik says to be recited sixteen times but I found once was enough. I've used this ritual with a small group and saw possibilities to include the Egyptian "call and response" componant in any future performance.

Hathor's can also say:
"May she give life, stability and dominion
and all health to us like the sun god Ra forever".

The corn mummy

"Everyone knows that among all the people of antiquity the Egyptians have the strangest uses of the materials of perfumery

... and also are the most peculiar in their uses of the most common of products" (D. H. Aufrère)

There's an account of the Khoiak festivals carved onto walls of the Osiris shrine on the roof at the temple of Hathor at Denderah. Similar rites were celebrated at every major temple in Egypt. Thus included the newly rediscovered sunken city of Thonis-Heracleion, which, rather like Pompeii, has preserved many cultic objects from this festival (see various works by underwater archaeologist Frank Goddio, especially *Sunken Cities*).

Plutarch's contention that "the death of Osiris occurred on the 17th (of the lunar month) when the full moon is most obliviously waning", seems to work. Actually the entire passion of Osiris is played out over the complete cycle of the moon. And in this holy month of Khoiak, approximately October in our modern calendar, important events happen on the 12th & the 16th day, when the sun and moon can appear together in the sky and when cult rites were enacted all over Egypt.

Here we find one of most important magical techniques bequeathed to us by antiquity. It's a rite that we can and many do still replicate in some form and is an instance of the highly important magick of statues. In this ritual sequence two small statuettes, each the approximate length of one's forearm (a cubit); are prepared in parallel over the course of the month. The two figures are Osiris-Vegetans and Osiris-Sokar.

Starting from the new moon, earth and water - the material for the Osiris Vegetans or germinating figure of Osiris are placed into a small mummiform planter. I use a small metal mummiform pencil case obtained from the British Museum shop. The seeds need darkness to germinate but should be ready to be a "corn mummy" by the appropriate day, in this case the 12th. Now exposed to sunlight, allow the corn mummy to continue germinating until the 22nd day, when in olden times it participated in a nautical festival on the river in which, Strabo wrote that, 36 papyrus boats took part, illuminated by 365 lamps, presumably, then, a night-time festival.

Parallel to this is a rite to Osiris-Sokar, who we might consider as an older form or precursor of Osiris. Sokar was the god of dead. Some say that this part of the ritual may not originally have had any association with Osiris but could be of the cult of Ptah, Re or even moon god Khonsu.

In both instances we see a connection being made between death and fertility. This Osiris-Sokar rite requires the construction of a second corn mummy but using a different technique. This mummy is also made on the 15th or full moon day; but now 14 different components are ritually prepared, each symbolising different parts of the dismembered god. They are first carefully measured out into 14 different containers, which included things such as incense, precious stones and earths, with special rites for each substance.

The recipe for the "precious unguent" as carved on the wall of the chamber of the temple of Edfu, known by Egyptologists as the *Laboratory*.

> "A location where the recipes for various unguents and perfumes used in the temple were precisely described – was common to all places supposed to have have one of the pieces of Osiris' body."

This following recipe describes the 14 parts. Unless otherwise stated, One part of each, actually 1 hin unit of liquid measure is equivalent to approximately 0.46 litres.[61] As this would make for quite a heavy mummy I would use smaller amounts but keep the same proportions.. I've not done this in truth yet but occurs to me this is a potentially combustible mixture and appropriate safetly precaustions will need to be in place, including fire control. Make a two part mold from plaster using a model of Osiris as a marquette. Calculate the final volume by measuring the displacement when submerged in water. For example, if the final volume is two litres, this divided into 14 would be approximately 143ml for each part: a much more manageable size! The recipe is as follows:

1. Bitumen, ground to perfection
2. Vegetable tar (a by-product the fir tree), then put on the heat to cook

add

3. Fine lotus essence, 1st quality
4. Frankincense, of 1st quality
5. Fine oil, (olive oil?)
6. Wax,

with

7. Fresh turpentine resin,
8. Dry turpentine resin
9. Extract of carob bean,
10. Aromatic Herbs and spices mixed in wine, 1/2 measure
11. Fine oil (another kind Almond)
12. True metals and minerals crushed into a very fine power Spread with
13. Honey

and incorporate with

14. Dry frankincense.

Assemble into one mass & apply on the day of the interment in [in the mould]

"The mixture was cooked and formed a blackish liquid with a predominant odour of bitumen."

After the component have been combined together they are kneaded into an egg, which is kept moist inside a special reliquary made of sycamore gilded with silver. On the 16th day it is pressed into a two-part mould.

This mummy, being still in construction, could not have participated in the boat festival mentioned in connection with the Osiris *Vegetans*. The egg is very suggestive of an unborn embryo. It is my contention that it is this object that is referred to as "headless", in for example the rubric from Denderah transcribed below. The theme of headlessness and the unborn, are part of the complex, astronomical and metaphysical mysteries of this cult, many elements of which far predate the emergence of the cult of Osiris.

One might expect Osiris to be dismembered into 15 rather than 14 parts, 15 being the number of days as counted in the original Egyptians lunar half month, rather than the later lunar days of the Greek astronomical schema. If there were a "missing" component to the corn-mummy, this would reiterate the fact that in the myth, one of the Osiris parts was never recovered; his phallus, eaten by the Oxyrhinchus fish. The goddess Isis was able to reconstitute it by magick.

This might also explain the remarkable erotic interchange between Ra and Osiris in the Temple of Opet (revival of Osiris) at Karnak. The original was mutilated by Victorian archaeologists. Osiris receives his missing part, the phallus from the sun god Ra. Sometimes it is his head he received although here some sort of euphemism or correspondence may be meant.

Meeks notes that in the famous Denderah account of this ritual, the "corn mummy" borne in the hollow plinth of a gilded wooden statue of the Cow goddess is said to be headless:

> "Concerning the cow "bearer" (remenit), she is made of sycamore wood covered in gold. A [corn] mummy with no head is inside, the venerated recipient; is a cubit in length. There are two mice on the plinth of gilded wood beneath her. It is a cubit long. A table of offerings is placed in front of her. She has a scarab on the top and a covering of sai [fabric], the

Atef crown on her head & an Usekh collar of flowers & lapis lazuli"

At the culmination of the festivities on the 30th day of the month, which would be Halloween in later ritual years, the corn mummy from the previous year is moved from the "upper" to the "lower" tomb. Finally a Djed pillar, a stylised tree, is raised, representing stability and resurrection. This is a very ancient ritual act, the raising of a pillar or pole of some kind. Some have suggested this kind of act is recognisable in one of the oldest ritual sites thus far discovered: Gobekli tepe in Anatolia.

Notes & Sources

Gaballa, G A and K A Kitchen "The Festival of Sokar", *Orientalia* 38 (1969) pp1-76 and plates. Allan Gardiner (1961) *Egypt of the Pharaohs* OUP.

5th Month (November – December) Neith

This month was often considered sacred to Min, whose festival was described earlier in connection with the second month. So rather than give Min a second bite of the cherry I've substituted some ritual material for an equally important deity, Neith, one of Egypt's oldest goddesses. Some say she was one of the consorts of Set, and that it is her arrow that protrudes from his flank; perhaps a message. Her forms are Cow, Beetle, Late Fish and Dwarf. Many of her attributes are set out in the hymns:

Hymn to the goddess Neith

To Adore Neith. Say:
1. You are the teacher of Sais
That is to say the earth (Tanen)
Among whom two thirds is masculine,
And a third feminine
Primal goddess mysterious and great,
Who was there at the beginning,
And inaugurates all things.

2. You are the celestial arch
In which the sun travels
The one who gives birth to the stars as long as they are,
And raises them on their portable shrines;
The breath which consumed the earth in the flame of her eyes,
The ardour taken out from her mouth;
The divine mother of Re, who shines on the horizon.
The mysterious one who shines with proper light.
3. You are the serpent goddess,

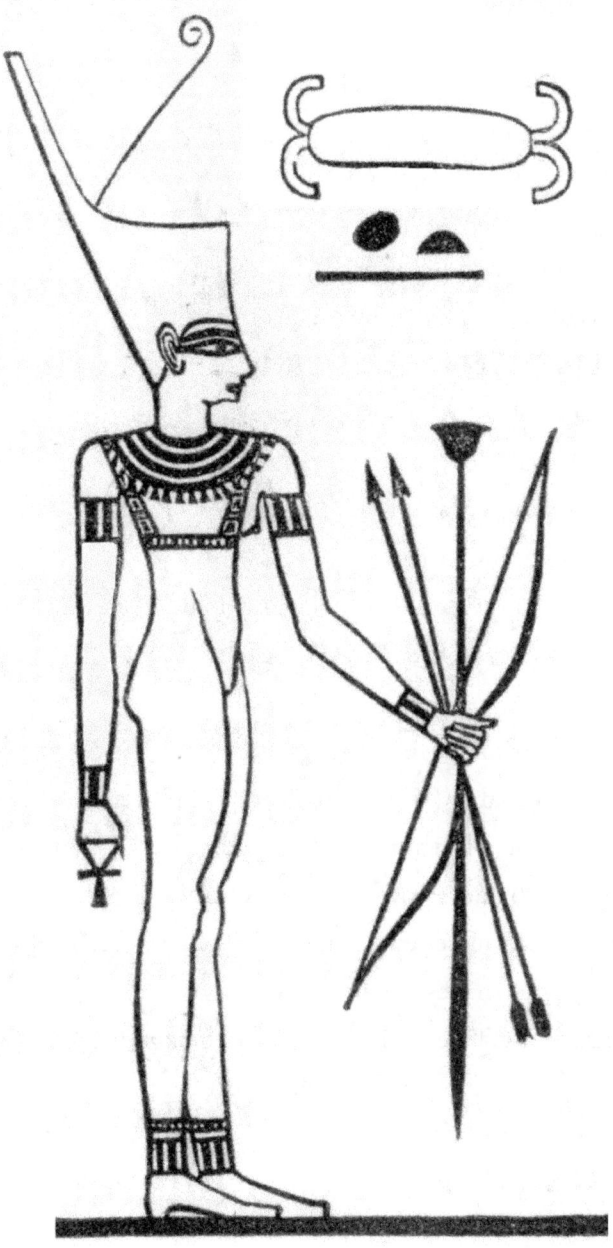

Neith, showing her bow. Top right is her talismanic sign, two bows bound together. From J G Wilkinson, *Manners & Customs of the Ancient Egyptians*, 3 vols (Murray 1837)

Manifested before all,
The protector of the entire land,
She who began to exist,
Before everyone else who has to be,
All who rule do so by her authority.

4. You are the one who made the lower World,
In its goddess form which reaches to
the borders of the universe,
In its material form as surface water,
In its name of "length without limit".
Mistress of the anointing oil
As well as rooms of cloth,
Goddess who divided the comb into five for its functioning
She who resides in the sky and the earth.

5. You are the expanse of water
Which made Earth (Tanen) and the primal waters (Nun),
And whom gave birth to everything that is;
(the one) who causes the inundation to flow in its time,
and the waters of renewal which gives a new life in its season;
(the one) who makes the vegetation sprout,
and creates the Tree of Life for living beings;
Raising the creative primal water (Nun)
Mehet-Weret, the Cow Goddess known as "the Great Flood"
Overcoming the one who rebels.

6. You are the mistress of Esna
Within the [mysterious] countryside
North of the [mound] of the two fledglings;

The one who nurses two crocodiles,
In their names Shu and Tefnut,
Guardian of their fortresses,
Who embraces the necks of two crocodiles
That is to say Re and Osiris
Both nestlings (children), sons of Re
in his chantry (Pi-Sahourê);
Who provides divine offertories for gods and goddesses.

7. Holy Cow.
Lady of southern place
The teacher of Re's country
In the middle of the [mound] of two nestlings;
Supporting the sky on your backbone,
Neith the great
Which gave birth to all beings,
And created grain [to nourish us]
Shu, son of Ra is maintained on your milk.
She nourished the "Seven Primordial Old Ones"
in the interior of the House of Gods
Rejuvenating Osiris lord of Life

8. You are the mistress of the brave
On the day of the fight,
You seize the bow and notch your arrow
Pushing back the hordes of rebels;
Overwhelming in her mightiness over the nine bows
The barbarians fall under your onslaught
Whosoever she favours will be king,
Horus, emblem of royalty eternally on their banners

9. You are the mistress of the sky,
Of the earth and the lower world,
Of the water and the mountains,
Your prestige everywhere elevated

10. You are the mistress of the palace
Protects the sovereign principal,
Maintaining its warriors,
And watching over the entire land
From the flood plain to the mountain top,
Great Uraeus serpent upon the forehead
of the gods and the goddesses,
Serpent of life that protects
And support benign governance
Through the body politic;
The Earth god revealing those worthy of support
So that the golden hawk
And humble lapwing are with her

11. Source of divine order
Ever watchful of intruders & impostors.
Kings depend on you for their power,

12. You are the mistress of the care-ers of the desert,
Lady of bracelets,
Teacher of travellers to the east,
Lady of Punt,
For whom the Fortress-of-the-Honeybee
is flooded with perfumes,
The smell of the cool olibanum,

Distilled drop by drop on curls on your hair
The white crown distinguishing your body
Gentle patroness of the living rock
Creatrix of every precious stone,
Of whatever purposes & function
You are venerated wheresoever they are mined
From Istéren to Rochet and Tefrer;
Lapis lazuli, turquoise and jasper.

Notes & Sources

El-Sayed, Ramadan (1975) *Documents relatifs à Said et ses divinités*, Cairo; El-Sayed, Ramadan (1982) *La Déesse Neith de Sais, Cairo;* Sauneron, S (1962) *Les fêtes religieuses d'Esna aux derniers siècles du paganisme*, Caire: Institut Français d'Archéologie Orientale.

6th Month (December – January)
Nwt – Rekhwer (Greater fire festival)

For this month I'd suggest a celebration of the very ancient star goddess Nuit. For this I have adapted a dramatic text from the Osireion at Abydos. It comes from the *Book of Nut* or is more recent renaming as "The Book of the Fundamentals of the Stars". I have rendered the original in a more user friendly manner without changing the fundamental meaning which concerns the cycle of rebirth. The prayer is either done directly to Nuit or the Milky Way, or as a ritual for three or more participants, Nuit, the Star goddess; Shu the god of the Atmosphere and Geb the Earth:

The Dramatic Text in the Cenotaph of Seti I

Nuit:
"Stars that sail out at night
To the limits of the sky outside of my body;
Shine and be seen.
In the daytime you sail inside of me,
And are not seen.
Enter with the sun god Ra
And go forth after him.
Travelling with him on my body
Supported by Shu
Who settles you in your places (in the night sky)
When the sun god Ra sets in the western horizon.
My head is in the west

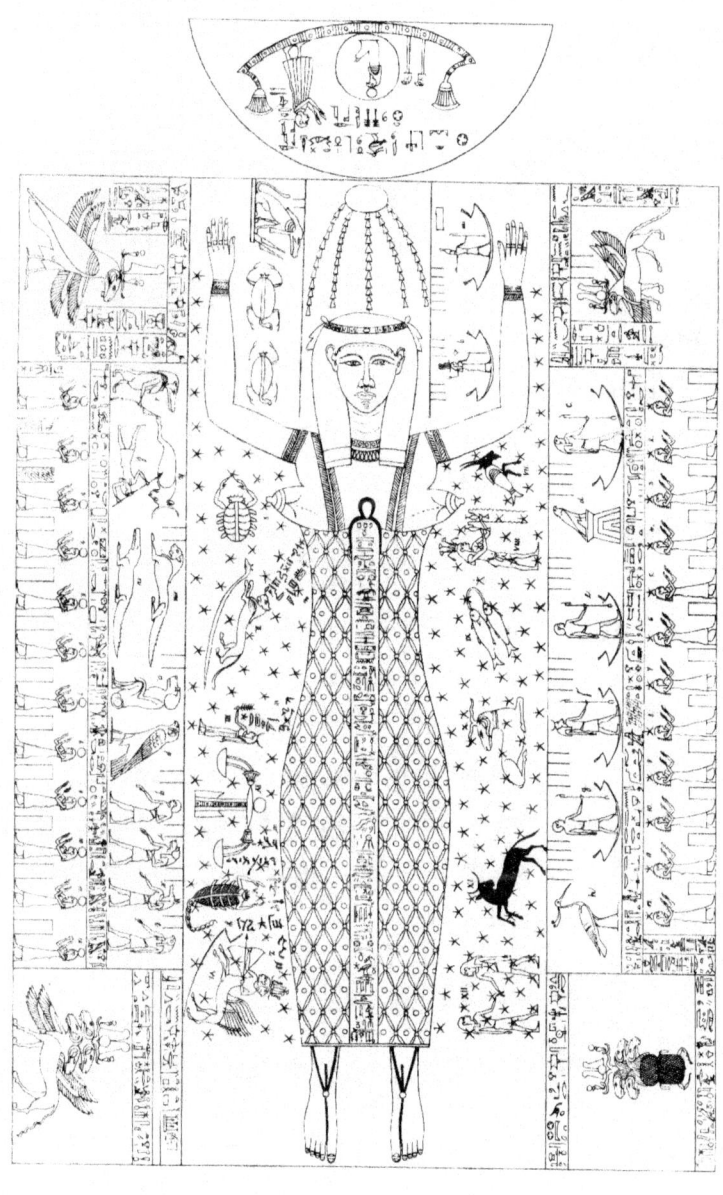

Nuit the star goddess, shown here surrounded by images of the planets, the four winds and the signs of the zodiac. Painting on inside of Heter's coffin, from Neugebauer O & Parker, R (1962) *Ancient Egyptian Astronomical Texts*, 4 vols, Brown University. Original now lost – Brugsch, *Recueil*

Enter my mouth
And I shall eat you!"

Geb:
"Sow who eats her piglets!" says earthy Geb quarrelling with Nuit, angry because she is always eating his children.

Shu:
"Let Geb beware! Says her father Shu, lifting her up, supporting her above himself, "Do not quarrel with Nuit for eating your children, for just as she gives birth to Ra everyday, so shall they live and go forth to their places from under her hind part in the East.
Not one of them has fallen since their birth.
The stars that go into the earth
Die and enter the Duat.
They stop in the house of Geb for seventy days.
Regenerated, loosing their impurity to the earth.
One does not speak the name of the one who is to be reborn,
During those seventy days.
For they have yet no identity
Until, as a shining star,
It rises at the end of the period of regeneration.
Nor do we name them among the 'living'
until all of its impurity falls to the earth
and like Sothis, it rises.
Then it is 'pure' (regenerated) and 'lives' again."

Nuit:
"The heads of gods are located in the east.

'one dies and another lives every ten days.'
They celebrate the First Feast, a birth day there."
"If their bones fall to the earth,
I give them back their head,
And their soul goes forth upon the earth."

"Tears fall and become as fish.
In a lake where the life of a star begins.
As a fish it grows and goes forth from the water.
From the sea it flies upward to the sky
From its former self it flies upward to the sky
From its former self rising as a star.
With other stars that go forth from the Duat
and withdraw across the sky."

Geb:
"I demand that the stars show their heads in the East!" Says Geb, prince of the Gods, again arguing with Nuit.
"Fish your own head out."

Thoth:
"Thoth commands it too, Fish out your own heads."

Nuit:
"Arise as stars I say, shining forth from the deep
Your burials like, those of men.
This period in the Duat just right for everything
That has to be done (for regeneration)."
"As souls you travel inside of the sky at night.
And then by day withdraw to the boundaries of the sky

Invisible to sight.
When seen by the living,
It is indeed as a star,
a piglet of your mother,
making its journey
and shining forth in the sky
in the hours of the night
Travelling the sky to the end."

"Thus all life is seen.
The stars go forth
outside of me, the goddess Nuit
Proceeding as they do and returning.
[The never-ending cycle of death and rebirth]
As the son succeeds the father
As new moon succeeds the full."

Notes & Sources

This ancient, and to many scholars, enigmatic drama is based on various sources, mainly Anne Sophie von Bomhard (2008) *The Noas of the Decades*, Oxford; Otto Neugebauer & Richard Parker (1960) *Egyptian Astronomical Texts*, London; Erik Hornung (1999) *The Ancient Egyptian Books of the Afterlife*, Cornell.

7th Month (Jan – Feb) Wepwawet/Anubis (Lesser fire festival)

The Harris Magical papyrus (pHarris) show how there is a long association between the Jackal god Anubis and a technique known as a vessel divination or inquiry. His name, Egyptian *Inpw*, can mean child, which perhaps explains why these kinds of spell often stipulate that a youth acts as medium.

Anubis is most often said to be the child of Osiris & Nephthys. The spell uses various elements often associated with the god Set e.g.: oasis water and this may be because in for example the Papyrus Vandier the god Set is able to take on the form of Anubis. The spell is for general divine intelligence about the future. It aims to make contact with the divine spirits that control the "decans" i.e. fate as the astrological 'hours' at the time of the conjuration.

If the information you require is more specific then the ancients recommend submerging an *appropriate* object in the water or burning it on a brazier or thurible. So for example in the pHarris, the earliest known version of this spell, an "egg" of ass's dung is cast into water to repel bad influences.

The following spell is from one manuscript augmented with lines from related sources listed in the notes. If you check these sources I hope you will agree I have not distorted the original meaning merely interpreted and in some cases with the contemporary practitioner in mind, shortened the speeches. This kind of spell is often said to come from a physician in the *Oxyrhynchus* nome. Herm-Anubis is another

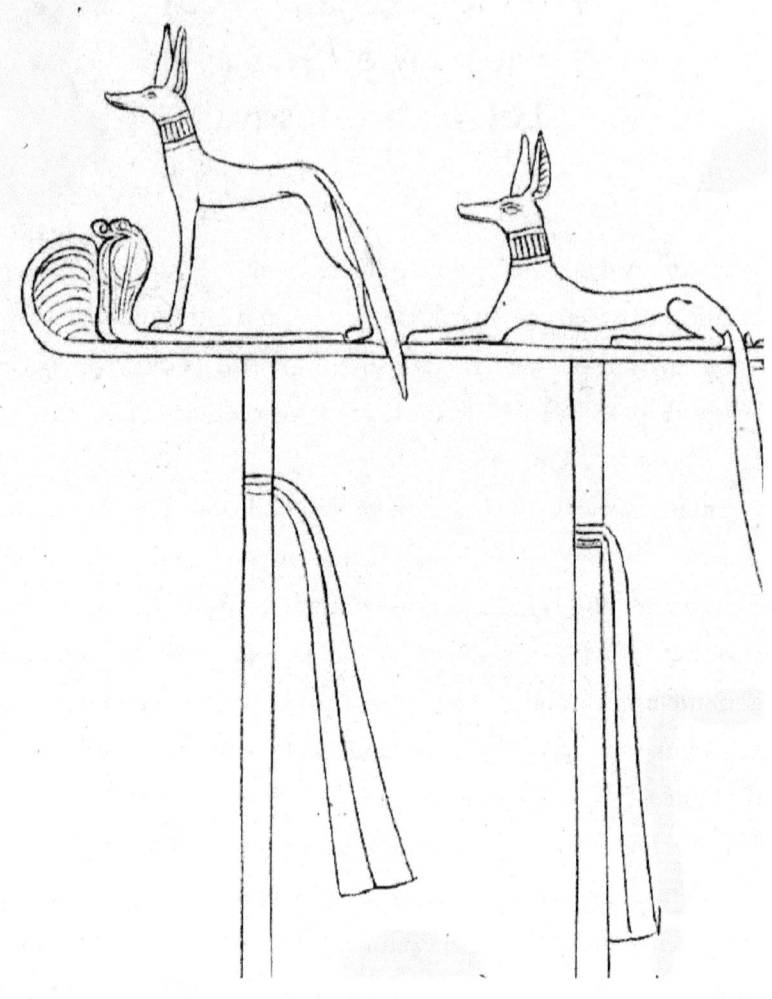

Ancient jackal deity Wepwawet/Upuaut 'Opener of the ways' from Temple of Sety I at Abydos drawn by Amice Calverley. His function was originally to open the field of battle.

Classic image of Anubis/Anpu, detail of painting from a private Theban tomb, From I Rosellini (Pisa 1832-44) *Monumenti dell' Egitto e della Nubia*

important aspect of the god. For comments on the Sethian associations of Oxyrhynchus see *The Bull of Ombos*.

This rite is for two people, the priest who acts as amanuensis or scribe and a medium. It develops into a dialogue between the medium and the god Anubis. In classical times, the medium was usually a virginal youth but for this reconstruction I have it as a sensitive medium. For equipment one needs a suitable bowl or chalice into which one places clear water or oil, preferably from one of Egypt's oases. In addition a table altar on which to place food and drink as well as a thurible or brazier to burn incense and other magical catalysts. Egyptian magicians used a special Anubis herb for this rite. This has been variously identified as Stachys or Woundwort, which has a long medical history as a mild antiseptic and eye medicine. An alternative could be Mentha Aquatica/ Water mint. It seems likely that the medium used an embrocation to open their inner eyes.

1. Start with the Tankhem opening as given earlier:

2. Priest: (opening address)
"Hail thou soul god, Anubis,
The son of the goddess Nephthys
Hail key-holder
Who sends the phantoms of the dead,
For my service in this very hour.
Hail Anubis loyal dog
Resting on a box of myrrh,
Your feet on the frankincense

When I make this libation

Anubis with a fair face
I see you great god
And with this masque (or mark) about my head
I am Anubis, master of secrets."

Priest:
"Oh Anubis, the edge of whose strap rests in Pelusium
Whose his face is like a spark
Put the light and breadth in my vessel
Open to me, O Earth!
Open to me, O Underworld!
Open to me, O primeval waters!
O protector of the necropolis at Abydos

Oh Gods who are in heaven
Who are exalted, come
And put the light and breadth in my vessel.

May we prosper for this vessel that was used by Isis
in her searching for Osiris
Powerful one of heaven, ABLANATHANALBA
The griffin of the shrine of the god who stands here today.

Then whisper:
"Oh good Oxherd Anubis,
My compeller, open the eyes of the medium so they may see.
O pure gods of the primeval water,
I am a child of earth by name,
Under the soles of whose feet the gods of Egypt are placed.
I am the one in the shrine

Of earth by name
I preserve the one in the shrine
With these forearms of real gold
The truth in my mouth is the honey of my lips.

Priest addressing the Medium:

"Open your [inner] eyes and tell me what you see?"

Medium:

[The following develops into a trance session. The text gives an idea of how this goes but in practice the participants would need to allow some flexibility. For example there needs to be a pause to allow the medium time to refocus and then whisper or otherwise signal they are beginning to see visions. They may say something like:]

"Be great, be great, oh Light"

Priest: (If necessary)

"Oh darkness, remove yourself from before him.
O light bring the light to me
Fate who is in the primal water
Bring the light into me
O Osiris who is in the divine bark
Bring the light in to me
O these four winds which are outside, bring the light in to me
O he in whose hand is the moment,
the one who belongs to these hours
Bring the light in to me
O Anubis, the good Oxherd, bring the light in to me

in order that you give me protection here today, for I am Horus,
the son of Isis, the good son of Osiris!
You should bring the gods for the place of judgement
and you should cause them to take care of my affair
so that my business proceeds
O those belonging to the avengers you should cause them
to do it for me"

Medium:
[They may repeat the simple sentence of before]:

"Be great, be great, oh Light".

Eventually they indicate when they can see Anubis
in their visions.

Priest:
Words before Anubis:
Oh RIDJ MYRIDJ,
Oh earth,
Great one of the earth
O this beautiful male whom Heset the daughter
of the Nemesis bore
Come to me, for you are this lotus flower, which came forth from
the lotus bud of Ra, which makes light for the entire land!

Hail, Anubis! Come to me!
O High one,
O mighty one O master of secrets for those in the Underworld
O Pharaoh of those in Amenti

O chief physician
O good son of Osiris
He whose face is strong among the gods
You should appear in the Underworld before the hand of Osiris
You should serve the souls of Abydos
In order that they all love through you
These souls, the ones of the sacred Underworld.
Come to the earth!
Reveal yourself to me here today
You are Thoth
You are the one, who went forth from the heart
of the great Agathodaimon,
The father of the fathers of the gods.
Come to the mouth of my vessel today
And tell me an answer in truth concerning everything
About which I am inquiring,
Without falsehood, therein, for I am Isis the wise,
the sayings of whose mouth come to pass.

[The original rubrik says repeat seven times which may be excessive but perhaps one could apply to one small section as this is an important symbolic instruction. Anubis then acts as psycho pomp or mediator between the medium and the other gods and spirits.]

Priest: (speaking with a calm, slow voice)
"Ask Anubis to go forth and bring the gods in."

Medium:
"It is done" (or similar).

Priest (with calm, slow voice)

"Awaken to me,

Awaken to me Fate (Pshai)

Awaken Mera

The great one of the five (i.e. Thoth)

TSITSIY TENNDJIY

Do justice to me

Thoth, may creation fill the earth with light

O Ibis in his noble countenance,

Noble one who pleases the heart,

Create truth,

O great god whose name is great"

[The priest now focuses on the table set in order to entertain the gods. On the table is wine [or beer] and bread. This table is an altar but also the elaborate *mesa* as used in 'shamanism']

Priest to Medium

"Ask Anubis to bring in the gods to sit at the table".

Medium:

"It is done."

Priest to Medium

"Tell them it is open for the gods. Let them eat, let them drink, eat more, drink more, let them make merry."

Medium:

"It is done."

[The medium consults Anubis to ensure the divine guests are satisfied and for an appropriate moment to make the specific inquiry. When Anubis says the moment is come, ask Anubis to make the appropriate god stand up. When Anubis says the god has stood up, you say to Anubis to clear the table taking away that which is on it.]

Medium:
"Agathodaimon of today, lord of today, the one to whom these moments belong. Let him tell Anubis his name"

When he stands and tells his name you continue
asking every thing you wish.

"License to depart":
"Farewell, farewell Anubis the good Oxherd,
Anubis, Anubis, the son of a wolf and a dog
NABRIS-HOT HT [or *senebty*]
The cherub of Amenti
King of those of the Underworld" (repeat seven times)

After which pour the contents of the chalice on earth
And clear equipment, extinguish lamps etc.

Notes & Sources

This spell is based mainly on PDM xiv 1 - 92 with additional material from PDM xiv 425, PGM iv 1390-1495; PDM xiv 435sq, PDM xiv 2/7 in H D Betz (1986) *The Greek Magical Papyri in Translation*, Chicago; Jacques Vandier (1961) *Le Papyrus Jumilhac*, CNRS; The *Harris Magical Papyrus* is published in *Facsimiles of Egyptian Hieratic Papyri in the British Museum : with descriptions, translations, etc.* by E.A. Wallis Budge; British Museum, 1910, Col vii. This collection has several other interested ritual texts connected with Apep, Isis, Nephthys & Sokar. As an alternative to the use of a full Anubis mask, which can be troublesome if not well constructed, I suggest a small symbol of Anubis drawn on your forehead over the third eye or worn as a headband.

8th Month (February – March) Renenutet (Greek Thermuthis) or Meretseger

Renenutet is an ancient serpent goddess associated with the harvest but also weaving and linen. Her usual form is that of a woman wearing the serpentine uraeus headdress, or a large snake wearing the solar disk and cow's horns. The association of snakes with harvested fields is perhaps a universal phenomenon, not to mention hazard that required some form of propitiation.

She is the mother of another mysterious serpent deity "Nehebkau". She may therefore share something with scorpion goddess Selket also said to be mother to Nehebkau. Both goddesses feed and nurture the future king. Selket is actually the non-venomous water scorpion, perhaps Renenutet is a non-venomous serpent.

Rubrik

Details of the cult practices are sketchy. It is probably an old harvest festival. One would expect a feast, possibly involving fire. This is also the birthday of the 'corn mummy' Neper. These are small dolls made of soil mixed with grain of corn, wrapped in linen and buried in the fields each year in association with the cult of Osiris.

These rituals may be connected with marking out the fields at the beginning of harvest. There is perhaps some overlap with the Sed or 30 year jubilee rite of the king. Some say this 30 year interval is modeled on the 30 day lunar month. Among public rites, the chieftain is required to circumambulate the fields. *Encircling* was and indeed still is an important magical technique. This was no doubt modeled on the custom by which Egyptian folk circumambulated their fields in order to drive out the "pests of the year" – ie "pests" understood as physical and metaphysical entities.

Using these sources as clues I have compiled a short ritual for Renenutet. This could be combined with the construction of a small "corn-mummy" to be buried in the ground at the rite's conclusion.

EGYPTIAN MAGICK ☙ 301

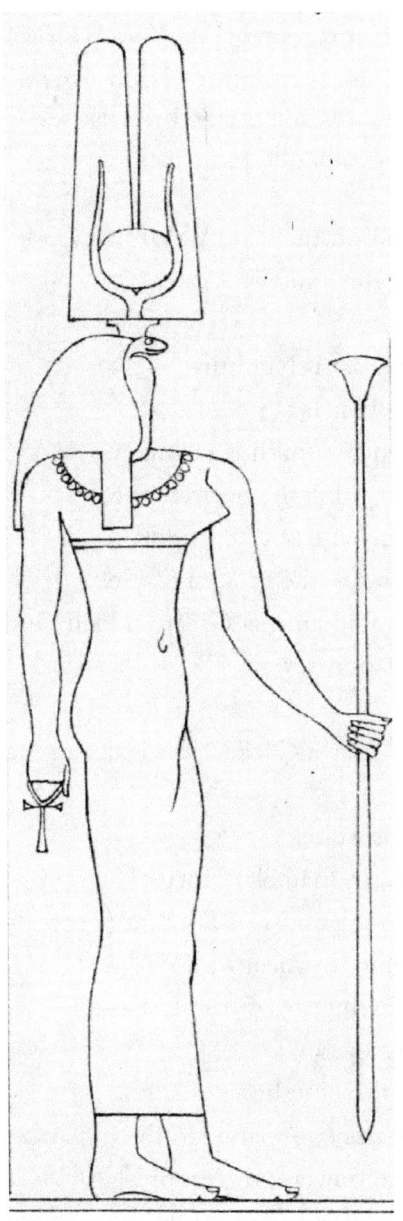

Image of Renenutet from Dendera, see Mariette-bey, Auguste (1870-1880)
Dendérah : description générale du grand temple de cette ville / Vol III PL75

1. The *Tankhem* / Heptagram opening given earlier is here especially relevant. The version I use is from the Greco-Egyptian magical papyri but others found in records for the Sed rituals (see Uphill in *Notes & Sources*) echo the same geomantic principles.

2. "I take my stand on the staircase of the south
on the festival of Renenutet"
The Abydos Formula
"Before me in the east is Nephthys
Behind me in the west Isis
On my left hand in the south is Horus
And on my right hand in the north is Set
For above me shines the body of Nuit
And below me extends the ground of Geb
And in the centre abideth the 'Great Hidden God.'
Then to each direction say:

" 'To the ground' I say as Hekaw the Elder magician"

3. How beautiful is Sobek,
He of Crocodile city, (namely) Horus,
The one who is in the midst of Shedyet (Crocodile city)
Who appears in glory by means of Wadjet,
Who is beautiful by means of his great eye,
Which is under his eyebrow.
Verily, she guides the nine bows
Even when she issues commands to the nine troops;
And she causes the powers of [Apophis],
Who is in the darkness outside, to flee
Even when she puts slaughter
And blood of her into her enemies
In her name of "blood-red."

Let the Coiled One awaken even in peace,

With the awakening of your spirit (Ba)
Being in a state of peace!
You [the diadem] have been established
On the head of Sobek, etc,
Even so that you might appear in his forehead
In your name of "Great of Magic."
Let the gods have fear of you,
And let the living and the dead fall upon their faces for you!

1. Awake in peace! Great Queen, awake in peace;
thine awakening is peacefull.
2. Awake in peace! Snake that is on the brow of a king,
awake in peace; thine awakening is peaceful
3. Awake in peace! Upper Egyptian snake,
awake in peace, thine awakening is peaceful.
4. Awake in peace! Renenutet, awake in peace;
thine awakening is peaceful.
5. Awake in peace! Uto (the Dawn) splendidly fingered,
awake in peace; thine awakening is peaceful.
6. Awake in peace! Thou with head erect, with wide neck,
Awake in peace; thine awakening is peaceful.
7. Awake in peace! Thou with head erect, with graceful neck,
Awake in peace; thine awakening is peaceful.
8. Awake in peace! Selket,
Awake in peace; thine awakening is peaceful.
9. Awake in peace! Scribe, who binds the papyrus bundle,
Awake in peace; thine awakening is peaceful.
10. Awake in peace! Who points to the place in the fields,
Awake in peace; thine awakening is peaceful.
11. Awake in peace! Royal Serpent,
Awake in peace; thine awakening is peaceful.

Another Invocation

Use a magick square of the 7 vowels

Thozo pithe etc (Thermouthe pythia)

> The doors are open
> And seven virgins
> Shall arise from the deep earth
> Their garments of purest linen
> Their faces those of serpents
> You are the fates of heaven
> Wielding golden wands
> Welcome

Hail thou seven fates of heaven
O noble and good virgins
O sacred ones
Hail thou chrepsienthaes
Hail thou meneschees
Hail thou mechran!
Hail thou ararmaches
Hail thou echommie
Hail thou tichnondaes
Hail thou erou rombriese

Hail thou seven
snake headed goddesses
The fates of heaven
The goddesses who hold the pole in its place

Thozo pithe etc (Thermouthe pythia)

Hail thou bear goddess,
Great one
ruling heaven.
Reigning over the pole of the stars.
Hail Highest one,
beautiful-shining goddess.
Whose element is Incorruptible .

Hail thous Composite of the all,
The all illuminating,
bond of the universe
You who stand on the pole, you who the lord god
appointed to turn the holy pole with a strong hand.

Thozo pithe etc (Thermouthe pythia)

(Say the following as a voice offering): I offer 4 drams of frankincense; 4 drams of myrrh; 2 ounce each of; Casia leaf; Of white pepper; 1 dram of bdelion; 1 dram of wormwood; 1 dram of vetch plant; 1 dram of Kefi; The complete brain of a ram; Combine these with mendesian wine; And honey. Take pellets of smokey incense and drop on a thurible of burning charcoal and scry into the smoke

Notes & Sources:

Broekhuis, Jan (1971) *De Godin Renenwetet*, Bib Classical Vangacumiana vol 19. English summary available; *The Edwin-Smith Surgical Papyrus*, col 18/15-16; *The Ebers Surgical Papyrus; Harris Magical Papyrus* (Col 10/1 – 11/1); Sauneron, Serge (1989) *Un Traité Egyptien d'Ophiologie* has six magical incantations to repel snakes. Red snakes here seen as manifestation of Set. The text includes a compendium of remedies, whose subsequent history is interesting in terms of medical alchemy – thus (p82) lists "sexualized" minerals – e.g.: "le mâle de galena". Sauneron, Serge (1962) *Les fêtes religieuses d'Esna au derniers siecles du paganisme*, Vol 5 (331 T 2 S); Khnum, Neith & Heka, Ptolemaic temple but extensive liturgy: Speech of Isis (p20&), Speech/Hymn of Thoth (p219); Birth of Apophis (p265); Uphill, Eric (1965) "The Egyptian Sed Festival Rites" *JNES* 24 p365-. Perhaps the nominal number of 30 dynasties is similarly modelled on the lunar month? The geomantic structure is recorded in scenes for Festival Hall of King Osorkon at Bubastis: The king takes his stand on the "staircase of the south" – South: Tjanen & Set; East: Isis & Nephthis; North: Atum & Horus; West: Kephra & Geb. Neville, E (1892) *Festival Hall of Osorkon II*; *Medinet Madi* – (Narmouthis) shrine to Sobek, Horus & Renenutet. Johnson, Sally B. *The Cobra Goddess of Ancient Egypt*. Raven, M J (1982) 'Corn Mummies' OMRO 63, 7.38

9th Month (March – April)
Khonsu "The wanderer"

The sun god Ra is all, more than just the visible sun, his Mysteries include the sun at midnight, the moon, his left-eye. Khonsu is the ancient moon god who gives his name to this month. To those that love him he is also the centre of the universe, thus Queen Cleopatra commissioned the following cosmological inscription for the temple of Khonsu at Karnac:

> Khonsu
> King of Upper and Lower Egypt
> Moon, Pillar of Heaven
> To your right I see the gods marching in
> Montu, entering your left eye on the 1st lunar day
> Atum, entering your left eye on the 2nd lunar day
> Shu, entering your left eye on the 3rd lunar day
> Tefnut, entering your left eye on the 4th lunar day
> Geb, entering your left eye on the 5th lunar day
> Nuit, entering your left eye on the 6th lunar day
> Thoth entering your left eye on the 7th lunar day
> Nephthys entering your left eye on the 8th lunar day
>
> To your right I see the gods marching in
> Osiris, entering your left eye on the 9th lunar day
> Isis, entering your left eye on the 10th lunar day
> Horus, entering your left eye on the 11th lunar day
> Hathor, entering your left eye on the 12th lunar day
> Sobek, entering your left eye on the 13th lunar day
> Tjenenet, entering your left eye on the 14th lunar day

Unusual image of Khonsu, from R V Lanzone, *Dizionario di mitologia egizia*, 3 vols. Lanzone says the original is among the Turin Egyptian Museum's fifteen thousand small objects – so still looking.

Iunyt, entering your left eye on the 15th lunar day

Cleopatra, the Queen, the lady of the two lands

stands to your left,

May your kindly face be gracious to me and to my beloved son

The Kings of Upper and Lower Egypt

stand to your left,

The sky is clear and the horizon

bears the form of the moon.

So that the left eye shines for everybody.

The sky is clear,

when the sound eye, born of Nuit, is elevated.

The following ancient invocation of Khonsu is another that makes use of a suitably filled cup; hold this in your hands to draw down the lunar blessings.

I am the one who appears shining and endures

My body grows old when I delay

For I am the serpent that came forth from the Nun,

I am the proud Ethiopian,

I am rearing serpent of real gold,

There is honey on my lips;

That which I shall say cometh to pass.

I am Anubis, the baby creature;

I am Isis and I will bind him,

I am Osiris the drowned who is bound.

Save me from every danger

Protect me, heal me, give me love, praise and reverence

Into my cup here to-day.

Come to me, Isis, mistress of magic,

the great sorceress of all the gods.

Horus is before me, Nephthys as my diadem, . . .

EGYPTIAN MAGICK ⚜ 309

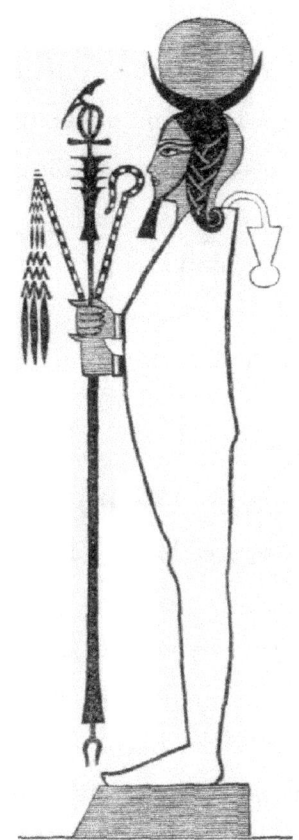

Khonsu, child avatar as part of the Theban triad with Amun & Mut. Illustration from J G Wilkinson, *Manners & Customs of the Ancient Egyptians*, 3 vols (Murray 1837)

Send the mighty lion sons of Mihos
Send the souls of god,
The souls of man,
The souls of the Underworld,
The souls of the horizon,
The spirits, the dead,
Come into my cup and tell me the truth to-day
Concerning that after which I am inquiring:
I summon all your souls and forms to the mouth
Of my vessel;
Let them talk with their mouths,
Let them speak with their lips,
Let them say about that which I ask
Come in to me,
South, North, West, East,
Every breeze of Amenti, for I am the fury of all these gods,
Whose names I have uttered here to-day,
Rouse them for me,
The drowned, the dead; let your soul and your form live for me
Even the fury of Apophis and her daughters I summon
from their places of punishment,
Let him make me answer to every word [about]
which I am asking here to-day in truth without
falsehood therein. Hasten,
quickly

Notes & Sources

For the unusual "Khonsu Theology" of Cleopatra III (161–101BCE) see *Epigraphic Survey, The Temple of Khonsu* Vol 2, Chicago University Press.

It is inscribed over the doorway to the inner sanctuary of Khonsu's temple at Karnac, first hypostyle hall, north wall, lintel.

10th Month (April – May)
Khentykhet – (Horus)

Khentykhet (Gr: Kentechtai) is an ancient lunar form of Horus, whose cult centre was Athribis in the Delta. There is a record of the visit of the Nubian Pharaoh Piankhi of 8th BCE to Athribis at the invitation of the local ruler that he "may see Khentykhet and worship his consort Khuyet offering an oblation of bulls, calves and fowl to Horus in his house." (BAR IV 867)

Khentykhet means "possessor of the divine body". He is especially associated with the crown and attributes of royalty including divine justice (Maat). In modern esotericism, the crown, in the wider sense of the head, signifies a person's self-esteem. Not surprising that this ancient ritual comes from a New Kingdom collection of spells for protection and general well being. This is the era of the Ramesside Kings, most famous of whom are Ramses II and his father Sety I.

Horus the moon (Khentykhet), is very much the chthonic counterpart of Horus the Sun (Khenty-Irty). So this ancient rite has strong lunar component and may be done whilst gazing on the full moon, drawing it down into one's crown or forehead. The spell mentions a special book from which one may recite the spell to the moon.

> Hail to you Horus
> who resides at Athribis
> Who, in the midst of all the gods;
> judges the two lands in your boat
> The jackal of the south,
> "Opener of the Ways" who strikes the rebel;
> Journeying in your shrine
> As it roams in ancient places.

Mnervis Bull who rejuvenates,
Great god, master of Nubia
For whom Punt was created
To whom the two countries were given
So that he can rejoice in your own name.

Keep me away from evil
Protect me from all things bad and pernicious,
Done against me, or to my detriment;
Deliver me from the destruction of Sekhmet;
Protecting me from her red darts.

I am the one who avenges my father;
My form is your form
My places are your places
My heritage also yours.

I am one with Thoth,
Who made the alphabet,
Wearing the Crown of Ra,
As master of Heiracleopolis.
I am Ra
"He who makes himself secret to those who are in the Nun",
Firing arrows at enemies,
To destroy the reactionaries.

Jubilations for Horus-Khenty in Athribis,
Travel in peace.
I come near you; hear my call;
Grant me a long and prosperous life,
In the places I call home,
As do you in your beloved town.

Khenty Khet – an ancient lunar form of Horus. Illustration comes from R.V. Lanzone, (1881-6) *Dizionario di mitologia egizia*.

Whensoever I read this book,
It is for me a favoured day.
I will not hunger or experience thirst;
Neither will I know sorrow.

My heart is not afflicted;
For I am not imprisoned
Neither is judgement delivered against me;
If ever I go to gaol,
I come out vindicated;
Adorations are offered to me as if I am a god;
From whom affection is never parted.

I will not be overcome by my sorrows;
And the plague of the year will not harm me
Nor oppression crush me down.

Notes & Sources

My primary source is Vernus, Pascal (1978), *Athribis : textes et documents relatifs à la géographie, aux cultes, et à l'histoire d'une ville du delta Égyptien à l'époque pharaonique* from which I've translated the invocation which itself comes from Borghouts, J. F. 1978. *Ancient Egyptian Magical Texts*. Leiden: E. J. Brill. I also took information from Cauville, Sylvie (1983) *La théologie d'Osiris à Edfou* (Cairo). The latter is a commentary on the monumental Chassinat, Émile (1892-1985) *Le temple d'Edfou* that is the standard source on the site. Breasted, James Henry (1906-7) *Ancient records of Egypt: historical documents from the earliest times to the Persian conquest / collected, edited and translated with commentary* IV p.867. Wepwawet "Opener of the Ways" = Greek Ophois/Ophais.

11th Month (May – June)
Ipet Hippo goddess

The feast for the hippopotamus goddess Ipet or Jepet ('her majesty') extended over two days but from New Kingdom times was celebrated in the first day of the month. There is a small temple of Ipet in the south-western corner of the temple complex at Karnak. She was also worshiped at Oxyrinchus and the Dakhleh Oasis along with her consort Set. She was an ancient Mother goddess, perhaps originally from Heliopolis, a tradition continued as birth goddess Thoeris. Her protective powers may also be invoked during sleep and in the dream landscape. Another of her names, especially in astrological texts is Reret "The Sow" and it is as well to recall that the Ancient Egyptians considered the Hippo to be a species of pig.

The following short hymn and spell was found on a small ostracon included in the published edition of Papyrus Turin:

> Awake and embrace the void
> Your heart strong enough for its joys
> and its worries
> Leave, and when you awake to life
> You will feel young again on the new day
> Rest, lie down assured of long good health.

> "Good night,
> the gods protect you,
> their protection is before you each day
> No bad thing approaches
> The demon (Apep) is repelled from your bed chamber
> Jepet the Great protects you in your long and powerful life."
> The day and night illumined,

Hippo Goddess from astrological ceiling of Senmut, Neugebauer O & Parker, R (1962) *Ancient Egyptian Astronomical Texts*, 4 vols, Brown University.

You shine forth
For she guides your steps on the right path,
And you know what is needed,
The god Ptah provisions you,
filling your storeroom,
With food and drink aplenty,
and in good measure.
Your diary and records all in order
and well composed.
The mistakes of the past forgotten,
The staff in your hand well made and sustaining.
Break bread with the wise,
Your cares all behind you.
Only reason lies before you,
The best is yet to come.

Praise be to TAWERET,
Bringing "perfection" in her beautiful name.
I praise her to the limits of the sky,
I desire her Ka, calming day by day.

Be merciful to me,
May I behold your mercy,
You, of perfect mercy!
Extend your hand to me,
Giving me life,
And granting me offspring!
Do not reproach me for my errors
You, in perfect mercy!
Even if my helpers slip up,
My peers still reward me.

I desire your great strength,

None knows you as I do;

I will say to the children and children's children:

Thee as guardian before her!

Joy my heart should seize,

Because on this day TAWERET is merciful,

My house prospers with her blessings.

May she give them day after day,

And I never say "Oh I have regrets!"

May she continue to give me health,

And my womb bear children safely,

[Or the future be secure].

My heart is glad every day, for sure

The good ones expel the evil,

And I am blessed.

Behold her people will live forever,

My enemies are fearful before you TAWARET!

Since your rage oppresses them

more than a mountain of iron,

Her mercy gives us life!

Notes & Sources

Jepet Hmt – most ancient form. Pleyte, Willem, *Papyrus Turin*, Brill, Ostacon p.1148 3-6 ; Daves, Norman G (1953) *Templi of Hiblis in El Khargeh*, Vol III; Bonnet, Hans, *Reallexikon* (RAAG) p530-535; Assmann, Jan, *Agyptische Hymnen*; Hornug, Erik & Theodor Abt *Knowledge of the Afterlife*; Jong, J Wde *Het Hat de Ipet* (Dutch with English summary).

12th Month (June – July)
RaHorakhty or Ra

The vast majority of Egyptian hymns are devoted either to Osiris or to the sun god Ra in his various avatars. What follows are two examples, the first an extract, just one section of the voluminous *Litany of the Sun*. This litany survives in many versions but the standard text is taken from an inscription in the tomb of Sety I ("Belzoni's Tomb") in the Valley of the Kings, and therefore dating to c1350BCE. This is followed by a long solar ritual from the Greek Magical Papyri / Theban Magical Library.

The first text gives us an idea of the esoteric doctrine of the Egyptian priests, which was clearly pantheistic, and certainly differed from the polytheistic worship of the common people.

The second part uses a version from the Theban Magical Library in restored to the "original" Egyptian idiom. This invocation is rather long but one soon gets used to it. Almost every line implies a philosophical attitude and in order for the spell to work you have to have satisfied yourself that you understand and agree with this implicite theology. So even if you never use this spell - reading it, especially as part of a Pagan meditational practice is an important spiritual exercise.

I've shortened this some as I suspect that over time parts that were once instructions have become incorporated into the words of power. The vibe is an address to the sun, both visible and symbolic, as the pivot of the whole celestial hierarchy.

The Litany of RA (1st Canto)

Title. The beginning of the book of the worship of RA in the West, (The heavenly region) of the worship of the United One in the West. When any

Above: Ra at sunrise as Kephra, sunset as Tum. Detail from door lintel in tomb of Rameses X. The lower image is a very early version of the same idea, the mountains of sunrise/sunset, east/west. Nagada I/Amratean predynastic pottery circa 4000BCE

one reads this book, porcelain figures are placed upon the ground, at the hour of the setting of the Sun, that is of the triumph of RA over his enemies in the West. Whoso is intelligent upon the earth, he is intelligent also after his death.

1 Homage to thee, RA ! Supreme power, the master of the hidden spheres who causes the principles to arise, who dwells in darkness, who is born as the all surrounding universe.

2 Homage to thee, RA ! Supreme power, the beetle that folds his wings, that rests in the empyrean, that is born as his own son.

3 Homage to thee, RA ! Supreme power, TANEN (The Earth) who produces his members (Gods), who fashions what is in him, who is born within his sphere.

4 Homage to thee, RA ! Supreme power, he who discloses the earth and lights the Ament, he whose principle has (become) his manifestation, and who is born under the form of the god with the large disk.

5 Homage to thee, RA ! Supreme power, the soul that speaks, that rests upon her high place, that creates the hidden intellects which are developed in her.
6 Homage to thee, RA ! Supreme power, the only one, the courageous one, who fashions his body, he who calls his gods (to life), when he arrives in his hidden sphere.

7 Homage to thee, RA ! Supreme power, he who addresses his eye, and who speaks to himself, he who imparts the

breath of life to the souls (that are) in their place ; they
receive it and develop.

8 Homage to thee, RA ! Supreme power, the spirit that walks,
that destroys its enemies, that sends pain to the rebels.

9 Homage to thee, RA ! Supreme power, he who shines when he
is in his sphere, who sends his darkness into his sphere, and who
hides what it contains.

10 Homage to thee, RA ! Supreme power, he who lights the
bodies which are on the horizon, he who enters his sphere.

Consecrating a ring, statue, etc., with the power of the sun god Ra

1. An address to the triple sun

I invoke and beseech the consecration,

O gods of the heavens

O gods under the earth

O gods circling on the middle region from one womb

O masters of all the living and dead

O heedful in many necessities of gods and men

O concealers of things now seen

O directors of Isis, Nemesis and Adrasteia who spend every hour with you

O senders of fate who travels around the whole world

O commanders of the rulers

O exalters of the abased

O revealers of the hidden
O guides of the winds
O arousers of the waves
O bringers of fire at the appropriate time
O creators and benefactors of every race
O Lords and controllers of kings
Come, benevolent ones, for the purpose for which I call you, as benevolent assistants in this rite for my benefit.

2. Assumption of the god form
I am an outflow of blood from the tomb of Osiris
[between] the palm trees
I am the faith found in men and I am he who declares the holy names, who is unchanging, who came forth from the abyss.
I am the sacred Phoenix bird
I am Helios
I am the god whom no one sees or rashly names
I am Shu the sender of winds
I am Tefnut the fire
I am Geb the earth
I am Nuit the mother of the gods
I am Osiris called water
I am Isis called dew
I am Set who defeats Apophis
I am Nephthys called spring
I am Harpocrates who came forth from the eye of the sun
I am an image resembling the true image
Therefore I beseech you
come as my helpers,

for I am about to call on the hidden and ineffable name, the forefather of the gods, overseer and lord of all

3. Hymn to the Demiurge

Come to me, you from the four winds,
god, ruler of all
who have breathed spirits into men for life,
master of the good things in the world.
Hear me, lord whose hidden name is ineffable.
The daimons, hearing it, are terrified -
the name is
BARBAREICH ARSEMPHEM-PHROTHOU
and of it the sun, of it the earth.
hearing, rolls over.
Hades, hearing is shaken
rivers, sea, lakes, springs, hearing are frozen
rocks, hearing it are split
Heaven is your head; ether body
earth feet and water around you ocean
O Agathos Daimon
You are lord, the begetter and nourisher and increaser of all

4. Hexametrical hymn to the Demiurge

Who molded the forms of the beasts of the Zodiac
Who found their routes
Who was the begetter of fruits?
Who raises up the mountains?
Who made the winds to hold to their annual tasks
What Aion nourishing an Aion rules the Aions?
One deathless god

You are the begetter of all and assign souls to all
and control all,
King of the Aions and Lord before who
mountains and plains
springs and rivers
valleys of earth
spirits and all things
High shining heaven
and every sea trembles.
Lord, ruler of all, holy one
and master of all.
By your power the elements exist
and all things come into being,
the route of the sun and moon,
of night and dawn
all things in air and earth and water and fire.
Yours is the eternal processional way of [heaven]
in which the seven lettered name is established for the harmony
of the seven sounds of the planets which utter their voices
according to the phases of the moon.
You give wealth, good old age, good children, strength, food.
You lord of life, ruler of the upper and lower realm,
whose justice is not thwarted,
whose glorious name the angels hymn,
who have truth that never lies,
hear me and complete for me this operation so that I may wear
this power in every place,
in every time, without being smitten or afflicted,
so as to be preserved intact from every danger
while I wear this power.

Yea lord, for to you,

the god in heaven,

all things are subject, and none of the daimons or spirits will oppose me because I have called on your great name for the consecrations.

5. Invocation of the deity

The gates of heaven are opened

The gates of earth are opened

The route of the sea is opened

The route of the rivers is opened

My spirit is heard by gods and daimons

My spirit is heard by the spirit of heaven

My spirit is heard by the terrestrial spirit

My spirit is heard by the marine spirit

My spirit is heard by the riverine spirit

Therefore give spirit to the ring

I have prepared

O gods whom I have named and called on

Give breath to the ring

Let its mouth be opened

so that it may breath and live

According to the Egyptian way: Ei IEOU - Oh Hail

According to the Jews: Ei IEOU - Oh Hail

According to the Greeks: Ei IEOU - Oh Hail

According to the High Priests of Egypt: Ei IEOU - Oh Hail

According to the Hindus - Ei IEOU - Oh Hail

Consecrate and empower this object for me,
for the entire and glorious time of my life.

Invoking the power of the sun

To use the ring or magical object there is a short invocation that one can recite whenever one has need of special power from the ring:

The gates of heaven are open
The gates of earth are open
The route of the sea
The route of rivers are opened
My spirit is was by all gods and daimons
My spirit is was by the spirit of heaven
My sprit is was by the terrestrial spirit
My spirit is was by the marine spirit
My spirit is was by the riverine spirit
Therefore give spirit to the mystery
I have prepared
O Gods whom I have named and have called on
Give breath to the mystery I have prepared.

Finish with a litany of 15 gods names. The text here is garbled, so I suggest some alternatives taken from the lunar days at the temple of Horus at Edfu:

EI IEOU Na (Oh Hail Red Serpent)
(pronounced Ai Ee-Ah-Ou with emphasis on the first syllable)
EI IEOU Shem (Oh Hail the stranger)
EI IEOU Irymeryef (Oh Hail the merry maker)
EI IEOU Wenet (Oh Hail The Hare Goddess)

EI IEOU Khnoum (Oh Hail)

EI IEOU Horus (Oh Hail his father's offspring)

EI IEOU Nehes (Oh Hail Goddess)

EI IEOU Thoth (Oh Hail)

EI IEOU Horus (Oh Hail avenger of his father)

EI IEOU Osiris (Oh Hail)

EI IEOU (Oh Hail) Amseti

EI IEOU (Oh Hail) Hapi

EI IEOU (Oh Hail) Tiamutef

EI IEOU (Oh Hail) Kebsenef

EI IEOU (Oh Hail) Iretef

Notes and Sources

The translation has been made from Edouard Naville, *La Litanie du Soleil* (Leipzig, 1875, avec un vol. de XLIX planches), where this text has been first translated into French with a commentary. Ring Spell from PGM XII 201-216 & 270-350. For Greek Helios as Egyptian Ra see Jacco Dielemann, *Priests, Tongues & Rites*, 2005 p159

13th Month (July – August)
Thoth
Extra lunar month as needed, ie approximately every third year
Or as alternative to Seth in first month

By a quirk of history more is known of the popular cult of Thoth than its "official" temple version. For example Turin's Egyptian Museum (the largest outside Egypt) houses a small votive stele found at workman's village of the Theban necropolis (Deir el-Medina). This object tells us that one swore an oath by the moon and if one broke that oath, it was to the moon one appealed. It's a very human document and gives a glimpse at the world behind the perfect image presented in most "official" Egyptian inscriptions.

Spell to be said before portable shrine set before an image of the lunar barque bearing the moon's disk between two horns with caption "Lunar-Thoth: The great god, the merciful":

"I NN (*your name*) servant of the moon say:
'I am that man who uttered an oath
falsely by the Moon concerning [any matter].
And he caused me to see the greatness of
his power before the whole land.
I will declare thy might
To the fish of the deep
To the fowl of the skies
So they shall say to their children's children,
Be aware of the moon!
O merciful one, thou art able to turn this away".

Thoth – from Nubian tomb in I Rosellini, *Monumenti dell' Egitto e della Nubia* (Pisa 1832-44)

1. Standard Adoration to Thoth

O Gods who are in the sky

O Gods who are on the earth,

Gods of the south, north, west & east

Come and witness:

Thoth appear glorious with his crown (*oureret*)

in Hermopolis

With the Two Lords, Horus & Set

Guiding the common people (*rekhyt*)

Exultant in the great house of Geb, the earth god

On account of his efforts.

Adore him, exalt him, praise him!

Felicitous Lord,

The guide of the masses in their entirety

All you gods and goddesses, behold!

Praise Thoth this day

Who founded your sanctuaries,

And devised the temple liturgy

On the primal sunset island.

2. Greeting to you, Thoth!

It is me, alone (here), who adores you.

Give me a home and property

So that I am grounded with possessions.

Let me live,

In the country of the living,

Made by you on the primal sunset island.

Give me love, blessings, benevolence and protection;

This person here of feelings, mind and heart,

Whether commoner, patrician or astral being etc.

Overcome my enemies in this life or the next!
Said by offrant of Thoth,
One who is justified before his adversaries
In the tribunal of the Gods
Over which Thoth presides,
Commanding the nine (Gods) of the Company of Heaven.

2. Prayer to Thoth

O Thoth, take me to Hermopolis
The city where the living is easy,
And I am placed before the Lord my god
And I go forth justified.
Where you provide all the necessities of life,
In bread and beer.
Come, O divine speech!
Thoth, you are behind me in the morning!
Guarding my mouth (when) I speak.

O great sixty cubit doum-palm
Which bears a fine crop,
Of luscious fruits within every
moist kernal.

O you who provide water in desert,
Come and save me, who keeps silent!
O Thoth, gentle fountain in the desert!
Untouched by human artifice.
The one that is hidden from the profane,
But flows for the initiate,
who comes silently to the well spring.

3. Prayer to Thoth

Praise be thou, O Lord of the house,
Baboon radiant of mane,
of sweet appearance and gentle charm,
beloved of everybody.
You of the *shrt*-stone
Shine on Thoth and illuminate
the land in all its beauty.
Upon your head is the crown of red jasper
and your phallus of cornelian.
Love emanates from your brow,
And when you speak you bestow life.
My threshold is blessed when the dog (*iw*) enters.
It thrives and has flourished from the time
that my lord has trodden it.
Be happy you of my street,
Rejoice all my neighbours.
Behold my lord, it is he who has made me,
thus my heart longs for him.
Thoth, thou shall be my companion,
and I shall never fear the (evil) eye.

4. Prayer of a scribe of Thoth

Come to me Thoth, august ibis,
Desired God of Hermopolis,
Scribe of the acts of the Company of Heaven.
Great in your city!
Help me to direct myself,
Making me skilful in our profession.
The best of all occupations.

It rises one up.

The respected scribe becomes great.

There are many you have thus helped;

Who are now among the best,

Your actions are strong and graceful.

You are the one who guides a person,

who lacks a mother's hand.

Fate and Renenutet are beside you.

Come and guide me.

An attendant of your temple.

Allow me to impart your knowledge,

Such that in any country where I am,

The multitude of people say;

Great is the knowledge of Thoth!

And they come, together with their children,

To be marked (branded) as scribes:

The good profession of the victorious Lord!

Happy the one who exercises it!

Notes & Sources

Claas J Bleeker, *Hathor & Thoth, Two Key Figures in Ancient Egyptian Religion*, Leiden 1973; Patrick Boyland, *Thoth the Hermes of Egypt* London 1922; Battiscombe Gunn "The religion of the Poor in Ancient Egypt" *JEA* III p 81-94. Adolf Erman, *Handbook of Egyptian Religion*; translated by A S Griffith; André Barucq & A F Daumas, *Hymnes et prières d'Egypt*, Paris 1980; Gardiner, A H, *Late Egyptian Miscellanies*, Bruxelles 1937. The terms feeling, mind and heart in the first prayer are translations of Hwt "to burn"; HAty = "thoughts, mind"; Ib = "heart".) The third hymn is translated by Ricardo A. Caminos in his thesis/translation of Allan Gardiner's, *Late-Egyptian miscellanies*. "The Evil Eye" is literally ꜥIrt – the "left eye of heaven, the moon".

8. Taboo Magick, Sacrifices etc

"Cannibalism is a predicament of the animistic hunter or gardener, who must live by consuming animals or plants which are essentially persons themselves" (Graeber & Sahlins, *On Kings* p16)

"Thus the weakened and shattered power of Typhon," ... still gasps and struggles", so the priesthood must "appease and mollify" which they do by means of "sacrifices". Sacrifice is a very ambiguous thing. Sacrifice brings to mind the ritual slaughter of an animal or, – including in some records - human beings. Although the latter is largely confined to a very remote history of humanity where it is known from archaeological or written records, usually occuring in desperate times. In almost all myths of the world, the gods eat flesh and drank blood. Human beings are even referred to as the "divine cattle" i.e. divine food. Thus is often recorded in religious scripture for the purpose of telling us why we no longer offer such sacrifice. Thus in the famous myth of the Divine Cow-goddess Hathor, she threatens to kill humanity entirely and proceeds to makes a good stab at it. She is diverted from this grisly task with the offer of a substitute that tastes like blood but is in fact beer. You can guess the rest. I hazard an opinion that every culture has a similar story.

The offering of an animal, other than human, is less contentious. The animal offered still shares in some of the characteristics of the god to whom it is offered. The animal is often an avatar of the god, e.g. goats are sacred to the sun god Ra, cats to the goddess Bast, the sacred Ibis to scribal god Thoth, Crocodiles to Sobek or the falcon to Horus. It is a curious double take that one would kill the sacred animal as an offering to the god whom it is thought to symbolise! However, cattle were also offered to all the gods if the moment was appropriate. It has long be the practice for magicians to find an alternative, such as incense or some, as it says in Crowley's Liber Al "The best blood is of the moon monthly". Or indeed orgasm is often considered sufficient (see NakedTantra).

Eating magic

This is a good moment to discuss the "eating magick", a ubiquitous religious practice, past and present. Indeed, it still is one of the world's most popular ritual acts. Think for a moment of the Catholic Mass in which bread and wine is shared. During Mass, (from the Greek "Messa" meaning barley cake) one is witnessing or participating in what may well be humanity's oldest rite. It was an ancient practice even before the early Christians "appropriated" or adopted it from their Pagan predecessors. It is common to many religions and long may it be so.

Whilst talking about the then popular variety of "eating magick", Plutarch tells us that people attending Egyptian festivals were offered, "round cakes in festivals of the months Payni and Phaophi, [and] as an insult, they stamp on them an image of a tied ass." Elsewhere he says the image is of a male hippopotamus, another common animal form of the same god Seth. With recent discoveries at Hierakonpolis as our guide, we must say that the hippo, male and female, was a symbol of royal prestige from the time of Egypt's earliest dynasties. Is this humiliating or is it, as in the case of the "sacred bread", eaten as a sacrament, like in many of the world's religions, sharing of the body and power of the god? Difficult to say

In H W Fairman's *The Triumph of Horus, An Ancient Egyptian Sacred Drama* published by Batsford in 1974, there is a reconstruction of the entire mystery play compiled from the texts on the walls of the temple of Horus at Edfu. This all dates from the first centuries of the common era but it re-enacts what seems to be an older prototype, dated to Egypt's first dynasty, as depicted in a seal impression from Abydos, where King Den harpoons a hippopotamus.

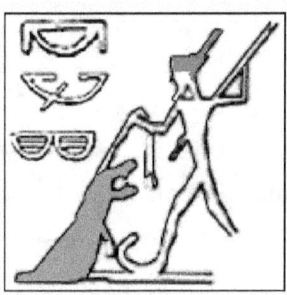

In the play's third act, a large cake, shaped as a hippopotamus is carried onstage and sliced up, dismembered into multiple portions, which are then laid on the altars of the heavenly company of gods with the words: "Let his foreleg be taken to Busiris, for thy father Osiris Onnophris the triumphant. Consign his ribs to Iyet for Haroeris pre-eminent in Letopolis ... "and so on."

There's no way of knowing whether it was a model cake made of plaster used in the original rite, or if it could have been really eaten. It's entirely likely that the public rite involved some ritual sharing of the offerings. If so it is another example of *eating magick*, which at the time of Plutarch's writing, was already an old tradition.

Given the popularity of eating magick as a religious activity in the classical world, one might consider whether this was framed as a way of receiving a god's blessing or whether eating was a form of destruction and final absorption of their power? Ptolemaic records contain requests from workers for time off to attend the "Typhonia" for one-and-a-half days before the month of Epiphi (approximate to our May). Their pilgrimage culminated in the immolation of donkeys. It is not always so clear what their mindset was. The acts are ambiguous, yes some of these accounts of "eating" Seth, seem all about humiliation or even triumphalism. But was there also a paradoxical placation of the god? It all depends on what the celebrant was thinking at the time.

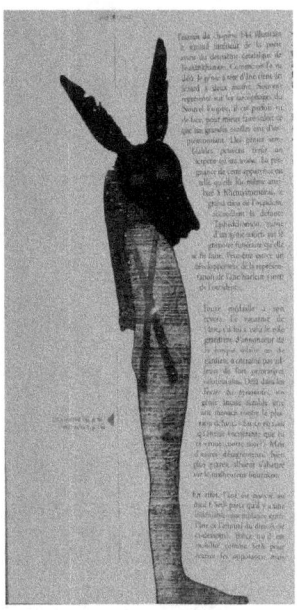

In his commentary on Plutarch, Gwyn Griffiths calls all of these ritual acts the "appeasement of power", that were performed to appease the power of the god who was still a force in the land.

The Book of Overcoming Apep or Apophis

A temple manuscript, originally from Karnak, provides another possible rubric for rites actually intended for overcoming Apep. Apep, Apophis, or sometimes even Apopis, is a supernatural entity that emerged during the chaos of Egypt's first Intermediate period between the Old and Middle Kingdoms (c2181-2055BCE).

The surviving manuscript is dated not later than 312-311BCE in the reign of Alexander IV of Macedon, son of Alexander the Great. Whilst this book, appears relatively late in the Egyptian timeline, experts agree it was likely based on older rites of a similar nature. In it we could well be seeing the paradigm for all works of magical *execration*.

Reading the extract below, it is easy to see an affinity between Seth and the deity Apep, whom he is often called upon to repel. This could simply be an instance of fighting like with like. The rites contained could easily be reversed to direct them at Seth himself, something that apparently often happened in temple rites.

Although the books themselves were written down at the beginning of Ptolemaic times, similar rites are attested from the first intermediate period between the end of the Old and the establishment of the Middle Kingdoms, a time when things fell apart, and the name of Apep first erupted into the discourse. But it seem likely there were precedents for this kind of magick from even earlier times, for example in the Pyramid texts, a chaotic, demonic serpent entity called 'Imy-nehed.ef ("He who

Painting from tomb of Ankhtifi

is in the sycamore tree") could menace the deceased, a ghost or "psychonaut", in the Pyramid texts, could equally be protecting them, difficult to say from the context:[122]

On the other hand, despite the late appearance of this book in the timeline, the gods Seth and Apep are clearly distinguishable. Seth invariably appears as the powerful emanation of Ra against Apep. Apep is the one who threatens us with non-being at important moments of transition. Seth's inner role is to protect us from complete dissolution in those moments of crisis and magick.

Some scholars say that it provides the model for other execration rites that were used against Seth, in particular at the temples of Horus at Edfu and Hathor at Dendera. We are here invited to believe that Egyptian priests of the late period had an ambiguous relationship with the god. They demonised him by day but were also very conscious of his usefulness in certain situations.

Hence Jacco Dieleman tells us that in the 4th century of our common era, in order to keep Seth's destructive powers ritually at bay, priests manipulated and destroyed small wax dolls or other inanimate objects as magical substitutes for Seth and his group of enemies in the daily temple ritual.

Here is the ritual they used:[123]

> "Seize Seize, O you employees to the orders, Bind, Bind, O you employees to the cords: bound is this vile enemy, Seth, son of Nut, and his associates, who have done evil, who have caused suffering, who have plotted suffering and injustice. The

---

122. K Kousoulis "Magic and Religion as a Performative Theological Unity: The Apoptropaic 'Ritual of Overthrowning Apophis'" PhD Thesis, Liverpool 1999 p41 see also Naii snake "Seed of Shu" (p41) and *s3-t3* "son of Earth"

123. J Dieleman *Priests, Tongues, and Rites: The London-Leiden Magical Manuscripts and Translation in Egyptian Ritual (100-300 CE)*, Brill 2005 (p 132).

eldest, who was appointed to rule before coming to the world, does not miss this. He made fun of the order of the universal master, of which was told by the One who created that which exists. He created evil before coming into the world, having aroused disorder before his name exists. Do evil to one who has caused evil"

This rite, being so important on so many levels, is examined in some detail in my earlier book *Supernatural Assault in Ancient Egypt*, p145-157. It was used to send "Evil Sleep" and if persisted with, could even bring death on the victim. The ritual for sending and also blocking "evil sleep" would be an important magical technique, then as now.

All of the above rituals derive from older paradigms. No doubt copies of them were preserved in temple libraries, some of which may well have dated back to the Middle Kingdom. So we can assume that the temple scribes could do a "cut and paste" job on an older ritual, in the process, substituting the name of Seth for that of Apep. From which we can learn a useful technique of magical "sampling" or "scratching"; take the "best" or most appropriate parts, discard those elements that you don't want or need, and Abracadabra, you have a new hit record.

It has to be said that there are parallels between mythology of Seth and that of Apep, example of which are not difficult to find. Take this passage from a longer spell where the spirit of Apep is seen in the the Thunderstorm:

> "[Thereby] shall Apep, the enemy of Ra, be overthrown in the thunderstorm, and Ra shall shine brightly, and Apep shall be overthrown in very truth".[124]

---

124. The Bremner-Rhind Pap "The Book of Overthrowing 'Apep" RD Faulkner, JEA Vol 23 No 2 (December 1937) pp 166-185) . Hieratic Papyri in the BM, series 3 edited by Gardiner (Bremner Rhind 10188) Contains Book of Overcoming Apopis – long set of spells from beginning of Middle Kingdom? [383.2 Lon G [Text, La Fol] but seems to be bound as one volume.] Verse 10

Elsewhere, notably in the Magical Papyri Seth is also called lord of the storm, although not uniquely so as the epithet is also one of broadly *typhonian* deities such as Bes.

"O dark's disturber, thunder's bringer, whirlwind,"
(PGM IV 154-258)

There are several possible explanations for this. Again, it might be yet more evidence of textual manipulation in order to make Seth and Apep *appear* to be the same god. Or it might be more of what I earlier called *fighting fire with fire*: Seth can defeat Apep, because only he has similar powers.

The Triumph of Horus, An Ancient Egyptian Sacred Drama, 1971 performance by Padgate College of Education in Lancaster.

The *Book of Overthrowing Apep* tells us that Apep is prone to roaring: "thereby shall be driven away the roarings[4] of the fiend". Seth is also known to roar. It brings to mind the archaic Indo-European deity Rudra, whose name means "howler". *Goetia*, the Greek term designating the conjuration of demons, also ultimately derives from the word for howl or wail.

We also learn from the *Book of Overthrowing Apep* that he is one of the "red ones". Red is quintessentially also the colour of Seth – "the red ochre god".

Gender

All classes of venomous snakes and scorpions were ascribed filial connection with Apep, and usually referred to as "sisters" although this in itself implies no actual cosmology.[5] Apophis is a genderless being for it is said of them "you shall not become pregnant, there will be no giving birth for you". The New Kingdom papyrus sometimes known as the *Cairo Calendar* or, as I prefer it, *Almanac of Lucky & Unlucky days* regularly refers to the "Children of Badesh" or of Apophis:

> AKHET (INUNDATION) SECOND MONTH, DAY 25 "it is the day of finding the children of Apophis, wrapped in the archiac way on their sides". [127]

There is another, extraordinary expression that occurs in a long

---

125. Peals of thunder (?).
126. Sister of Apep – spI11, 144-6 in L Borghouts *Ancient Egyptian Magical Texts* (Brill 1978).
127. AKHET (INUNDATION) SECOND MONTH, DAY 25 "it is the day of finding the children of Apophis, wrapped in the archaic way on their sides."

cup divination from the PGM XIV 239-295 line 263-265, for the moon god, Khonsu:

> "Even the fury of Apophis and her daughters I summon from their places of punishment, Let him make me answer to every word [about] which I am asking here to-day in truth without falsehood therein." [128]

The Book Of Overthrowing Apep [129]

Here Begins The Book Of Over-Throwing Apep, The Enemy Of Ra, The Enemy Of Un-Nefer (Osiris), Life, Strength, [and] Health [*Be To Him*]! Which Is Recited In The Temple Of Amen-Ra, The Lord Of The Throne Of The Two Lands, The President Of The Apets,[130] Throughout The Day Daily.

---

128. There is another, extraordinary expression that occurs in a long cup divination from the PGM XIV 239-295 line 263-265, for moon god Khonsu: translation from F Li Griffith & H Thompson The Demotic Magical Papyrus of London and Leiden 3 vols (london Grevel 1904). Apophis appears in this spell under the name Wonte ie Pessiwonte "daughters of Wonte" & this is identified as a name of Apophis in the great lexicon compiled by Erman & - where the name has the Apophis serpent as its determinative:

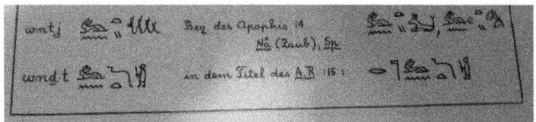

see also PGM XIII line 264: "Stay, for you are Aphyphis" (Apophis) - spell to kill a snake
129. ibid
130. I.e., Karnak, the Northern Apt, and Luxor, the Southern Apt

I. 2. The Chapter Of Spitting Upon Apep.

Say the [*following*] words:

Be You spat upon, Apep.

Be You spat upon, Apep.

Be You spat upon, Apep.

Be You spit upon, Apep.

Ra rests with his Ka (i.e., double), Per-Aa (i.e., the Pharaoh) rests with his Ka (i.e., double). Ra comes, the mighty one! Ra comes, (3) the victorious one! Ra comes, the exalted one! Ra comes, the one equipped [for battle].

Ra comes with rejoicing, Ra comes in beauty, Ra comes as King of the South, Ra comes as King of the North, Ra comes with divine (4) offerings, Ra comes with triumph, and Per-Aa (i.e., the Pharaoh) shall come. Life, Strength [and] Health [be to him]. You have destroyed for him all his enemies, even as he has over-thrown Apep for you. He has slain for you the fiend Qettu. He ascribes praise to your might. (5) You are adored by him in all your risings wherein you shine upon him, even as he overthrows for you all your enemies throughout each and every day.

[…]

There follows a very interesting passage showing the use of wax dolls or images. It was a common technique within Egyptian magick, and one that we seem to have been inherited. Wax was supposed to be especially appropriate for use in this kind of image magic on account of it being completely consumed in the flames, thus leaving no remnant that could be latched onto by a malign spirit as a vehicle for a return to menace the unwary practitioner.

VI. The Chapter Of Placing Fire Upon Apep.

Say the [*following*] words:

Fire be upon you, O Apep, enemy of Ra. The Eye of Horus has gained the mastery over the accursed soul and shadow of Apep, the burning radiance of the Eye of Horus ate into the enemy (1) of Ra, the burning radiance of the Eye of Horus shall eat into all the enemies of Per-Aa (Pharaoh), Life, Strength, [and] Health [be to him]! both living and dead.

And you shall recite the [*following*] words of power when [the figure of] Apep is put in the fire, and shall say:

Taste You [the fire], perish, O Apep. (2) Get you backwards and retreat, O enemy of Ra, fall headlong, get backwards, retreat, be gone. I have driven you back and have cut you in pieces. Ra triumphs over you, Apep. [Repeat] four times.

Taste you [*the fire*]. [*Repeat*] four times.

(3) Back, Sebau Fiend, destruction be to you. I have heaped fire upon you and I have made you to perish, and I have doomed you to evil. An end and destruction be to you, taste you the fire, an end to you; you shall have no further being (4). An end and destruction to you, an end to you, taste you [*the fire*] and come to an end. I have caused Apep, the enemy of Ra, to be destroyed. Ra triumphs over you, O Apep.

[*Repeat*] four times.

Per-Aa (Pharaoh) triumphs over his enemies. [Repeat] four times.

Rubric: (5) NOW after [the figure of] Apep has been defiled by you with your left foot four times, You shall say as you stand before Ra with your two arms bent [raised in homage] as soon as he has risen

Ra has triumphed over you, Apep. [*Repeat*] four times.

Ra has made himself to triumph over you, Apep, in very truth.

To effect the destruction of Apep this (i.e., the above) chapter must be recited. It shall be written upon a strip of new papyrus in ink of a green colour, and [recited over] a figure of Apep made of wax (7) whereon his name has been written in ink of a green colour.

The figure shall be laid upon the fire that it may consume the enemy of Ra.

And one shall place a figure of Apep in the fire at daybreak (or, sunrise),

At noon also,

At eventide when Ra heart (8). is in the Land of Life (i.e., the West),

At the sixth hour of the night (i.e., midnight),

At the eighth hour of the day, when evening is about to come

And afterwards at every hour of the day and of the night

On the day of the festival (9).

By day,

By month,

On the sixth day festival each month,

on the fifteenth day festival each month, [full moon]

And likewise every day.

[*Thereby*] shall Apep, the enemy of Ra, be overthrown in the thunderstorm, and Ra shall shine brightly, and Apep shall be overthrown in very truth. (10)

And when the figure of Apep has been burnt in a fire made of khesau herbs, the remains (i.e., ashes) thereof shall be soaked in wine and then thrust firmly into a fire.

And you shall make a repetition of this ceremony at the sixth hour of the night (i.e., midnight), (11) and at daybreak on the fifteenth day of the month (?).

And when the figure of Apep is placed in the fire, one shall spit upon it a very great many times at the beginning of each hour of the day until the shadow comes round. And as for what shall be done after these things, on the sixth day festival (12). each month, at daybreak, You shall place a figure of Apep in the fire, and shall spit upon it, and shall trample it into the dirt with your left foot; thereby shall be driven away the roarings[47] of the fiend "Stinking Face," and you shall make a repetition of this act (13), at daybreak on the fifteenth day of each month; thereby shall Apep be repulsed and hacked in pieces at your Sekti Boat [O Ra]. And you shall make a repetition of this ceremony when lightnings blaze in the eastern pares of the sky, when Ra sets (14) in the Land of Life (i.e., the West), in order that the red ones (i.e., fire-fiends) may not be allowed to come into being in the eastern pares of the sky. And you shall repeat this ceremony many, many times to prevent a rainstorm coming on in the sky, and also to prevent (15) the occurrence of a thunderstorm in the sky. And you shall repeat this ceremony many, many times to [prevent] rain and to make the disk of the sun to shine, [for thereby] shall Apep be overthrown indeed. The doing of these things is a protection to a man on earth and in the (16). Other World (Khertet-Neter), for thereby will power be given unto him to [attain to] dignities which are above him, and he shall be delivered from every evil thing in very truth. May I see [this] happen to me!

The whole book is published in *Seth & the Two Ways*.

The rubric [verses 6-16] says the rite was to be performed several times a day. At dawn, noon dusk, midnight (sixth hour of the night) and sometimes throughout the night. The rite also acts as a protection against storms, presumable both those of dust and of rain. If you've ever experienced an Egyptian storm you will understand how elemental and awe-inspiring they are in power. Such storms articulate a metaphorical connection between civil disorder and the biosphere. It is an attractive idea, that social disorder and biosphere disorder are intimately connected.

The Evil Eye

Apophis is dangerous to the sun god Ra, and other gods because he has the power of the evil eye, first recorded in a prototype of *Book of the Dead*. In the Coffin Texts, it is written:

> "Now when it is the time of the evening, he will turn his eye towards Re'. /
> A standstill comes about among the crew /
> and a great bewilderment during the course. /
> Seth will bend himself/
> within his reach. "Ah!" he says to him by way of magic. "I stand within your reach! The course of the boat passes off in a regular manner! You who see from afar, /
> just close your eye!" /
> I have ensnared you - /
> I am a robust male! /
> Cover your head; /
> when you are safe, I am safe! /
> I am somebody whose magic is great; /
> there has been given (something) to me against you!" /

"What is this?" "Something useful, / O you who creep on your belly" /
... ' etc. [131]

Ra seems to be particularly vulnerable to serpents. *The Book of Overthrowing Apep* is the culmination of a long tradition of such rites. Several of which reference the famous myth whereby Isis reveals a morally ambiguous side to her character, when, in order to supplement her already great magical power, she places a venomous snake in the sun god's path:

> "Re has swooned he says "I have trodden on something hot. My heart is afraid, my flesh creeps. The useful member in me obeys me not. "Tell me your name, your mother and me let lay a spell upon you. "I am lion, I am the lion pair, I am the phoenix, which came into being by itself, I am one of millions whose name is unknown. For if the poison go up on high, the Bark of Re will fonder on that spine of Apophis which coils up (/) when it meets the dew' 'flow forth, you scorpion'"[132]

In most instances, the sun-boat encounters a snake at sunset and must do battle daily with an avatar of Apophis, although the name given differs from text to text. The meeting takes place always at twilight, a magical time. The snake has the power to enchant the crew using just the power of his or her eye. Only Seth can withstand him. And the

---

131. P I Kousoulis PhD "Magic and Religion as a Performative Theological Unity: The Apotropaic 'Ritual of Overthrowing Apophis' ", University of Liverpool 1999 (19)

132. P ChesterBeatty VII, RT 5/2-5 Other versions of similar spell found in same Papyrus. They allude to the notorious incident described in PchesterBeatty XI (BM 10692) "The Story of Isis & Ra with other magical Spells . pp116-118. *Hieratic Papyri in the British Museum* 3rd series, Chester Beatty Gift 1935 edited by Alan Gardiner.

reason Seth can stand up to the snake, although this is nowhere stated in the spell, is because he himself is said to possess a "dreadful" eye.

For example is another from the collection of ancient spells published by J. F. Borghouts:

> "The raging of Seth is against the 'Akhu demon', the grudging of Ba'al is against you. The raging of the thunderstorm - while it thirsts after the water in heaven ... then you will taste the things the sea tasted through his hand"[133]

Although Seth was also known as "Lord of the Storm" in the earlier Pyramid age, as in Pyramid text 261:

> "Address to the spirit as it leaves the burial chamber. The storm-lord, the one with spittle in his vicinity, Seth – he bears you: he is the one who bears Atum" [134]

Spell to cause evil sleep[135]
PDM xiv 675-94 [PGM XIVc 15-27]

The rite was to be completed twice a day, at sunrise and sunset. It is repeated over four days causing the victim to suffer from evil sleep - 'nektek bin' (*nktk bin*). If the process were continued for seven days,

---

133. J F Borghouts *Ancient Egyptian Magical Texts*, Brill 1979 spell 23 & fn 59 & 61

134. PT Spell 247 J P Allen, *The Ancient Egyptian Pyramid Texts*, 2nd edition sbl 2015. Possibly also spell 311 "I will blow away the deluge for you, drive away the clouds for you, and break up the hail for you."

135. NKTK BN in Demotic. NKTK meaning sleep, which I would say was a synonym for the evil dreams discussed at length in Szpakowska, Kasia (2003) *Behind Closed Eyes: dreams and nightmares in Ancient Egypt*, Wales. The most commonly used word for dream was rsw.t, a noun with no verbal form - signifying that a dream was a concrete vision rather than an activity of the sleeper.

the victim would die (this later feature is written in code for obvious reasons). Dream sending was an important skill for the Egyptian magician. We may not wish to emulate the intention here but be aware that a great deal of the modern magick is situated in the imaginal world and that of dreams, so we have to be familiar with the principles.

The spell invokes Seth-Typhon to accomplish its aim using a technique known in the classical times as a diabolè—literally that which 'tears apart' as opposed to the symbolic—'that which unites'. The appropriate god is provoked or antagonised even desecrated until he or she becomes sufficiently angry that they send a 'demonic' emissary to trouble the victim in their sleep.

Instructions:

While facing the rising or setting sun, the practitioner should place the head of a donkey between his feet and position his right *hand* in front of, and his left hand behind, the animal's head. While he is seated on his heels above the head, he has to recite the invocation. Before starting the rite, he has to anoint his right foot with yellow ochre from Syria, his left foot and soles with clay, and to put donkey's blood on one of his hands and the two corners of his mouth. As a phylactery, he should bind a thread of palm fibre to his hand and a piece of male palm fibre to the head and phallus. The accompanying Greek invocation runs as follows:

> I call upon you who are in the empty air,
> You who are terrible, invisible, almighty, a god of gods,
> You who cause destruction and desolation,
> You who hate a stable household,
> You who were driven out of Egypt
> and have roamed foreign lands,
> You who shatter everything and are not defeated.

> I call upon you, Typhon <u>Seth</u>;
> I command your prophetic powers because
> I call upon your authoritative name,
> to which you cannot refuse to listen,
> then some barbarous names of power including:
> IÔ erbÊth IÔ pakerbÊth IÔ bolchosÊth etc
> Come to me and go and strike down him, NN, (or her, NN) with chills and fever. That very person has wronged me and he (or she) has spilled the blood of Typhon in his own (or her own) house. For this reason I am doing this (add the usual ie more details in your own words)

The rite and the invocation are linked together through the Egyptian god Seth, who was identified, at the latest from the fifth century BCE onwards, with the Greek deity Typhon, whom Zeus had punished for insurrection by throwing him into the Tartarus. The rite evokes a connection with Seth by means of the manipulation of the head and blood of a donkey, which animal was the symbol *par excellence* of the god Seth in Egyptian temple ritual throughout the Late and Greco-Roman period.

The reversed nature of the rite manifests itself most explicitly in the donkey's head. According to an account of Herodotus, "Egyptian priests never offered an animal's head up to the god, but cursed it and took it outside the sacred precinct of the temple."

> "After leading the marked beast to the altar where they [Egyptian priests] will sacrifice it, they kindle a fire; then they pour wine on the altar over the victim and call upon the god; then they cut its throat, and having done so sever the head from the body. They flay the carcass of the victim, then invoke many curses on its head, which they carry away. Where there is a market, and Greek traders in it, the head is taken to the market and sold; where there are no Greeks, it is thrown into

the river. The imprecation, which they utter over the heads, is that whatever ill threatens those who sacrifice, or the whole of Egypt, fall upon that head. In respect of the heads of sacrificed beasts and the libation of wine, the practice of all Egyptians is the same in all sacrifices; and from this ordinance no Egyptian will taste of the head of anything that had life."
[Herodotus, *The Histories*, II, 39]

"By making use of the head of a donkey, the rite does not only establish a close relationship with Seth, but also it defines itself as a rite opposed to the rules of regular temple ritual, which is in accord with Seth's role as an enemy to the ordered world. When the practitioner applies the donkey's blood to one of his hands, he trespasses in the same way another rule of Egyptian temple ritual. Because blood was seen as impure, the flowing of the sacrificial victim's blood symbolized the triumph over enemies in regular temple ritual. In this particular case, the practitioner does not cast the blood away, but smears it on his hand and, in the act, identifies with the enemies by way of contiguity."

"Next to Seth, the rite is also concerned with the sun god Ra, since the invocation has to be recited to the sun, while the practitioner faces the rising and setting sun disk. Daybreak and evening were probably considered opportune moments for this rite, because they are the beginning and end of the sun god's nightly travel through the underworld, where he has to enter into battle with the forces of chaos and evil, who attempt to bring the sun boat to a standstill in their effort to subdue the forces of creation and rejuvenation. By reciting at these critical moments between light and darkness, the practitioner takes full advantage of the intensified activity of the forces of disorder. More-over, according to pharaonic sun theology, the god Seth, part of the sun boat's crew as a servant to Re, exerted his destructive powers now to combat the snake Apophis, the sun god's arch-rival in the underworld. Seth and the sun god were consequently believed to be in each other's presence at these moments."

> "The Greek invocation develops the Sethian elements of the rite further by calling the deity the god of cosmic upheaval, who is hostile to the social order and dwells in foreign countries. As outsider to the divine pantheon, the social world and the land of Egypt, he is the appropriate candidate to take up the anti-social task. In the final lines of the invocation, the practitioner prompts the deity to come to his aid by accusing the victim of having 'spilled the blood of Typhon in his own (or her own) house' (line 19-20)." [136]

As the ancients knew only too well, in the right hands, even a poison can become a medicine and vice versa. Kasia Szpakowska writes with great insight in *Behind closed eyes : Dreams and nightmares in the ancient world view* that "a dream is something seen not done" and is more like a vision, spectacle or memory. The action occurs in a special realm, similar or identical to the otherworld, where spirits and the dead also reside. Although Szpakowska does not discuss the kind of dream sending evidenced in this particular spell, this is a very important insight. The adept Miryam Devi has identified what could be a problem in the mechanics of ritual here and it is that, on the face of it, the ritual would almost certainly give the *sender* bad dreams but it's not obvious how this would have any effect on the intended *victim*. The answer may lie in the intention or belief of the magician who devised and sold the spell in the first place. He or she almost certainly did beleive that the bad dreams of the sender would generate a vision that the victim could not help but

---

136. Dieleman, Jacco (2005) *Priests, Tongues and Rites - the London-Leiden Magical Manuscripts and Translation in Egyptian Ritual* (100-300CE), Brill. pp130-135

also see. So as the case of what we call the *placebo* effect, it is the self-belief of the physician that makes the *medicine* work.

Nephthys Magic

> Oh, Nephthys, daughter of Nut, sister of Seth, she whose father sees a healthy daughter, beautiful of face. Beautiful of face.* I am the divine power in the womb of my mother Nut.
>
> Spell to be said on the birthday of Nephthys

Nephthys is the introverted sister and counterpart of extrovert Isis. She is much more a representive of the dark, saturnine personality, so although in cult of divine kingship she shares many crucial functions with her sister Isis, she would be associated with the descending night boat of Ra, whereas Isis stands in the ascending day boat. She personifies selfless help to others, often in the form of healing, mothering and nursing. She has important functions in association with birth but more as midwife than actual mother.

She is the sister and wife of Seth, and this an awareness of her former alliances is always in the background. Even so, she is never hostile to Osiris and according to Plutarch, bears him a son, Anubis. In reality she represents the archetype of the childless women - by reason of her extreme youth or age derived lack of fertility. The ancient Egyptians probably had a different attitude to childlessness than elsewhere in the ancient world. They were certainly more favourably inclined towards adoption.

She is rarely seen apart from her sister Isis, with who she sings the famous lamentations to the stricken Osiris. She has thus changed sides and this desertion may be part of the motivation for Seth's murderous

---

*   Duplication is in magical spells to add emphasis.

rage against his brother Osiris. She is also one of the mourners and sustainers of the deceased, and as such can represent death and decay.

Her name means 'housewife' and this 'tamed' nature is reflected in her hieroglyph which shows the groundplan of a house with a symbol for mistress which also looks like a cleaning bowl.

Mercer says she is sometimes called lady of the west, also associated with the goddess of fate and also the headless goddess of the west called 'justice'.

Unlike Isis, there is far less cultic material on Nepythys although there is evidence of a small priesthood. She features heavily in the Pyramid Texts, for example the *Cannibal Hymn*. This later text alludes to an otherwise unknown piece of her mythology, whereby she is said to lack a vagina but is otherwise very beautiful. The only other reference to her in Old Kingdom literature is the *Memphite Theology*.[137]

Although a shadowy presence in official literature, she may well have had a more lively existence in the popular magical tradition of the folk (Rekhyt). She is featured in the Ramessium Papyri – found in a magician's box along with several other interesting artifacts. From this, we can surmise that she has a hidden magical side as the Red Goddess - more closely aligned to Seth. And indeed the *Greek Magical Papyri* contains at least three rare but extremely interesting invocations of Nephthys in her more Sethian mode. The example below is fairly revealing of her character type as maid and crone:

---

137. The sometimes rather grandly termed *Denkmal Memphitischer Theologie* being the text found on the Shabaka Stone now in the British Museum. Allen, J P (2000) *Middle Egyptian: an introduction to the language and culture of the hieroglyphs,* Cambridge. This text alone, is enough to place Egyptian thought squarely in the line, at the beginning of western philosophy. (p173).

Apollonius of Tyana's old serving woman:

Take Typhon's skull [Ass] and write the following characters on it with the blood of a black dog:

"⌐ ⁊ ⌐ ☉ ⫯ SABERRA"

Then, going to a suitable place, by a river, the sea, or at the fork of a road, in the middle of the night put the skull / on the ground, place it [under] your left foot, and speak as follows:

The formula: "ERITHYlA MEROPÊ GERGIRÔ CHÊTHIRA ANAPEROUCH...LYRÔPHIA GÊGETHIRA LOLYN GOUGÔGÊ AMBRACHA BI... AEBILÊ MARITHAIA MPROUCHE ABÊL ETHIRAÔ AP... ÔCHORIÊLA MÔRÊTHIRA PHECHIRÔ ÔSRI PHOIRA AMERI...PHÊ. OUTHÊRA / GARGERGIÔ TITHEMYMÊ MÊRAPSÊCHIR AÔRIL.

Come, appear, O goddess called Mistress of the House. (Nephthys)"

After you say this, you will behold sitting on an ass a woman of extraordinary loveliness, possessing a heavenly beauty, indescribably fair and youthful. As soon as you see her, make obeisance and say: "I thank [you], lady for appearing to me. Judge me worthy of you. May your Majesty be well disposed to me. And accomplish whatever task I impose on you."

The goddess will reply to you, "What do you have in mind?"

You say, "I have need [of you] for domestic service."

At that, she will get off the ass, shed her beauty, and will be an old woman. And the old woman will say to you, "I will serve and attend you."

After she tells you this, the goddess will again put on her own beauty, which she had just taken off, / and she will ask to be released.

But you say to the goddess, "No, lady! I will use you until I get her."

As soon as the goddess hears this, she will go up to the old lady, and will take her molar tooth and a tooth from the ass and give both to you; and after that it will be impossible for the old woman to leave you, unless perhaps you want to release her. From that time forth, you will receive a bounty of great benefits, for everything that your soul desires will be accomplished by her. She will guard all your possessions / and in particular will find out for you whatever anyone is thinking about you.

Indeed, she will tell you everything and will never desert you: such is her store of good will toward you. But if ever you wish, there is a way to release her (but never do this!). Take her tooth and the ass's tooth, / make a bonfire, and throw them into the fire, and with a shriek the old woman will flee without a trace. Do not be prone to release her, since it will be impossible for you to replace her.

But do release the goddess, when you are sure that the old woman will serve you, by speaking as follows: "menerpher phie prachera lylori / melichare nechira." When the old woman hears this, the goddess will mount the ass and depart.

The phylactery to be used throughout the rite: The skull of the ass. Fasten the ass's tooth with silver and the old lady's tooth with gold, and wear them always; for if you do this, it will be impossible for / the old woman to leave you. The rite has been tested.[138]

---

138. PGMXIa 1-40 translated by Hubert Martin, Jr. in Betz (1986). For other rare invocations of Nephthys, see PDM xiv 1219-27 Nephthys as a healer (as opposed to Isis's role as maker of magick -- and fevers caused by seizure of the south wind; PDM LXI 100-105 The Red cloth of Nephthys.

THE SEVEN SPELLS
OR UTTERANCES OF NEKHBET

Memories recorded via myth imply that pretty much every culture of the Near East, where they had once practised human sacrifice, record the point when they stopped doing so. They often framed this as an instruction from their god or gods. In its stead they usually substitute perhaps a bodily modification such as circucision or, more commonly, an animal sacrifice.

Thus, some of us learnt in "Sunday school", how Abraham set out to sacrifice his first-born Isaac but was stopped from doing so at the last moment when god instructs him to instead sacrifice a Ram.

In Egypt the corresponding "polemic", if that is what it is, could be found in the *Story of the Heavenly Cow*, and the blood lust of goddess Hathor, or in some later versions of the myth, the lion goddess Sekhmet. Her rage at the insult to the All-father Ra, in which she sets out to slaughter of the "human cattle", is only sublimated when she is induced to drink as much beer as she can hold, which is a lot. To this day, votive offerings of beer are flavoured with red ochre, whose metallic tang is so reminiscent of blood. Experts assume that human sacrifice did occur in archaic Egypt and is known to have persisted in special circumstances, usually in what we might call conflict zones or occasionally via outbreaks of communal violence aimed at the people of Seth, who became the victims on the altars of the antagonistic god.

Thus in Plutarch one reads how: "In Eileithouias-polis they used to burn men alive, as Manetho has recorded, calling them Typhonians, and they used to remove and scatter their ashes with winnowing fans. But this was done openly and at a fixed time, in the dog days."[139] "The

---

139. Plutarch, *Isis and Osiris* 73d-3

gods are joyful with the offerings of Sekhmet [on this] day. Establish the cakes of light (pAwt) and repeat the offerings. It will be pleasant; to the heart of the gods and the spirits."

The dog days are the time in the hot summer months commencing with the dawn rising of Sirius, the most sultry and uncomfortable time of the year in Northern Climes and indeed especially so in Upper Egypt. It would be a time when the unsavoury power of Seth were most apparent, hence the idea of punishing his "people".

Eileithyia, or Ilithyia after whom the Greeks named this Egyptian settlement, was the goddess of childbirth and midwifery. The Native name would be **Nekheb** from Nehbet the white vulture goddess, hence the modern town of Elkab, which is same name expressed in Arabic. The vulture as a hieroglyphic sign means mother, and as a goddess she is indeed associated with childbirth.

She is also a powerful protector of Egypt's dangerous southern border and it is in this aspect that the story of the Typhonian sacrifice likely arises. Nehbet, Goddess of the south, was identified with Selene by Greeks.

ια´. Τί γῦπα γράφοντες δηλοῦσι.

The "Seven" Serpents & their utterances

The seven utterances of a god become other gods. We see this pattern in several Egyptian monuments and it is an idea that finds its way in the

Greco-Egyptian Magical Papyri (PGM). The excavation of the temple that must have dominated the interior of the citadel revealed a remarkable piece of Sethian themed battle magic. It also seems to be an instance of an important grouping of serpent demons, who are closely related to Seth. I would remind the reader of the number of times the sevenfold cluster of components arises in connection with the God Seth, whose constellation is, after all, the sevenfold Ursa Major, the Starry Plough. Working this in ritual has shown this to be the Egyptian equivalent, perhaps even source of the seven headed dragons that prowl or are widely remembered in the universal mythos. It is the serpent in each of the following tableau on which one should focus as the core, the 'riders' being there to explicate its character.

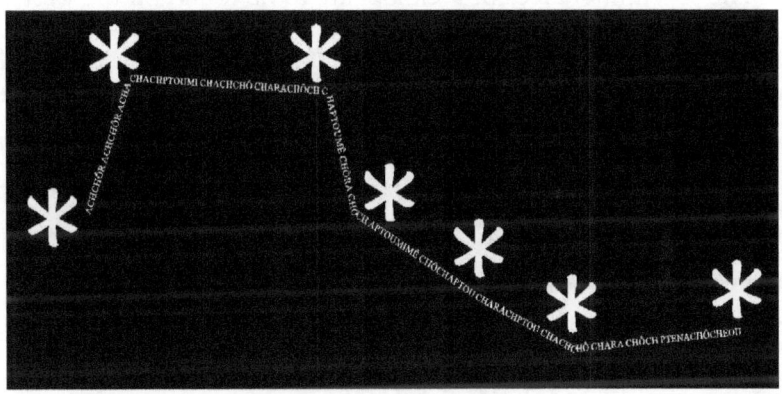

I've written about this earlier in connection with the seven signs of deliverance in the Greco-Egyptian magical papyri and their possible iteration in the Arabic magick as the seven seals, shown here:

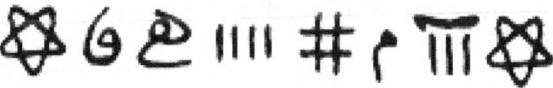

This rite I am about to describe exists is several versions although that at Elkab seems the most complete. Others are to be found in the temples of Edfu, Philae and Denderah. This in itself is rather remarkable, as each of these three shrines has strong sectarian associations with the deities Horus, Isis and Hathor; respectively. All three of these deities could be thought of as the enemy of Seth. These temples are all late period Ptolemaic constructions, although built on foundations of older temples.

The Belgium Egyptologist Jean Capart discovered a crypt at Elkab during his mission to excavate the citadel in the dig seasons of 1937-1940, immediately prior to the second world war. The temple of Nekhbet is situated on a prehistoric mound, enclosed by massive mud brick walls that surround the sacred precinct and the associated township.

The seven utterances of Nekhbet are to be found on the west wall of the crypt in the most recent part of the sanctuary. The blocks are marked with the cartouche of Saitic warrior king **Psammetichus** I ("Psamtik"). This king won his country's independence from Assyria. His name was later replaced with that of Amasis II, who built the crypt. It faces east to the mouth of Wadi Hillal, an important gateway to the Nile from the Red Sea, approximately 80km south of Luxor.

A few kilometres into the wadi is what must surely be the original sanctuary of the Vulture goddess, the "rock of the vultures" which is covered with inscriptions dating from modern times back into the prehistoric age.

The seven utterances of Nekhbet, as shown in the freeze overleaf, are the rubrik of a "typhonian" ritual of defensive magic, with the intention of repelling external attack from Egypt's vulnerable borders. The "grimoire" is to be read from left to right:

THE TEXT

1. [Seth] Aa pehti, "great of strength, the 1st arrow of Nekhbet, save the king from the slaughterers of Sekhmet".

2. To the twins Horus-Seth, Abductor of the heart that pleases and the Unique.

"Health to you, of powerful sight, criminal master who makes massacres, save the King from any wound, (give him protection

Reconstruction of the eastern wall of the crypt from Capart's publication.

EGYPTIAN MAGICK & TABOO 367

against) your impure followers. For you are the unique, protector the gods."

3. "Master of the tent - the one who does not listen."

"Oh grand god, master of eternity, with the terrible face, of which none cannot deflect the harm, master of prestige, great are your roars, putting terror into the heart of the gods, save King Psamtik from any sickness during the course of the year."

4. "Redden face, whose face is inflamed, scratching with your nails."

"Salutation to you, grand god … powerful, whose power projects as far as you will it, (master of terror), the strongest, the executioner when comes on the day of the slaughter. Save the son of the sun Psamtik. Save him from any wound, caused by thy flame; you are the son of Sekhmet during the season where she dominates, you are Khonsu, the joyous, son of Bast."

5. "The one that is in the papyrus bush in the midst of the Nile making carnage."

"Salutation to you, of the sacred forms, salutations to you mysterious master, who makes wounds, creates disorder and produces ruin; put your heart to the task and save the pharaoh from the wicked."

6. "Creator of disorder (in the middle of your redness)."

"Salutations to you, sole generator of forms, great bull, master of the inundation (?) ... of which we ignore the surge (?) coming under the form of wind without being seen; let us go, save the pharaoh."

7. "Red bull, generator of trouble" ...

"Salutation to you the very strong, maker of warfare, master of the axe, with the piercing arm, repelling the enemy from the prow of the barque of Ra, protect you the pharaoh"

"Nekhbet, the white of Nekhen, with the raised talons of iron ... the progenitor of the gods, mistress of the palace of the south. Commands my seven messengers to make it so."

Reconstructed image of Goddess Nekhbet, the white of Nekhen, with the raised talons of iron ... the progenitor of the gods, mistress of the palace of the south.

Sex and Death

Seth a god of death. One who according to Te Velde seeks to abolish death by killing his brother Osiris, also a god of death and of the underworld.[140] Seth is[141] the "destructive demon of death" who gives a coffin (good) to Osiris but also then tries to dismember the body (bad). Thus the *Book of the Dead*, a composition written after the Pyramid Texts, and therefore when the theological balance had swung against archaic gods like Seth, one reads: "deliver me from this god, who seizes souls and licks that which is rotten, who lives on offal and is in darkness and obscurity, who terrifies the weary – it is Seth"

In the new dualism of Seth and Osiris – Seth kills the god of death (Osiris), from which life arises; Seth is life who causes death."This would mean that he is the demonic initiator, who leads his brother to life through death by violence."

---

140. Ph Derchain: mythes et dieux lunaires en Egypt. Te Velde (1967 : 43q) follows his theory as of Contendings as lunar story. Ritual of filling eye take place on 6th rather than 15th day. Light (eye) & sexuality (testicles) are elsewhere seen as antagonistic principle – as in inner illumination v sexuality etc. (although Egyptian would not see sexuality as degenerative). The reasons may be different but the connection between light and semen is there, perhaps "Gods and the world" although Horus emerges as leader."We see neither necessity nor a decisive reason for tracing the religious symbolism of the eye and testicle to blinding and emasculation during acts of war between prehistoric Egyptians. Eye and testicles form a stock pair of symbols, and give the impression of stemming from a single, grandiose religious conception. This would also imply that the contrast between Horus and Seth, might be primary, and not a secondary historical-political development, or a commixture of a separate Horus religion and a separate Seth religion." p53

141. Te Velde (1967)

Sacred "Prostitution" & Celibacy

Herodotus wrote that Kheop's pyramid was built by proceeds of him prostituting his daughter Hetepheres, one stone per trick – a tall story, I think.

The Greek author Strabo wrote a voluminous *Geography* during the reign of emperor Augustus when a *pax romana* made it relatively safe to travel throughout the extensive empire. He visited Thebes (Luxor) in Upper Egypt and records how the once great capital had, since Homer's time, declined to a collection of villages on either side of the river. Although not mentioned by name one can assume that on the west bank of the Nile these are Qurna and Bayrat. Strabo's account is marred by what some say is a "remarkable example of the perverted meaning of a religious custom, by the ignorance of the Greeks and Roman writers".

These remarks are from early 19th century explorer and pioneer Egyptologist Gardner Wilkinson. His work, still remarkably current and readable, is perhaps one reason why Egyptologists, unlike other historians of ancient history, have never really accepted the existence of sacred prostitution in Egypt.

For Strabo wrote that for "Zeus (Amon) whom is held in the highest honour, they dedicate a maiden of greatest beauty and most illustrious family (such maidens are called "pallades" (virgin-priestesses) or pallacide (harlots) by the Greeks); and she prostitutes herself, and cohabits with whatever men she wishes until the natural cleansing of her body takes place; (menstruation) and after her cleansing she is given in marriage to a man; but before she is married, after the time of her prostitution, a rite of mourning is celebrated for her."

Stephanie Budin, in her recent study of the topic opines that previous scholars have misunderstood Strabo, what he is is really only recording the existence of local virgin priestesses, female temple functionaries, perhaps prophetesses. There is apparently nothing in his language to imply they were also "sacred prostitutes". Stephanie Budin's more neutral retranslation of the passage reads:

> "But for Zeus, whom they [the Thebans] honour most, a beautiful girl maiden of most illustrious family serves as priestess, [girls] whom the Greek called pallades; she serves as a functionary (prophetess) and accompanies whomever/attends whatever [rites] she wishes until the natural cleansing of her body; after her cleansing she is given to a man/husband but before she is given, a rite of morning is celebrated for her after the time of her religious service." [142]

I suspect this is a garbled account of the existence of the Tombs of the Divine Votaresses that can still be visited within the walls of the sacred precinct of Medinet Habu. The entrances to these tomb-chapels are conspicuous and face the Small Temple of Amun, the god whom these women all served. In my opinion, what one reads in Strabo is a memory of the existence of these high-ranking priestesses in Egyptian religion. Their cult was obviously still a living memory when Strabo visited and one can speculate that their tombs-chapels continued to receive cult offerings of some sort. Did their spirits continue to inspire those who served the god Amun in an Egypt under Roman rule? Priestesses of one kind or another had an active role in temple life although, as with their male counterparts, the end was nigh. Perhaps in difficult times they felt an affinity with their ancient forebears?

A votary is an uncommon word in English meaning someone who is devoted to the service of the deity, usually a monk or a nun. In ancient

---

142. Stephanie Budin (2008) *Myth of Sacred Prostitution in Antiquity*, Cambridge jii 45 b

Egyptian the term used is "Duat Neter"- meaning divine adoratrice. Approximately thirty such tombs have been discovered in the temple precinct. None of them is intact. They cluster in three groups – the most significant are a dozen or so buried in crypts associated with the tomb-chapels of the divine votaresses. A second group of less elegant tombs are near the enclosure wall of the small temple of Amun and the third group lie beneath the floors of rooms in the main temple. Where names are known they are all women.

There are three Egyptian terms used to designate these special priestesses. The earliest, "divine consort" (Hemet Neter) is first encountered and is perhaps an innovation of 18th dynasty. The word *hemet* means womb (see N40 in the standard sign list). To us the most famous bearer of this title is Queen Hatshepsut (circa 1479-1458BCE), who was married to Amun and at the same time was favourite wife of king Thutmose II. She also bore the title "hand of the god" (djedet neter) and "divine votaress" (duat-neter). She was not celibate or if so perhaps only so on sacerdotal days. Her role was something to do with the fertility of the god Amun-Min. Was this, as some speculate, some sort of gross sexual stimulation of the ithyphallic god? Gay Robins doubts the necessity of manual stimulation for a god almost permanently aroused. She prefers to focus on the other possible connotations of "hand of god" as someone who holds executive power on behalf of the king – like the "hand of the king" in *Game of Thrones* perhaps?

Over time the lifestyle of the divine adoratrice evolved and changed. By the time of what Egyptologists designate Egypt's Third Intermediate period (1000-700BCE) no single dynasty ruled the whole of the land. What we call dynasties overlapped. In 25th and 26th dynasties the institution of Divine Adoratrice was revived at Thebes (Luxor). Amun's divine consort were now royal princesses who never married. Their husband was Amun. They were treated like queens and had royal titulary.

The succession passed from adoptive "mother" to "daughter" – coronation followed the mother's death.

She exercised some executive power as representative of the king in the Theban state. She also had great priestly power on a par with the high priest at Karnak, until that post was itself abolished around the time of Soror Niticris.

Above ground the stone structures of the chapels of the Votaresses have interconnecting doorways. This suggests some interaction between the different priestesses both during and after life. One can imagine the newly adopted priestess served firstly as understudy to the older woman during the latter's final years of life. The new priestess was responsible for continuing the cult of her predecessor in the corresponding tomb chapel and this no doubt included consulting the Ka of the deceased. Her function was complex, serving the cult of Amun but also that of her departed predecessor, making daily food offerings and channelling the messages of her ghostly ka spirit, perhaps also making prophesy. Each priestess had her own chapel-tomb, some of the oldest were of mud brick, although these were swept away in the 19th century clearance (déblaiement). The easternmost of these would have been the most ancient.

From the above arrangement, we gain insight into how a group of priestesses interacted and one can deduce quite a lot concerning the mechanics of ancient religious practice. One thing that seems obvious is the need for the living priestess to interact with her dead ancestor, presumably for on-going inspiration. This mirrors the way every Egyptian interacted with their own ancestors and how most tombs was designed to facilitate such a dialogue.

In both instances the living offer food and other supplies to the dead. Every important Egyptian temple was linked to a priestly scriptorium or "house of life" – perhaps this too enabled interaction between living and dead priests, a relationship they may have been initiated into between living mentor and student? It's a "technique" that one can envisage would still work in a contemporary religious setting such as one finds in neo-paganism.

Both accounts, then are wrong or garbled but they lead us into some useful and interesting aspects of Egyptian magic and how it regards sex and death.

Sacred Sexuality

Egypt actually takes quite an earthy approach to the mysteries. Erotic or sexual-magical literature is a recent discovery in Egypt. Take for example is an ancient Egyptian "spell kit" written on a Ptolelaic ostraca that reads:

"For our good fortune:

The singers will come, the priests of *Tayy* who renders joyful the countenance of all who come to worshipped Nehemanit within the temple,

Nehemanit who dwells in the marsh.

When they are drunk, they will see the mer.et goddess by means of the vessel, Drink, truly, eat truly, Drink, eat, sing, get drunk. Those who proclaim Ai, those who proclaim Tay. She will not let drunkenness be far away for them on the day. (As for) the critics, his rejoinder (is) Ai has said "evil Indeed! Easting in the fullness of bounty is (to) their backs"

continues

"They say "may she be radiant" in a state of ecstasy. Ai will put them in a place of seeking – since they take care of them – in the hands of her corporation on a festive day. May it be granted, the emergence of Ai. Let him drink, let him eat, let him make love before *Tay*. "Tay, Tay" he says, namely the one who desires a companion, he who multiplies divine offerings, as he invoke Tay. "Let your voice come to me in accordance with the state of my heart. I do not neglect your vessel, Tayy, I will drink. I will feast, I will sing, I will become drunk. I will see the face of Ai daily."

Who are the Two goddess named in these invocations - Nehemanit and Ai ?

They are best seen as one goddess with a double nature – sex and death if you will. One side benevolent the other violent, ferocious, leonine, who cuts Apep in pieces. These dualities are more commonly represented by Sekhmet and Hathor or Sekhmet and Bastet.

The Goddess Nehemanit

Goddess of music and singing. So she is the goddess who brings joy whose name means "she who saves the one who is robbed" or "she who removes the claw/Talon" from the oppressor or "The beautiful saviour". Note that in Egypt, female musicians are often portrayed as wearing hardly any clothes. They sometimes also have a tattoo of Bez as patron. We could imagine this might have something to do with these objects found in a tomb of a priestess of Goddess Hathor, which may indicate the deceased's continued sex life in afterlife, also found in male tombs – called the "Bride of the Dead"

Bes is connected with female sexuality – some ostraca show prostitutes with Bes tattoo, under his protection perhaps. Monkeys are also associated with sexuality

The Goddess Ai

This ferocious aspect of this goddess is rarely attested under the name but she was worshipped at Herakleopolis in Middle Egypt .

Ai – aios – eye as in hand or actor of the god. Ai and Nehemanit both known as the eye of Ra which is why it is best to think of one goddess in two aspects here. Like the uraeus energy that can either blast with its heat or arouse the recipient.

Herakleopolitan Ai is the more ferocious, violent, lionine energy who threatens to burn miscreants in her ovens. Nehemanit is more benign, patroness of music and dance. In some versions of the dance, a dancer may even imitate the monkey as Bes or perhaps the Ape of Thoth.

Fig. 10. — Le dieu Bes dansant.

Trance

One of the words used in this spell, *syhyh*, means ecstasy but in a sense that reverberates through the ages – including the Coptic *cizi* (deranged)– enchantment, possession, to be deranged, to shine.

Timing

The evidence shows this kind of ecstatic ritual was a regular occurence, although the one under discussion coinicided with what's called the Emergence, an annual barque festival on the river. This could be the well attested "feast of drunkenness" on 20th Thoth – performed in honour of Hathor of Denderah. The occasion for this feast was the "return of eye" after its winter sojourn in Nubia. Nubia is again interesting as it was thought by the Egyptians to be an exotic place full of magicians, and no doubt this attitude persists today in respect of Sudanese practitioners. There is also the famous Bubasteia mentioned in classical sources. The festivities began in twilight, and climaxed deep in the night, with the arrival of goddess in a supernatural vision at sunrise.

Hathor Returns to Medamud – the venue

It very much looks as if every temple had a special chamber set aside for this kind of ritual activity. Musicians are described in hymn to mother goddess Mut at Northern Ptolemaic gate to her temple at Karnak – the carving shows the king himself playing the tambourine (see Sauneron). The open courtyard at Philae was also such a venue. A particularly informative text shows dancers at the temple of Medamud where a special Hymn for the "return of far wandering eye of the sun" is written in vertical text next to dancing figure of Bez. The musicians accompanying the procession are labelled "Those who placate the malevolent one" The special room in the temple is set aside for the return of the distant goddess Hathor who is both the Sun and Sothis star.

This ritual chamber is referred to as the *marsh,* which, as it happens, is also a euphemism for sexual activity of all kinds. The tomb inscriptions refer to "wandering in the marsh" with this obviously in mind.

Because the Egyptian temple in Egypt is a microcosm, where the marsh is also a liminal space between the land and the outside world, this is the place where one first encounters the goddess upon her return (Smith).

But the rite could also occur in private houses where Hathor is known to appear in personal dreams, thus in the bedroom, no doubt incubated by these practices. I'm mindful that there is no impermeable barrier between private and temple spaces, both realms are related.

Activities

Drunkenness, intoxication, music, and eroticism were closely connected in ancient Egypt. Their common expression of a "a happy day" involved all of the above. Herodotus wrote in his history (II.64) "The Egyptians were first to make matter of religious observation not to have intercourse with women in temples not enter a temple without washing after being with a woman. And indeed a text from Edfu reads "do not sing in his domain or inside the gods house! Do not enter the women's quarters!". But this rule doesn't seem to have been universal and indeed the existence of the rule suggests is was often broken (see Lisa Manniche, *Sexual Life in Ancient Egypt*).

Naturally those who love the goddess are pleased to see her when she returns. They fall into an ecstatic trance and see her face. This practice has a tranquillising, narcotic and also stimulating hallucinogenic effect on her followers. The goddess is placated by pleasing her physical and sensual needs; the latter worshippers do vicariously by having sex.

The following example is from one of many fragmentary accounts that exist, spread across various scholarly articles and books:

> "Yes let us drink, and let us eat from the banquet!
> Let us rejoice, rejoice and rejoice again!
> May Bastet come to our feast!
> Let is become drunk for her at her feast of drunkenness"
> Then he [the priest] was silent, he paid homage to the crowd,
> did obeisance and blessed them before Bastet.
> As the people heard his words (groans?),
> Their faces exulted, their bodies rejoiced
> Bliss reached them as
> Joy rose in their hearts,
> They called out and screamed.
> They clapped their hands "complete the joy""
> and Bastet has come, mollified.
> We have reached ... in drunkenness.
> She has brought joy to us in the world.
> She who love truth is her with truth."

> "On the day when I saw her beauty
> and my heart passed the day in her festival,
> I saw the mistress of the two lands in my sleep
> and she gave joy to my heart.
> Then I was happy through her offerings
> without any wish being unfulfilled"[143]

---

143. Richard Jasnow & Mark Smith " 'As for those who have called me evil, Mut will Call them Evil' Orgiastic Cultic behaviour and its Critics in Ancient Egypt" *Encoria Zeitschrift fur Demotistik and Koptologue* Band 32, 2001/2011 : 25. Darnell, J. (1995)."Hathor Returns to Medamûd". *Studien Zur Altägyptischen Kultur*, 22, 47-94. Ryholt, K. (1997). *The Carlsberg Papyrus Collection*. Copenhagen: Carsten Niebuhr Institute, University of Copehagen.

From this account we might suppose that a priest and priestess performed a sexual act, nearby, perhaps even publicly or symbolically?

Sex and Religion after the pharaohs

The PGM abounds in sexual magick but often of an abusive nature, ie. compelling others to have sex or exploiting their vulnerability in that regard. There is however one example that seems similar to the above older tradition we discussed earlier this is PGM XXXIV. Some say this is a lost fragment of an ancient novel. Professor Richard Parkinson, there was a time when it was otherway round, scholars doubting the existence of narrative myth in Egypt, saying that fragments were all parts of magical spells. He says that surviving tales show both styles of literature exist. We have learnt, there is no impermeable line between story-telling and sorcery.

> " … [the sun] will stand still; and should I order the moon, it will come down; and should I wish to delay the day, the night will remain for me; and should / we in turn ask for day, the light will not depart; and should I wish to sail the see, I do not need a ship; and should I wish to go through the air, / I will be lifted up. It is only an erotic drug that I do not find, not one that can case, not one that can stop love,. For the earth in fear of/god, does not produce one. But if anyone has it and gives it, I beg, I beseech him: "Give! I wish to drink, I wish to anoint myself."

> "You say that a handsome phantom keeps appearing to your daughter, / and this seems unreasonable to you. Yet how many others have fallen in love with "unreasonable bodies". (PGM XXXIV 1-24)

Dream books, some for men and some for women gives additional insights into inner lives and sexuality. Dreams were and still are the primary theatre of magick.

The Egyptian Liturgy

OPENING

Hekas, Hekas, Este Babaloi
"Love and do what you will"

Face North and try to see the constellation Ursa Major.
Draw down its power and say:

0. Guardians of the House of Life at Abydos
   Before me in the East: Nephthys
   Behind me in the West, Isis
   On my right hand in the South is Seth
   And on my left hand, in the North, Horus
   For above me shines the body of Nuit
   And below me extends the ground of Geb
   And in my centre abideth the 'Great Hidden God'

   Mnemonic:
   [FAther GEt GAme to FEEd the HOt NEw hOme]

1. Now turn to the East.

   Make the "Horus Fighting" gesture.

   [Breath in and in one perfect movement, form both hands into fists and raise them up and to the left of your head, stretch your right hand and arm in front of you and bring the left hand and arm to join it. As you finish the intonation, bring both hands back to the centre of your body]

   Vibrate the first vowel long and hard - AAAAAAA - as in fAther

2. Now turn to the North

Make the gesture "Horus Fighting" and vibrate the second vowel EEEEEEE, E as in gEt as above.

3. Then turn to the West

    Make the "Horus Fighting" gesture
    and vibrate ÊÊÊÊÊÊÊ, Ay as in GAme

4. Turn to the South

    Make the "Horus Fighting" gesture
    and vibrate IIIIIII, EE as in fEEd

5. Return to face the East

    Now bend over and reach out to the Earth
    vibrating OOOOOOO, as in HOt

6. Then gradually unfolding, come up and place your hands on your heart and vibrate YYYYYY - Ew as in NEw

7. Finally stretching up to the heavens
    vibrate Ô Ô Ô Ô Ô Ô Ô O as in HÔme.

    Now make the sign of the (invoking) pentagram in the air in front of you and vibrate

    >   Aa, Eye, EE, Ou, Uh (Ay EAO - Oh Hail) Nephthys
    >   Aa, Eye, EE, Ou, Uh (Ay EAO - Oh Hail) Horus
    >   Aa, Eye, EE, Ou, Uh (Ay EAO - Oh Hail) Isis
    >   Aa, Eye, EE, Ou, Uh (Ay EAO - Oh Hail) Seth
    >   Aa, Eye, EE, Ou, Uh (Ay EAO - Oh Hail) Geb
    >   Aa, Eye, EE, Ou, Uh (Ay EAO - Oh Hail) Nuit
    >   Aa, Eye, EE, Ou, Uh (Ay EAO - Oh Hail) Hidden God

8. Repeat "Abydos Arrangement" (0)

POSSIBLE LINES FOR DRAWING DOWN THE MOON

I draw down the bright blue Moon from the sky
though brazen cymbals crash and thunder
to keep her in her place;
even the chariot of the Sun,
my grandfather, grows pale at my song,
and I drain the colour from the dawn for my potions.

SHORT INVOCATIONS, PRAYERS, VALEDICTIONS, MALEDICTIONS ETC

"live long and prosper"
(*Ankh wedja seneb*)
Source: *Contendings of Horus & Seth* (1.6)

"Your shrine is empty"
(*Karya ka shawe*)
Source: *Contendings of Horus & Seth* (3.9)

Offering formula (Osiris version)

"An offering that the King makes
To you Osiris, Lord of Djedu
Great God,
Lord of Abydos
All good things on which the soul lives,
bread, beer, beef, fowl, alabaster & linen

(*Hotep Di Nesew*
Osir neb djedw
Neter Aa
Neb Abdu
Di-ef peret-herew
ta heneqet, ka, aped, shes, menhet)

Offering formula (Sethian version)

"An offering that a king makes
To Set, Bull of Ombos
Great God
Lord of the sky
And heaven's gate
standing at the prow of the sun boat.
A voice offering,
In bread & beer (and linen)
And all things pure & good
On which the God lives"

(*hotep di nesew,*
Set neb nubt,
Neter Aa,
neb peret

Def peret her

te heneqet,
het nebet
neferet wabit
anehet neter im)

Source: "Egyptian Interest in the Oases in the New Kingdom and Colin A. Hope and a New Stela for Seth from Mut el-Kharab" Olaf E. Kaper" *Ramesside Studies in Honour of K A Kitchen*

Maat mantra
"Never did (I) do any evil thing against the people"
(En zep ire khet , djewer remetet)
Source: Tomb of Redi-nes at Giza (G 5032)

"The snake is in my hand and cannot bite me"
Source: Coffin Text 885 ancient words to ward off evil, quoted in Ritner (1993)

General "negative" invocation form:
Be not unaware of me . . . (eg Oh Seth)
Source: Ramesseum Dramatic Papyri (Sethe 1910)

Invocation of Mut
"For those who call me evil, Mut will call them evil"
(Na I Ire dje ben rehorey, dje mewet ben errew)
Source: Ancient Papyrus

Final Words on Egyptian magick

Why would anyone in the twenty-firsth century be interested in the ideas of so long ago – we can argue about how long. Current philosophical thinking would probably maintain that the growth of 'do it yourself' religious movements is evidence of a strong irrational current within the modern world – an argument against the notion of intellectual progress and a counterpoint to the belief in progress based on scientific thinking (see John Grey, *Now History is Over*). This assumes of course that humanity's spiritua; quest is not a rational endeavour, except where represented by state and orthodox religion. But I contend that occultism and magick is rational and that an interest in reviving ancient cults is part of the process any self-aware person goes through. They must, of necessity, make for themselves a history, a chain of causes and effects that have brought them to this moment.

Nowadays there are so many contradictory accounts of the past, you must still make a choice, otherwise you are destined to vacillate between one account and another. The more you look at it, the more it sometimes appears that the writing of history is some form of game we play with ourselves. You must make your own synthesis, your own way through.

Some like to describe the activities of magicians as 'post-modern' in the sense of taking ideas and themes from an ancient, seemingly moribund past, and giving them a new content, making them work or become relevant for now. Some of us understand instinctively that there are certain preoccupations that were shared by the Ancient Egyptians and ourselves. It has taken the best part of the last century for the whole intellectual community to focus on the nature of consciousness. At first it seems that consciousness (and indeed unconsciousness) was the discovery of modern minds. But slowly the realization has dawned that these issues have been addressed long and hard in other cultures, often very ancient ones. Now the question is finally revealed as an interesting one, the search is on for data, perhaps any data, from our long past, that casts any light on the psyche and its progress. For example the Jungian psychoanalyst Charles Poncé wrote that the Egyptian creation of the otherworld beyond the horizon is parallel to the modern psychotherapeutic creation of the unconscious.[144]

If you are the kind of person who thinks this way, then your personal philosophy may demand that you seek the oldest ideas available. You may find yourself inexorably drawn, as many before have been, to the writings and artefacts of ancient Egypt. One way to understand how a complex thing is, is to look at how it begins. Santillana's hypothesis is that the origins of human consciousness lie in the contemplation of the shifting fortunes of the stars – or more especially in the unravelling of the mysteries of the precession of the equinoxes. Poncé took the less controversial line that contemplation of the revolutions of the northern

---

144. Charles Poncé, *The Archetype of the Unconscious and the Transfiguration of Therapy - Reflections on Jungian Pschology* (North Atlantic Books, 1990).

constellations were what first gave us rationality, in the sense that the world then fulfilled the function of a clock.[145]

Of course the constellations are an illusion, an act of magick, mental constructs or to use a less loaded term they are, abstract entities. In reality the distance between them could be colossal but their virtual magnitude makes them appear as a group. Constellations are humanity's earliest exercise in virtual reality or if you prefer abstraction. It is interesting to speculate how much ancient peoples shared similar views of the heavens. Some of the constellations shown on Egyptian star maps cover vast tracts of space and are probably peculiar to them. Others, such as those found in the zodiac are recognised by people as widely diffuse as ancient Greece and South America. Constellations do seem to have an intersubjective quality.

One phenomenon often observed with some precision, was the northern constellation. the Egyptians called *Meskhetyu* and which in the modern era is known as Ursa Major or the Plough. And it seems a likely fact that this was a skill they did not invent but one that they learned from their predynastic and Neolithic ancestors. This constellation was known by the ancient Egyptians as one of the imperishable stars. There's an obvious spiritual thought – when I die, I go to the imperishable stars – they do not perish.

> 'Oh my mother Nuit
> stretch yourself over me
> so that I may come to lie in the imperishable stars
> that are in you and I shall not die' – *Coffin Text*.

---

145. Giorgio de Santillana & Hertha von Derchend, *Hamlet's Will - an essay investigating the origins of human knowledge and its transmission through myth* (Godine 1969)

Of course not all ancient cultures are star gazers. People who live in deep forests (or brightly lit cities) have precious few opportunities for accurate star watching, due to the absence of a clear horizon. It would be a bold anthropologist who would speculate on the difference in consciousness and intellectual history that the absence or presence of an horizon might engender. But leaving that question aside for other minds, let us merely underline the fact that star-gazing needs a horizon, such as the sea or treeless landscapes. Perhaps we have stumbled on the beginning of one of the first major abstractions of our intellectual history – the concept of an horizon and of something that lies beyond.

Magical hermeneutics

It might seem to you that the approach I recommend to this material is a mixture of mystical inspiration and research. This kind of approach is not without precedent as it is the normal methodology of theology. Interestingly this is given the technical name Hermeneutics, which basically means to interpret. As I understand this discipline, the interpretor enters into the very thing he or she is attempting to explain, so in some sense the arguments are circular and from a formal point of view not objective. It is rather like the idea that one has to believe in order to know. I suppose in the final analysis one judges this kind of thing on pragmatic grounds. So the interpretations, however generated, hold together and make sense of the material and do they yield predictions that are later corroborated by other lines of thought.

I started as a believer and practitioner of magick. The variety of magick that influenced me was not mainstream, even in the terms of the pagan community. I was drawn to the fringes of magical belief and I felt an affinity with the outsiders of mythology. Every mythology has its outsiders, in the Abrahamic tradition it is Shaitan, Satan, Iblis, the Devil or whatever. I was drawn to their Egyptian manifestations.

An interest in supposed 'evil' or dark archetypes is not such an unusual thing in the modern world although it can put one in bad company. It seems to be that a great deal of the thrust of psychoanalysis is about confronting and integrating forces that at one time in our history would have been best ignored or even suppressed. One of the many analytical tools used by magicians is the tarot deck. I was very struck by some of the differences between cards designed before the popularization of Freud's theories and those created afterwards. This difference is most noticeable in a card such as the Devil. In the pre-Freudian decks, the Devil represents sexual instinct but seen as a negative force that enslaves humanity and obstructs further spiritual progress. In decks after Freud, such as Crowley's *Book of Thoth*, the devil represents rampant sexuality, but now seen as a potentially liberating force, the instincts are no longer seen as negative forces in our psyche, but as very positive.

So I looked again at the history of the Devil and this naturally enough brought me to the source of many of our ideas about evil, as they were first written down, many thousands of years ago in dynastic Egypt. Anyone for whom this is all familiar territory may be expecting me to introduce the strange god form known as Seth, who according to most standard accounts of Egyptian religion is said to be the personification of evil. Assume for a moment that ancient cultures actually had a concept of 'evil'.

The oldest personification of 'evil' is a serpent 'deity' called Apophis or Apep. As far as I can tell there was never any ancient cult of Apophis. He or she was probably not the demonised god of another rival cult. The most common account of Apophis is as a cosmic serpent that is so large and chaotic that it threatens the journey of the sun and can only be derided by the collective actions of all the gods, including Seth. For example an earthquake or perhaps some cosmic catastrophe such as a meteorite hitting the earth. The greatest evil of which the Egyptians, and perhaps we can conceive, is the end of all this, as it will all end in umpteen million years time when our own sun finally does succumb to Apep and burn out. Evil then is that which threatens our human existence with extinction. That's assuming that we haven't managed, by our own efforts, to bring either our existence and maybe that of other lifeforms, to an untimely end.

Egyptian religion is quite sophisticated although this was not the opinion of the Egyptologists of the early part of this century. Before the translation of hieroglyphs in the 19th century, what was known was at second hand from the accounts of ancient Greek philosophers and historians and these, we were told, needed to be treated with a big pinch of salt. Even so, the ideas of ancient Egypt were, to use the words of the advertising copywriter, full of eastern promise. What emerged was, for many, so perverse, that the study of these things ideas was virtually abandoned. From the standpoint of the modern mind, the texts do not seem to be very systematic.

Nowhere is this more evident than in the ancient Egyptian's attitude to the 'evil' god Seth & magick. Once again we encounter something unique, a god who starts good and becomes bad. (By the way that is another first for the Egyptian theologians). What I call theology is really nothing more than the efforts of the Egyptian priests to construct a family history of the gods that were most important to them. Even a cursory look at the material shows that the Egyptians were polytheistic and saw themselves as completely surrounded, almost submerged in divine forces. They recognised hundreds of gods and goddesses, although there was obviously some kind of hierarchy, if only because some of these forces have vast amounts written about them, whilst others must of necessity remain obscure for the simple fact that the only thing we know of them is their names mentioned in maybe one or two places. Our psyche is seldom influenced by one pure force, there are conflicting and rival gods at work. At the very least we might expect male and female forces to be there. If some mystics do encounter the One, it can only be in the world beyond gender and as it exists in the abstract realm of pure spirit – but this is not the world we most of us move in or have the clearest understanding.

The Egyptians cut through the proliferation of gods by imposing on it a family structure they called the 'company of heaven' and we call an Ennead or Ogdoad. These families of gods form a magical or symbolic system which is the nearest they got to our concept of theology. The most famous of these families are those of Heliopolis (the On of the Pyramid Texts), Memphis (Thinis) and Hermopolis (Egyptian Hmnw or Town-of-the-Eight). These are the systems of which records have survived, although it is fairly safe to assume that the priests of other urban centres also had their favoured views of the holy family.

The Temple of Seth

I was led to investigate a totally different Ennead, that of Abydos, the cult centre of Osiris in the ancient world. Although my reasons for avoiding the more well trodden theologies may seem capricious to some, I soon learnt that the Abydos system is acknowledged as an important if neglected cosmological view.

Apart from Seth's capacity for violence, Seth also represents society's libido in all its forms. That Seth should be the personification of raw sexuality, shows that these people recognised both the necessity and occasionally, negative aspects of sex. Seth was seen as both a lover of women *and* of men. Whereas other deities, such as Isis, may well be brought into play to represent fertility and fecundity, Seth is hardly about reproductive sex at all but almost solely about the raw power of sexual desire itself – or if you like, non-reproductive and recreational sex, both of which were important aspects of ancient Egyptian society. It is in this area of the power of sexuality that Egyptians show streams of thought closest to our own modern sensibilities. After a long hiatus, the second half of the twentieth century witnessed the rediscovery of the ability to control our fertility and enjoy and use sexuality for its own sake.

Modern magicians mostly agree that magick has no dogma, there is no one view of what the activity involves. It seems clear that magick is a part of, perhaps the origin of all religions. Even so scholars of ancient magick such as Hans Dieta Betz have advanced the thesis that magick can be seen as a unified religious view in its own right.

> 'We should make it clear that this syncretism is more than a hodge-podge of heterogeneous items. In effect, it is a **new religion altogether**, (my emphasis) displaying unified religious attitudes and beliefs. As an example, one may mention the enormously important role of the gods and goddesses of the underworld. The role of these underworld deities is not new to Egyptian religion or, to some extent, to ancient Greek religion; but it is characteristic of the Hellenistic syncretism of the Greek magical papyri that the netherworld and its deities had become one of its most important concerns. The goddess Hekate, identical with Persephone, Selene, Artemis and the old Babylonian goddess Ereschigal, is one of the deities most often invoked in the papyri. Through the

egyptianizing influence of Osiris, Isis and their company, other gods like Hermes, Aphrodite, and even the Jewish god IAO, have in many respects become underworld deities. In fact, human life seems to consist of nothing but negotiations in the antechambers of death and the world of the dead. The underworld deities, the demons and spirits of the dead, are constantly and unscrupulously invoked and exploited as the most important means for achieving the goals of human life on earth: the acquisition of love, wealth, health, fame, knowledge of the future, control over other persons, and so forth. In other words, there is a consensus that the best way to success and worldly pleasures is by using the underworld, death, and the forces of death.'[146]

I think modern magicians would agree with a great deal of that although they may vary as to their opinion on the exact nature of the underworld. Some, must ascribe real existence to its gods and goddesses. Many magicians experience a direct communion with entities that they perceive as existing independently of their own thoughts.

Others experience the presence of the divine in a more emotional way. As Poncé comments, if one adheres to a doctrine of correspondences between the gods and parts of your own body, a common enough magical view, then the activities of the gods will be experienced as emotions. I have to confess that I share a great deal of this view, some of my most potent, even destructive, encounters with divine forces has been through my emotional life. It is almost as if I am taking on the persona of a particular god or goddess, this seems to draw certain people into my orbit and this leads to unexpected life experiences

---

146. Hans Dieter Betz, *The Greek Magical Papyri in Translation* (University of Chicago Press 1986) Vol I, P. xlvi-xlvii

and emotional involvements, some of which seem parallel to the mythology of the god invoked.

The notion of the underworld emerges first into religious discourse in the writings of the ancient Egyptians. It is the world beyond the horizon, and this we have already commented, is strangely similar to the modern concept of the unconscious. Magicians soon learn that there are powerful links between this world beyond the horizon and the mundane world in which they exist. Some sorcerers have proved to their own satisfaction, that the unconscious is more effective at achieving certain things than the world of physical cause and effect.

Part of the training of any magician involves the assumption of a belief system. Mostly the magician adopts as a belief system the material of the magical tradition itself – which in this particular corner of the universe is the Hermetic tradition, an identifiable magical tradition, whose roots lie in ancient Egypt. Although the magician adopts the system on trust, a suspension of disbelief if you like, he or she hopes that after a period of total immersion in that system it will, as it it were, go live.

Some find joy in supporting other virtuoso practitioners whose results are tangible and interesting. And yet others hope that spiritual development might eventually come in the course of time. Magick, if you like, becomes a way of life.

A lack of ability to make progress in the greater, more 'gnostic' aspects of magick is no obstacle to success in the lesser forms of magick, including results magick or the casting of spells and sometimes curses. The fact is that many of the techniques of 'results' magick, such as construction of talismans, seem to work regardless of the operator's degree of mystical attainment. This kind of activity is fairly common amongst modern magicians, as indeed it was in ancient times. Some might object that the ability to work results magick is predicated upon mystical advancement. For example, the magical acts of tantrik magicians of South Asia is said to be dependent on the execution of quite complicated daily magical devotions. I like that idea but think that most magicians would admit that a great deal of results magick seems to work *regardless* of the inner state of the operator. Also it has to be said that magicians, certainly in the past, will often fulfil a magical task on someone else's behalf, even if they have doubts about their own ability to really make it work!

The above considerations apply to the magical community now and I think is quite likely that they applied to the magical communities of the past. Under the rule of Roman Emperor Augustus, magicians and witches had become enough of a nuisance to the state that Augustus passed laws that began a long period of book burning and general repression. This was long before the rise of Christianity, so one wonder's what they had done to bring this on themselves. And one also cannot but reflect on the decline in status of the workers of miracles, from the time of Egypt's golden age, when magick and religion were synonymous. The reaction was so strong that even the Egyptian language, once used by ancient magicians, became a dead language and those buildings which bore its inscriptions sank below the sands of the desert, only to re-emerge after several millennia of dreamy sleep.

2000 years on, the time is right for the beginning of a new cycle, the age of Aquarius may also be the time of the rebirth of magick although in some radical new form.

Magick is a rational and intellectually respectable pursuit. Try to live with its tensions and take an experimental approach that avoids some of the worst pitfalls. Afterall, there are aspects of any intellectual tradition that may be unpalatable but it is only the fanatic who would reject the whole enterprise because of some questions of value.

Lets not forget that modern science has some powerful critics, worried by some of its methods, eg: vivisection or its application such as military conquest.

One approach is by the construction of magical thought experiments. I use this term to mean that one makes certain assumptions and then immerses oneself into the magical tradition by learning about it history and techniques, seeing if you can make them work. Magicians start work using an elemental (indeed elementary system); over time their magical symbolism switches to the use of 'planetary' forces, and given enough time, their focus will turn even more outward (or is it inward?) to the realm of the fixed stars, felt by some to be the most subtle form of cosmic energy that has any influence upon us.

The use of thought experiments and visualisation has nothing intrinsically occult about it. Anyone approaching a complex system of ideas would be well advised to form some sort of mental model that they can view in their mind's eye from several perspectives. They can walk through it if you like, seeing how it functions in various imaginary situations.

The model or system I am developing increases my knowledge and enables me to make inferences and predictions. The major early discovery was in the symbolic significance of the cardinal direction North in mythology, indeed in the own psyche. Consideration of the implication of northern alignments and northern symbolism has emerged as a 'secret' key, not only to Egyptian magick but often becomes the connecting link across cultures. I couldn't say whether this is really a magical secret or something that is fairly obvious to anyone who looks at the magical tradition itself.

The experiment continues. The essence of this kind of magick is orientation. All magick worth its salt, seems, sooner or later to lead the operator to a consideration of themselves and their relationship to the cosmos. Whether this be by the use of astrology or the acquaintance with the other patterns of the stars as they flow around us or the rites of passage of the year. Magick attempts to place the individual at the centre of his or her universe. It is not so much that the position of the constellations and planets at birth determines the temperament and constitution of the subject. It seems more likely that the person already has these things hidden within their psyche. They are sensitive and react to cosmic forces, even if they are unaware of the full range of possibilities.

A useful concept here comes from the Tantrik tradition, itself with obscure connections to Egyptian magick. In Tantrism a great deal of emphasis is placed on deconditioning. Tantrism starts with a concept of the person, fully formed and possessed of temperament and constitution, given by birth and upbringing. Many elements of this conditioning are felt by Tantriks to be inimicable to the spiritual progress of that individual. Bad habits and social mores have crept into the psyche unnoticed and the Tantrik seeks to examine these traits one by one, stripping away what is unnecessary or arbitrary. What remains, so the theory goes, it the essence, and this essence is spiritually free and perfected. One of the techniques of Tantrism is the ritual cycle. This is at odds with the erroneous view that magick is deterministic, it is not.

Through this kind of stellar magick, the operator gains insight and is able to align his or her psyche to the cosmic forces around them or at least take account of possible sub-conscious forces. Magick aims I suppose, at the perfection of the self by the study of the self. Magick also aims at the perfection of wisdom, which can only come when all of the complicated chains of causes and effects is cognised either in full or part. The mystical mind claims to be able to cognise such a complex model. How to express this might be another matter, but it is the opinion of the present author that such insights are possible. It is up to you whether you choose to follow this path or construct your own version based on hints given by the magicians of the past. That's the fun, I hope you enjoy the journey.

Select Bibliography

J P Allen, *The Ancient Egyptian Pyramid Texts*, 2nd edition SBL 2015.

Assmann, Jan. The Mind of Egypt : History and Meaning in the Time of the Pharaohs. New York: Metropolitan, 2002. Print.

D H Aufrère, Encyclopéedie religieuse de l;universe véegétal – Croyances phytoreligieuses de l;Égypte ancinne ed Sidney Aufrere "Parfums et onguent liturgigues. Presentation des recettes d'Edfou" p213-263 (243-246) Montpellier 2005 vol 3

R Shumann Antelme & Stéphane Rossini *Secrets d'Hathor* Translated as *Sacred Sexuality in Ancient Egypt*, Inner Traditions

Michael A Aquino *The Temple Of Set* Draft 11 edition 2010

Michael A Aquino *The Church of Satan* 6th edition 2009

John Baines (1996 : 360) "Conceptualising egyptian representations of society and ethnicity" *The study of the ancient Near East in 21st Century: William Foxwell Albright Centennial Conference* edited by Jerrold S. Cooper and Glenn M. Schwarez. p360

Baldick, Julian Black God – *The Afroasiatic Roots of the Jewish, Christian and Muslim Religions*, IB Tauris 1996

Hans Dieter Betz, *The Greek Magical Papyri in Translation* (University of Chicago Press 1986) Vol 1, P. xlvi-xlvii

S G F Brandon (1969) *Religions in Ancient History* NY Charles Scribner

J Borghouts *BOTD 39 From Shouting to Structure* Harrassowitz p40. 26.16

J F Borghouts *Ancient Egyptian Magical Texts*, Brill 1979 spell 23 & fn 59 & 61

Bremner-Rhind Pap "The Book of Overthrowing 'Apep" RD Faulkner, JEA Vol 23 No 2 (December 1937) pp 166-185) .

F Li Griffith & H Thompson The Demotic Magical Papyrus of London and Leiden 3 vols (london Grevel 1904). Apophis appears in this spell under the name Wonte ie Pessiwonte "daughters of Wonte" & this is identified as a name of Apophis in the great lexicon compiled by Erman & - where the name has the Apophis serpent as its determinative:

Camilla de Biase-Dyson (2013 : 193-230) *Foreigners and Egyptians in the Late Egyptian Stories* , Brill.

E L Baumgartel (1947& 1960) *Cultures of Prehistoric Egypt* & (1970 : 124) *Naqada Excavation: A Supplement.*

J F Borghouts "The Evil Eye of Apopis, JEA Vol 59 (Aug 1973) pp 114-150 p114 .

Book Of The Dead 39.8, trans TG Allen, Chicago 1974.

P Boylan *Thoth The Hermes of Egypt* OUP 1922

Stephanie Budin (2008) Myth of Sacred Prostitution in Antiquity, Cambridge jii 45 b

Jean Capart (1940-) Fouilles D'el Kab executee par la fondation Egyptoloqoque Reine Elisabeth, Parc du Cinquantenaire a Bruxelles 2 vols

Jean Capart, "Les Sept Paroles de Nekhabit" *Chronique d'Egypt* N0 29, 1940

E Chassinat, Le mystere d'Osiris au Mois de Khoiak II Caire 1968

Colt, Jonathan, *The Search fo Omm Sety* (Rider)

Eugene Cruz-Uribe "Sth Aa Phty 'Seth: God of Power and Might' " *JARCE* 45 (2009) pp 201-226

Darnell, J. (1995). Hathor Returns to Medamûd. Studien Zur Altägyptischen Kultur, 22, 47-94.

Rosalie David, *Temple Ritual at Abydos* 1973:

Rosalie David A (Anne Rosalie), *A guide to religious ritual at Abydos*

J Dieleman *Priests, Tongues, and Rites: The London-Leiden Magical Manuscripts and Translation in Egyptian Ritual (100-300 CE)*, Brill 2005

Donadoni, *La decorazione della Tomba de Sethos I* [at valley of kings?]

Stephen Edred Flowers, *Hermetic Magick – the postmodern magical papyris of Abaris* (Weiser 1995)

Faulkner "The God Setekh in the Pyramid Texts" in *Ancient Egypt* March 1925

David Frankfurter *Religion in Roman Egypt* Princeton 1998

Gardiner, A.H. (1935) Hieratic Papyri in the British Museum (HPIBM) series III vol 1, text

Gardiner, A.H. Papyrus Chester Beatty I, pp 8-26 & pls 1-16

Gardiner A.H. (1932) *Late Egyptian Stories*, Bruxelles

Gardiner, A H, *Temple of Sethos I at Abydos*.

Gaster, T H, *Thespis, ritual, myth and dram in the ancient near east*, Anchor 1961.

Frank Goddio & Aurelia Masson-Berghoff *Sunken Cities: Egypt's Lost Worlds*, BM 2016

Henry Frankfort (1948) *Kingship & the Gods*

Grafton-Milne J & Crum, WE, *The Osirion at Abydos*, with sections

Kenneth Grant (1972) *The Magical Revival*, Muller, London : 47 & Glossary. American Edition Weisers (1973).

Kenneth Grant & John Symonds (1972) *The Magical Record of the Beast 666* (Duckworth, London)

Kenneth Grant, (1973) *Aleister Crowley and the Hidden God* (Muller, London)

Gwyn Griffiths *(1966) The Origins of the Cult of Osiris*

Gwyn Griffiths (1960) *The Conflict of Horus & Seth: a study in an ancient mythology from Egyptian and Classical sources*,

W Hartner, 'The Earliest History of the Constellations in the Near East' and the motif of the Lion-Bull combat.' JNES 24 (1965), pp. 1-16, 16 plates.

Hieratic Papyri in the BM, series 3 edited by Gardiner (Bremner Rhind 10188) Contains Book of Overcoming Apopis

Theogony of Hesiod, translated by Hugh G. Evelyn-White, [1914]

Richard Jasnow & Mark Smith "As for those who have called me evil, Mut will Call them Evil" Origiastic Cultic behaviour and its Critics in

Ancient Egypt" Encoria Zeitschrift fur Demotistik and Koptologue Band 32, 2001/2011

Barry Kemp (2006) *Ancient Egypt: Anatomy of a Civilisation* NY

Kaper, Olaf E. (2003) *The Egyptian god Tutu : a study of the sphinx-god and master of demons with a corpus of monuments* (Peeters)

K Kousoulis "Magic and Religion as a Performative Theological Unity: The Apoptropaic 'Ritual of Overthrowning Apophis" PhD Thesis, Liverpool 1999

Anton Szandor LaVey (1969) *The Satanic Bible*

Anton LaVey, The Satanic Witch (formerly: The Compleate Witch) retitled, pii (Feral House 2002)

Mark Lehner (1997) *The Complete Pyramids*, Thames & Hudson.

B Lesko "Women and Religion in Ancient Egypt" in Diotima http://www/stao.org

Rita Lucarelli "The Donkey in the Graeco-Egyptian Papyris" in Crippa, Sabina & Emanuele M Ciampini Langiages, *Objects and the Transmission of the Rituals : An Interdisciplinary Analysis on Ritual Practices in the Graeco-Egytian Papyri (PGM)*

Gerald Massey (1907), *Ancient Egypt The Light Of The World A Work Of Reclamation And Restitution* In Twelve Books

D Meeks *Masked God, Headless God* CNRS 1991 Unauthorised translation by Len Warner, NY on Scribd –

Gareth Medway (2001) *Lure of the sinister : the unnatural history of Satanism*, New York University Press

Manetho, English translation by W G Waddell (1940)

Mogg Morgan *The Ritual Year in Ancient Egypt.* (2011)

Montserrat, D. (1996). Sex and society in Græco-Roman Egypt. London: Kegan Paul International.

Murray, Margaret, 'Astrological Character of Egypian Magical Wands' *in Proceeding of Society of Biblical Archeology*

Percy E Newberry "The Set Rebellion of the 2nd Dynasty" in *Ancient Egypt* 1922 211-225

Omm Sety (Dorothy Eady) and Hanny El Zeini, *Abydos: Holy City of Ancient Egypt*, LL Company, 1981.

Omm Sety, *Omm Sety's Abydos*, Benben Publications, Society for the Study of Egyptian Antiquities Studies [SSEA] No 3, Edited by Daniel M. Kolos. Canada? 1984

Richard Parker *The Calendars of Ancient Egypt* Chicago 1950

Richard Parkinson Voices from *Ancient Egypt: An anthology of Middle Kingdom Writings*, Oaklahoma 1991

Richard Parkinson & Max Carocci & Kate Smith, (2003) A Little Gay History, Desire & Diversity, across the World BM Books 2003

Alexandre Piankoff (1974) *Egyptian religious texts and representations*, Vol 4, Mythological papyri (Papyrus Her-Uben B) Bollingen

Plutarch's *de Iside et Osiride*, translated b J Gwyn Griffiths (Cardiff, University of Wales Press 1970)

R Radin *The Trickster*, with commentaries by K Kerenyi & C G Jung London 1956

Donald B. Redford, (ed) (2001 : 599) *Oxford Encyclopedia of Ancient Egypt*.

Edmonds, Radcliffe (2003) 'At the Seizure of the Moon: the absence of the moon in the Mithras Liturgy' in *Prayer, Magick, and the Stars in the Ancient and Late Antique World*, Edited by Noegel, Walker & Wheeler, Pennsylvania State University Press. isure of the Moon"

Robert Ritner (1993) *The Mechanics of Ancient Egyptian Magical Practice*, Chicago University Press.

Gay Robins (1983) "God's Wife of Amun in the 18th Dynasty" in Images of Women in Antiquity edited by Averil Cameron & Amelie Kuhrt

Giorgio de Santillana & Hertha von Derchend, *Hamlet's Will - an essay investigating the origins of human knowledge and its transmission through myth* (Godine 1969)

Strabo, Geography 17.46 translated by Jones 1959 [1932]

Schumann-Antelme, R., & Rossini, S. (1999). Les secrets d'Hathor : Amour, érotisme et sexualité dans l'Égypte pharaonique (Champollion). Paris: Éditions du Rocher.

Te Velde (1977 [1967]) : 3) *Seth, God of Confusion: A study of his role in Egyptian Mythology and Religion*, Brill

John Douglas Turner, *Sethian Gnosticism & the Platonic Tradition*

H C Youtie "Heidelberg Festival Papyrus" in *Studies in honor of A C Johnson : Roman Economic & Social History* p178-208

Glossary

Acacia: tree associated with Seth and Osiris. An artifact in the Metropolitan Museum of Art shows Tawaret (Hippo), together with Mut (Mother) emerging from an Acacia. The seed pods have an astringent, antibacteriological properties and were used in Egyptian medicine for uterine complaints and infections. (see Allen J P 2005)

Alexandrian calendar has an additional epagomenal day every four years to arrest the forward shift of dates.

Amon: originally a wind deity, who rises in Ramesside theology, to be, together with Ra, King of the Gods, much as in later hermetic theology, the 'pantocrator' stands above the 'lesser' gods. Prototype is represented as a human being (at times ithyphallic), wearing a mortarboard crowned with two plumes or, at times, with a ram's head, the animal dedicated to him. With the goddess Mut and the god Khonsu, they formed the Theban Triad. He was also identified with the god Ra and venerated under the name of Amon-Ra. The cult's principal location was in Thebes.

Anath: Canaanite-Phoenician goddess of fertility and victory

Ankh-tawi: Necropolis near Memphis, Ptah, south-of-his-wall was lord of Ankhtawy, Bast was called Lady of Ankhtawy

Anubis: a jackal-headed god who presided over mummification and accompanied the dead to the hereafter.

Apep, Apophis, demon of non-being, the opponent of Ra. His companions referred to as the 'children of Bedesh' and 'children of the storm' in Cairo Calendar

Astarte: Canaanite goddess, called *Lady of Heaven* by the Egyptians.

Atef: the double-feathered crown of Osiris

Ba: 'soul' – after death, the person live on in this form not on earth but in the tomb and the community's memory. Ba is the characteristic manifestation of a entiry, divine or human. Bears comparison with Hindu: 'Linga'.

Barque of the Millions of Years: Ra's Manjet boat, with which he sailed through the 12 provinces of day. For his night journeys, Ra used his Mesket boat.

Bebon (bAbAwj) also Baba:.Baboon god and demon of sexual potency and prowess with red ears and features of Seth. Names in various texts including Plutarch and Almanacs of Lucky & Unlucky Days. See Kees, Horus & Seth II 47-48

Bousiris: from the Egyptian, meaning 'City of Osiris'. A city in Lower Egypt where the worship of Osiris was born.

Castles for millions of years: On the west bank of the Nile at Thebes, the Pharaohs of the 18th, 19th and 20th Dynasties had large religious monuments built, which were improperly called 'funerary temples'. In reality, they used them, during their liftime, to worship the deified pharaoh associated with Amon, the main Theban deity.

Chaîne Opératoire - methological concept devised in the 1960s by André Leroi-Gourhan in which the sequence of construction and deconstruction is analysed for information about the culture behind an artefact.

Cheth = CTh or Seth in etc. A secret name of power.

Cippus: Latin term meaning post or stake. In archaeology: 'a small low column, sometimes without a base or capital and most frequently bearing an inscription.' (OED: Gwily, J ,1842, An Enclyclopedia of Architecture: historical, theoretic and practical.) Used in Egyptology in reference to the Horus 'Cippi' - an image of 'Horus among the crocodiles.' The inscription describes an episode whereby Isis, during their sojourn in the Delta marshes hiding from Seth, cures the infant Horus of the effects of scorpion bite. Water collected in these Cippi is considered magically potent to ward off the effects of scorpion stings.

Coffin Texts: a term reserved for those spells which are peculiar to the early coffins and do not recur later, not at least until the Saite period, when some of them were sporadically revived. These Coffin Texts contain excerpts from the earliest Pyramid Texts, usurped by the nobility of the IX-XI dynasties for their own benefit (Gardiner: 1927:13).

Critical edition: a special edition of a text, edited from several sources to produce a final scholarly edition. This so-called 'critical edition' may not correspond with any of the extant 'street' editions of a text, and for this reason is viewed by some as a distortion.

Cubit: approximately half a metre

Damanhur: 'Town of Horus', argued by some to be the original Behadit in the western delta, until its transfer to Edfu as the 'Behadit' of Upper Egypt.

Dead (western): the Land of the Setting Sun: this is the Kingdom of the Dead.

Dendara: the capital of the sixth Nome of Upper Egypt, and its necropolis contains tombs dug between the predynastic period and the end of the Old Kingdom. This site's renown is due to the famous Temple of Hathor, which dates back to the Greco-Roman period. Dendara was dedicated to Hathor, one of the oldest Egyptian deities, represented as a cow or a woman with cow's ears.

Decan: 36 stars on the belt of the southern ecliptic, whose rising was used to mark the passage of the 'hours' during each cycle or 'week' of ten days.

Egyptian: A language of the Hamiti-Semitic group which includes Semitic, Berber, Cushitic and Hausa)

Epagomenal: see Intercalary.

Ennead: (psdt) 'The company of heaven', 'companions of the sun & moon', A group of more or less nine deities, such as the company of *Heliopolis* - Atum, Shu and Tefnut, Geb and Nut, Osiris and Isis, Seth, Nephthys.

Êsenephus = s.t-nb.t Hw.t = Isis & Nephthys - in 'garbled' version of PGM

Griffin: The griffin is an important avatar of Seth appearing on talismanic wands made from hippo ivory - the name is 'teshtesh' in Middle Egyptian.

Leibovitch once remarked: 'that as "dieu sauveur" Seth is a griffin. On the one hand the griffin is a guardian angel, on the other an avenger, pursuing its enemies at furious speed or crushing them underfoot, as appears from the many illustrations in the articles by Leibovitch. It might be that at Beni Hasan these two functions are divided over the falcon-headed griffin and the Seth-animal, and that the occurrence of griffins with a falcon's head or the head of the Seth-animal is not altogether arbitrary, but is connected with the duality of the gods Horus and Seth in mythology.' J. Leibovitch, *Le griffon I, BIE* 25 (1943), p. 188 and fig. 5 quoted in Te Velde.

Harpoon: the main weapons used for hunting hippos.

Head: 'reserve', a substitute for the mummy's head, placed in the tomb of the deceased in case the latter is destroyed (see Hayes 1953 : 109).

Histeriola: divine precedent for a spell.

Hathor: cow-headed deity (sometimes depicted as a woman with cow's ears) protected women and the dead, as she was likened to the Goddess of the Kingdom of the Dead; she was also goddess of music and intoxication.

Horus: god of the sky and protector of the pharaoh to whom he was likened. Horus could be depicted as a falcon-headed man. As the son of Osiris and Isis, he was often represented as infant (Harpocrates) with a finger held to his lips; a gesture rather paradoxically interpreted in the Hermetic Order of the Golden Dawn, as 'the sign of silence.'

Iathath = (ie Seth). In the Greek Magical Papyrus (Betz 1986). The black 'blood' of Seth.

Ideogramme: a pictorial sign, that has no phonetic value but nevertheless helps define the meaning or sense rather than the sound of a word. Incidentally where the ideogramme follows one or more phonogrammes and ends the word, it is known as a determinative. The ideogrammes are historically the oldest part of the Egyptian language, the phonograms later prefixed to it for the sake of clarity (Gardiner 1926).

Intercalary: twelve lunar months of 30 days equals 360, which leaves five extra or intercalary days, on which the priests of Heliopolis assigned the birth of five gods, almost as a supplement to their own theological system. The five gods said to be born on these days were: Osiris, Isis, Seth, Nephthys and Horus the child. This schema is known from Pyramid Text 1961 and Plutarch, *Isis and Osiris*, 12. Mercer (1949 : 277) states that the priests of Heliopolis had invented this calendar by 2781BC.

Ipet Hemet: Hippo or perhaps Hathor?

Jeu, Books of and Jeu the Hieroglyphist of the so-called 'Headless One' ritual of PGM (known in contemporary magick variously as the 'Bornless One', 'Liber Samech' and 'Preliminary Invocation of the Goetia') . *The Books of Jeu* are Coptic / Gnostic texts found at Nag Hammadi.

Kiki: seemingly the burning oil from the castor oil plant (ricinus communis) used in lamps.

Khmun: Hermopolis Magna in Middle Egypt, cult centre of Thoth.

Ladder of Seth: means by which the king's soul rises to the stars. Made of iron that has fallen from the heavens. Jacob's ladder may also be a meteorite (see Wainwright).

LPH: abreviation used by Egyptologists for stative formula: 'Life, Prosperity and Health' - Anx(w) wDA(w) snb(w) - 'alive, sound and healthy' or 'Life, prosperity and health' in older translations.

Maat heru: speaking true, which will get you through the gates after judgement.

Maat: divine personification of the cosmic order, secondarily connected to the concepts of truth and justice. She wears an ostrich plume on her head, the transcription of her name.

Min: in origin a sky god - one of whose forms is as a white bull tethered to axial pillar as cult object.

Mut: the wife of Amon, she was venerated in Thebes. Originally depicted as a vulture, she later took on a human form.

Neolithic: of or relating to the cultural period of the Stone Age beginning around 10,000BC in the Middle East and later elsewhere, characterized by the development of agriculture and the making of polished stone implements.

Neter: god or the divine.

Nehes: Nubia; (later Kash: Kush), according to Baynes & Malek (2000) the derivation of 'Nubia' may be from 'Nub' - meaning gold.

Neith: goddess of the hunt and war, whose cult centre was at Sais.

Nome: one of forty-two administrative districts, significantly also the number of the judges of the dead. Interestingly each Nome coincides with one of the enormous temporary lakes caused by the annual Nile flood (Butzer 1976).

Nomen: the King's titulary consisted of five great names. The family name, called the nomen by Egyptologists, is introduced by epithet 'son of Ra'.

On: Heliopolis

Onnophris: Osiris as known in the tradition of the magical papyri and Christianity, about whom is said: He brings peace to the lands in his name of Sokaris, mighty is his reputation in his name of Osiris, he persists until the ends of eternity in his name Onnophris.

Onomastica: words lists detailing divinity and geography. See final book of Apuleus' *Golden Ass* for an example, where it says her true name only known to the Egyptians and Ethiopians.

Onuris: Anhur, god of hunt and war, resident at This. He returns the Eye of the Sun as his consort Mehit.

Osiris: the husband of Isis; after having been killed by his brother, Seth, he fathered a son, Horus, who, grown to adulthood, avenged him. He is represented with his crown (atef), his scepter (bequa), and his flail, (nekhekh).

Pronomen: King's first cartouche or throne name.

Pars pro toto: 'part stands for the whole'. Ie type of time reckoning based on the observation of a single event to represent the whole cycle. For example the Slavonic *Leto* means the 'summer' and 'year'. It may seem obvious to us in temperate climes that there is only one summer per year, and therefore we could say 'she is a maid of eighteen summers' and we would all understand that.. But in some equatorial regions there is no winter or summer and there are two wet seasons! Some old traditions ignore or lump together whole segments of the year - hence the old Roman year of ten months.

Petosis: an Hellenistic astrologer who made an association between the Northern Constellations and the Lunar days. Source: Neugebauer & Parker (1962 III : 216). Most reference books say this Petosis is the occupant of the famous Hermopolitan 4th century BC tomb, but N&P cast doubt on this and indeed the theories of Petosis. The late text to which they refer is not quoted in their monumental work but may be in Neugebauer's 'Egyptian Planetary Texts' *Transactions of the American Philosophical Society*, Vol XXXII part II, Jan 1942 209-50.

PDM = Papyri Demotika Magicae

PGM = Papyri Graecae Magicae – Preisendanz's (qv) sobriquet, although he omitted the Demotic spells as of less interest and therefore ensured they disappeared from scholarly discourse for the best part of a century.

Pharaoh: Egyptian word for king is 'nsw' - 'pharaoh', as used in the Hebrew Bible is probably derived from 'per'o' - king's house.

Preisendanz, Karl, editor of the PGM in two volumes, 1928 & 1931.

Pre-Harakhti: a combination of Re and Horus!

Ptah: the God of Memphis, brought the universe into being along with the hieroglyphic pictogrammes, the most primitive level of the Egyptian language. These were later simplified and reduced to a short list of alphabetic signs by Thoth, the god of scribes. Ptah, the husband of the Lion Goddess, Sekhmet, was depicted wearing a mummy's shroud, holding in his hand a scepter. He was later likened to another Memphis god of death, Sokaris, and was worshipped in his syncretic form of Ptah-Sokaris.

Pylon: a monumental temple entrance, consisting of a portal between two enormous trapezoidal monoliths.

Ra, or Re, as Egyptian sun-god Ra. Ra was beholden to Seth for defending him against the demons who assailed him on his daily journey through the skies.

Rekhyt: the plebs, others say the followers of Seth

Sais: centre in western delta, where local rulers, decendents of 25th dynasty, became important in the conflicts of the 8th century BCE.

Sekhem: 'power', 'sign of power' hence 'image' or 'statue'. The Ba (qv) returns or is installed in the mummy / corpse / statue giving power. Assmann discussed this in relation to the hermetic doctrine 'as above, so below'.

Sekhmet: lion-headed goddess, sometimes crowned with the solar disk. She protected the royal power; she can be likened to Hathor, Bastet and Isis.

Shed: 'save', 'rescue', 'saviour' - used especially after the traumas of the Amarna period. The Egyptian aspect of the semitic god Reshef - or young saviour god used as an epithet of Horus.

Shen: the coil of rope known by the french term 'cartouche' - the Egyptian term derived from word meaning to encircle. Symbol of eternity and protective device around the name of the king.

Sycamore, Lady of the Southern: epithet of Hathor at Memphis, she had assisted Horus when blinded by Seth.

Tê: the underworld

Teshtesh (see Griffin)

Thebes: during the 18th Dynasty (ca.1550 - 1295BC), the city of Weset was founded by Amenhotep I; better known by its Greek name, Thebes, it became the heart of the country. It was at this time that the Great Temple of Amon in Karnak became the country's most important religious centre and the royal necropolises were excavated in the Valley of the Kings and the Valley of the Queens. *Theban Triad*: Amon-Ra, Mut and Khonsu.

Index

Symbols
Numbers 32
Midnight 60
12 provinces of day 410
Thirteen 36, 58
Fourteen 81
Twenty-eight 82
Three hundred and sixty five 59
42 sins *183*

A
Aa pehti, "great of strength" 365
Ab-du (see Abydos: 'The Desired Mountain') *177*
ABLANATHANALBA 142
Abraham 52, 361
Abramelin 50, 51
  Book of 102, 136
  Daemons & egyptian decans 108
ABRASAX 59, 141, 159
Abydos *21*, 28, 66, *176*, *181*, *185*
  Arrangement 8, 32, 68, 119, 139
  Formula 302
  Mysteries 94
Abyss 222
Acacia. *See* Trees: Acacia
Acrophany 145
Acrostics "crosswords" 112
Adultery. *See* Curse: Adultery
Afterlife 377
Agriculture *179*
Ahmes I *190*
Ahmes II (Amasis) *193*
Ai 377, 378
Air
  Empty 353
Aiwass 51
Akh 160

Akhenaton *196*
Akhet 96, 344
Akhw
  Demon 352
Al Buni 151
Alexander
  IV of Macedon 339
Alif 151
Alpha 150
Alphabet
  Demotic 143
  'soul' of 122
Amduat 28, 68
Amenhotep I 416
Amenti (The West) *184*
Amon 409
Amon Ra *11*, 164, *201*, *203*, *204*
Amon-Ra 42
Amulets 33, 139
Anastasi, Jean d' (1780?-1857) 55
Anat 78, 409
Andjty *182*
Anhur 414
Ankh 146, 409
Ankh-tawi 409
Anklet
  Tale of. *See also* Shilappattikaram : the tale of the Anklet
Anthropology 45
Anticlockwise 126
Anubis *11*, 41, 59, 114, *180*, 289, 357, 409
Apep 339, 340, 345
Apollo 148
Apophis 24, 25, 39, 67, 409
Apuleius 214
  Apology 214
  The Golden Ass 212, 214, 223
Arabic magick 171, 363

Arachi or Araki (place)   106
Ares   57
Argenteum Astrum   *10*
Arrow   365
Asclepius   92
Ash   31, 168
Asiatic   45
Ass   *212*, *214*
Assassination   73
Assault   342
Assmann, Jan   90, 122
Associated   300
Astarte   49, 50, 78, 409
Asterisk   150
Ate   409
Aten   *21*
Athame   150
Atlantis
   Myth of   137
Atum   39, *206*
Ay   *196*
Ay EAO /"Oh Hail   128, 167
Ayurveda (the science of longevity)   *205*

B

Ba   26, 98, 225
Ba'al   352
Baba/Babai   410
Babylonian   162
Badesh   344
Banebdjedet   409
Baptism   *216*
Baptistry   *219*
Baraka   98
Barbarous words   141
Bardon, Franz   108
Barrett, Francis   52, 161
Bast   337, 369
Bastet   416
Bata   9
Battiscombe-Gunn   159
Battle   363
Bear   *14*, *18*
Bebon   410

Bed   *219*
Bedroom   380
Beer   43, 46, 78, 410
Beetles   51
Bennett, Alex   50
Berber   411
Bes   *195*, 343
Betz, Hans Dieter
   "Greek Magical Papyri"   120
Bez   377
Bible   47, 101, *191*
   New Testament   26
Big Dipper (see Ursa Major)   *15*
Binding   32, 54
   Bound figure   36
Birds   57
Birth   26, 28, 39
Bisecting
   Of harmful hieroglyphs   66
Bitumen   275
Black
   God   *403*
Black box   100
Blood   39, 50, 52, 353, 355, 359, 412
   Impure   355
   Libel   52
Blowing   32
Blue Lily (Nymphaea caerulea)   257
Blue Lily (nymphaea caerulea)   *216*
Boat   24, 410
   Night   357
   Solar barque   28
Boats   *213*
Body   58
   Fluids   39
   Phallus   353
   Reversal   354
   Teeth   360
Book of Caverns   224, 225
Book of Gates   28, 29, 166, 168, *216*, *218*, *220*, *222*, 224, 227
Book of Job   *13*
Book of Nut   284

Book of Primeval Old Ones   136
Book of Revelation   155
Book of the Dead   94, 224
Book of the Law   48, 50, 52, 53, 54
Books of Jeu   146
Books of the Afterlife   144
Bornless or Headless ritual   146
Bow
   Nine bows   55
Bowl magick   57
Brain disease   47
Branding   29
Breaking   32, 66, 69
   Red pots   71
Breast   58, *213*
Breath   39
Bride
   Of the Dead   377
Brighton Museum   31
British Museum   *174*
Bronze   66
Bruno, Giordano   56, 95
Bryony   25
Buddha   *205*
Budge, Ernest   *175*
Bull   *12*, 70
   Leg   76
   of Meroe   410
   of Ombos   245, 387
Burial   32
   Execration   36, 64
Burning   32, 65
Busiris   410
Busiris (now Abusir el Malek)   *182*
Buto   78
Buttocks   58

C

Cairo   117, 163
Cakes of Light   48, 53, 161
   Cereal offering   47
Calendar
   Lunar

Calibration   239
Calverley, Amice   34
Canine cemetery   *194*
Cannibalism   43, 50, *179*, 336
   Cannibal Hymn   44
Canopic jars   410
Caraka Samhita   27
Cardinality   103
Carob   275
Cartouche   37, 410
Casaubon, Meric   224
Castle of the old Woman. *See Qasr el-Aguz (lit. the castle of the old Woman*
Cattle   69, 336
Celtic   41
   Taliesin   41
Cenchreae   *213*
Cenotaphs   *178*
Chalcedony   158
Chamber   379
Chaos   60, 355
   magick   51
Charaktêres   145, 146
Chemmis   78
"Cheth" (Hebrew)   133
Child   114
Children
   Adoption   357
   Childlessness   357
   Youth   357
Christ-Osiris   158
Christian   *214*
   Coptic   70
   Magick   *214*
Circumambulation   32, 37
Citadel   363
City of the Pyramids   *173*
Clearance   375
Cleopatra   306
Coffin
   Texts   67, 70
   texts   **410**
Coins   *213*
Colour

Flashing 98
King" scale 128
companions. *See* Smaiut
Compulsion 58, 77
Constellation *11, 12*
Contendings of Horus & Seth 29, 33, 53
Contraception 78
Copper 58
Coptic 379
Corinth *213*
Corn mummy 272, 300
Corpse 226
Corpus Hermetica 91, 98, 160, 162, 224
Cow 40, *219*, 276
  Story of the Heavenly 361
Crime 43
Crocodile 57
Crowley, Aleister 48, 88, 146
  Liber ABA - Magick *10*
  Liber Al 41, 50
Crown
  Atef 409, 414
  Red. *See* red: crown
Crypts 374
Cunnilingus 40
Cupid and Psyche *213*
Curse 36
  Adultery 47
Curse of the Pharaohs *186*
Cyphi 216

D

Daemon 148
  – Aiwass 114
  Language 112
Dahleh *189*
Dahshur *176, 189*
Daimons 60
  Guardian spirit 80
Damanhur 411
DAMNAMENEUS 142
Dance *15*

Of Yü *14*
Dark nights 160
Dawn 160
Day
  Break 355
Dead
  Land of the 32
Dead. the 411
Death 63, 371
Death mask 227
Decans 108, 289
Decapitation 32, 67, 354
Dee, John
  "Monas Hieroglyphica" 132
Defensive magic 364
Dehn, Georg 102
Deir el Medina *217*
Deir el Shelwit *217*
Demon
  Emissary 353
  Of death 371
  Of non-being. *See* Daemon
Demons
  Frankish 31
  Headless 81
Demotic 167, 170
Dendara 411
Denderah 276, 379
Depuydt, Leo 238
Desert *220*, 228
Diabolè/diabolic 353
Dieleman, Jacco 341
  "Priests, tongues, and rites" 121
Diet *215*
Disease & medicine
  Healing 357
  Phylactery 353, 360
Dismemberment 58, 67, 81, *216*, 276, 371
Djed pillars 411
Dog
  Black 359
  Days 362
  Star (see Sirius) *11*

Domitian, Emperor   148
Donkey   339, 353, 354, 355
   Ass   359
   Typhon's skull   359
'Doomsday' book. *See* Papyrus Wilbour
Door   129, 131
   Ka   99
Dragon   363
Drawing down the moon   386
Dreams   42, 121, *208*, *213*, 356, 380
   Incubation   *194*
Drunkenness   376, 379, 381
Duat   160, 243

E
Eagle   31
Easter / Jewish Passover   116
Eating   337
Edfu   274, 338, 380, 411
Edu   *182*
Egg   289
Egypt   *174*
   "alphabeth", "kabbalah"   170
   First Intermediate period   *186–211*
   Image of heaven   131
   Religion   *11*
   Temple   *217*
   Temple of the world   97
   Weeks   *215*
Egyptian
   Determinative   36
Eidolon   112
Eight sabbaths   *188*
Eileithouias-polis   361
Emerald Tablet   82
Emery, Walter   *182*
Encircle   37, 68
Enemy
   Captive   *201*
   Clubbing   *202*
Enigmatic writing   145
Ennead   412
Epagomenal days   411

Ephesian letters   141
Epiphany   *213*
Equinox   116
ERESCHIGAL   59
Eroticism   380
Evan-Pritchard, E E   30
Evil   80, 355
   Eye   350
   Sleep   342, 352
Execration   340
Executioner   368
'Exquisite Corpse'   35
Eye   155, *220*, 352

F
Faience   71
Fakhry, Ahmed   *176*
Falahin   *196*
Falcon   337
Farrell, Nick   118
Feast   69
Feasts/festivals
   Fire (Rekh-nedes)   284, 289
ferryman. *See* Nemty
Fetish   87
Fire   68, 347
Flail   414
Flint   36, 65
   Knife   66
   Miniature   67
flint   9
Folk   100
Foreleg   13
Fortress   64
Fortune, Dion   42, 134
Fourteen   *180*
   Parts   276
Frankfurter, David,   122
Frankincense   275
Frazer, J G   30
Freeform   89
Fries, Jan, Living Midnight - three movements of t   *16*
Funeral

Rites 38
Spell 38
Yours 63

G

Games
  Bead 45
  Mehen 45
Gardiner, Gerald 188
Gardiner, Sir Alan 30, 159
Gate 222
  opening 229
Geb 38, *179*
Gender 58
Genii, Djinn or Genius 107
Geomancy 65, 104
  Culture of 70
Germinating 273
Ghosts *189*
  Handsome phantom 382
Glass 68
Gnosis 63, 163
Goats 37
God-form
  Assumption of 41
Goddess 316
Goetia 75, 344
Gold 55, 414. *See also* Nemty
Golden Ass, The. *See Apuleius: The Golden Ass*
Graeco-Roman *194*
Graham, Lloyd D 147
Grant, Kenneth *11*
Great Bear (Ursa Major) *11, 12, 15*
Great Wagon *15*
Greek
  Magick 121
Greek Magical Papyri 55, 92, 358
Grimoires 162, 364
Guardian
  Angel 106
  Desert *222*

H

Habu village *217*

Hades 59
Hadit 36. *See also* Horus: Behadit
Hag 113
Halloween 277
Hand 374
Harpokrates 412
Harris Papyrus *192*
Hassan, Selim *176*
Hathor 40, *214, 217*, 245, 261, 379, 411, 412. *See also* seven Hathors
  Horned mirror 40
Hatshepsut 374
Hausa 411
Hawk
  Falcon 55
Headless 276
healer 360
Healing 194
Heb-sed *183*
Hebrew 47
  Goddess 50
Heka 25, 26, 34, 62, 87
Hekate 159
Hekayet 265
Heliopolis 163, *190*
Helios 60, 158, 246
Heliotrope 158
Hell 54, 68
Heptagram 118, 119, 126, 138, 302
Her-Uben 24
Herakleopolis 378
Heri-Hor *192*
Hermes Trismegistus 91
Hermetic 162, *213*
  Texts 146
Hermopolis 164, 333
Herodotus 355, 380
Heruifi 168
Hetepheres 372
Hetherington, Patrick
  Olympic flame 89
Hexagram 118

Hibiscus   *218*
Hidden God   8, 80
Hierakonpolis, "Citadel of the
   Hawk."   134
Hieroglyph   40
Hierogrammatos   *218*
Hinduism   30, 128
Hippopotamus   65, *182*, *183*, *219*, 316
Histeriola   39, 412
Holy family of gods   163
Honey   275
Horemheb   *196*
Hornung, Erik   29, 225
Horus   11, 60, 67, 68, *181*, *203*, *209*, 338, 412
   At Edfu   95
   Behadit   36, 411
   Cippi   44
   Fighting   126, 384
   Golden   55
   New moon   239
   Over the Crocodiles   44
Hours   227
House of Life   57, 68, 119, 144, 241, 375, *384*
Howler   344
Human
   Sacrifice   *179*
Hyksos   *190*

I

IAI. *See also* ass: ass-eared IAI
Iamblicus   94
Iathath   412
Ideogramme   412
Ilithyia   362
Imaginarium   101
Imbas Forosna   41
Imperishable Stars   11. *See Ursa Major*
Inaros   26
Incense   51
Individualism   80
Infertility   *189*

Initiation   63, 80, 83, *215*
Intercourse   380
Invocation   117, 386
   Of Mut   388
Ipet   316
Iron   37, *209*, 369, 413
Irrigation   *179*
Iseum Campensis   *223*
Isis   *11*, 67, *179*, *205*, 305
   Pelagia, "mistress of the sea"   213
   Temple of   57
Isis and Nephthys
   Lamentations   357
Islam   147
Israel   95

J

Jackal   *181*, 289
Jasper   158
Jesus   39, 146
Jeu the Hieroglyphist, Ritual of   146
Judgment Hall   *183*, *184*
Jung, Carl   42

K

Ka   26
   Going to   114
Kantarah   *196*
Karma   *184*
Karnak   *217*, 276, 306, 416
Kentritis   41
Kephra   *223*
Kephri   *206*
Khapesh   76
Kharga   *189*
Khasekhemiu   31
Khenti-Amentiu, whose name means
   'President of the   *178*, *185*, *188*
Khentykhet   312
Kheop   372
Khephra   159
Khepra   26
Khi-Rho   146
Khmun   413
Khnum   36, 54, *203*

Khoiak   273
Khonsu   *204*, *217*, 306, 369, 409
Khufu (Cheops)   *185*
Kiki   411
Kites. *See Birds: Kites*
Knives
   Throwing   66
Knot of Isis   168
Knucklebone   *19*
Kom el Sultan (The Sultan's
     Mound)   *185*, *190*, *191*
Koptos   83
Kush   411

L

Laboratory   274
Ladder. *See* Seth
   Jacob's   413
Lady of Heaven   409
Lakes
   temporary   414
Language
   Code   353
Lead   36, 59, 62, 66, 67
Legend of Isis and the Secret Name of
     Ra   39
Leopard   29, *219*
Letter
   To the dead   71
Libellos   162, 165
Liber AL   161
Liber Resh   159
Liber Samech   63
Libyan   45
   Plateau   *218*
License to depart   298
Licking   32, 39–85
Lion   29, 31
Lisht   79
Liturgy   383
Louvre   *194*
Lucius   212, *213*
   Asinine disguise   214
Lunar   *180*. *See also Moon*

Lute   122
Lycopolis   57

M

Maat   94, 268, 312, 413
   Maat heru - speaking true   413
   Mantra   388
Magician
   Elder   28
Magick   56, 87
   Ah hekau/'great of magick'   29
   Coup d'etat   72
   Definition of   30
   Eating   43, 46, 50
   Elder Magician   28
   Eucharist   50
   Harem Conspiracy   72
   Hermetic   83
   Image   32, 54–85, 61
   Invocation   353
   Lethal   73
   Love spell   61
   Mechanics   30
   "sampling"   342
   Sleep   42
   Squares   111
   Text   35
   Vocal spell   33, 35
magick. *See* histeriola
Makaras   *181*
Maledictions   386
Malinowski, B   30
Malkuth   101, 128
Manetho   361
Manjet boat   410
Marsh   376, 380
MASKELL – MASKELLO   145
Mass   337
Mastabas   129, 239
Master   369
Masturbation   39
Matanga sorceresses   *205*
Mathers, Macgregor   118
Medamud   379

Medicine   35, 39
Medinat Habu   136
Megaliths   133
Mehit   414
Memory   356
   archaeological   101
Memphis   26, *178*
   Theology   358
Mena-Narmer   *178*
Menstruation   52, 372
Mentuhotep III (11th dyn)   106
Meret   377
Merit-neter, 'God'loves-her'   *200*
Meroe. *See also* Bull
Meshketyu   76
Mesket boat   410
Meskhetyu   *12, 391*
Meteorite   37, *394*
Meteorites   413
Microcosm   380
Middle Pillar   119
Midwife   *218*
Mim   152
Min   *204, 209*, 257, 278
   Feast of   117
Mirgissa   64, 68
Mithras   *12*, 76, *214*
   Liturgie   *12*
   Liturgy   41
Moirai   60
Moisture   39
Moon   41, 53, 58, 94, 160, 330
   Calendar   101
   Chandrakala   83
   'day of rams'   82
   First visibility   239
   Full   238
   Kalas   75, 82
   Lunar days   82
   Lunar month   171
   New   171, 219, 238
Motherhood   357
Mounds
   Primary   95

Mouth   33
Mudra   57
Mummy   275
Murray, Margaret   *11*, 31, *188*
Musee du Louvre   61
Music & Musicians   377, 379, 380
Musical scale   122
Mut   *204*, 409, 413
Mut-Sekhmet-Bastet-Wadjet   139
Mystery
   Cult   *212*, 214
   Play   *187*, 338

N

Nag Hammadi "gospels"   146
Nails   67, 368
Name
   Mutilated   73
Nanefer (-ka-Ptah)   27
Narmer   *183*
   - Mena   *182*
Necropolis   *220*, 416
Nefer-hotep   *190*
Nehes   414
Neith   278, 415
Nekhbet   361, 370
Nekhekh - flail   414
Nemty   29
Nemys   41
Neolithic   46, 50
Neper   300
Nephotes   246
Nephthys   8, *11, 119, 179, 223,*
   241, 261, 359, *384. See also*
   Red: Veil of Nephthys
   Crone   358
   Domestic service   359
   Housewife   358
   Nursing   357
   Old woman   359
   Red cloth of   360
   Sister   357
Neterew   413
New Kingdom   *191*

New Testament   147
Nif-Wer channel   *198*, *207*
Night journey   *223*
Night Shadow   113
Nightmare   42, 356
Nile   *12*, 103, *198*, *211*
Nine squares or chambers   153
Niticris   375
Nome   29, 414
nomen   414
None   243
North   *13*, *211*
Northern tradition   80
Nubia   25, 45, 55, 64, 379, 414
Nuit   41, 76, *179*, *223*, 284, *391*

O

Occult Renaissance   132
Ochre   40, 65, 344
Offering
   Formulae   386
   Table   129
Ombos   35, 64, 68. *See* Naqada
Omm el Gaab   *188*
Omm Sety (Dorothy Louise Eady)   *173*, *176*
Omm Sety's Abydos   *407*
On   414
Oneness   168
Onnophris in Sais   414
Onuris   414
Opening the Mouth   97, 167
Opet   *217*, 276
Oracle   32, 62, *191*, *195*, *197*
Order of the Golden Dawn   88
Orientation   *211*
Orion   *14*
Orpheus   121
Orphic   91, 142
Osireion   100
Osireon   *183*, *185*
Osiris   *11*, 28, 67, 78, 94, *177*, *179*, *181*, *182*, *188*, *191*, *202*, 226, 268, 273, 414
   Tomb of   *188*
Ostracae   72
Ostrich   413
   Egg   35
Otherworld   *15*
Ouphor   98
Ouroboros   158
Oxford   88
   Bowl   71

P

Pagan   *215*
   Mystery cults   *214*
Pagels, Elaine   148
Palermo stone   257
Palestine   50
Palettes. *See* Narmer
Palindromes   112
Panishi   26
Panopolis   257
Papyrus   56
Papyrus Harris Magical   289
Papyrus Jumilhac   68
Papyrus of Khonsu-Renep   34
Papyrus Ramessium   37, 358
Papyrus Salt   32, 119
Papyrus Vandier   289
Parts   274
Parvati   *205*
Passsover or Easter,   102
Paternoster   112
Patmos   148
Paul the Hermit, Saint   107
Peake, Anthony
   "The Daemon"   112
Pechart   35, 37. *See also* Medicine
Pega   *188*
Pentagram   118, 149
   Inverted   149
   Lesser Ritual of the   117
Pentawere   72
Pepy II   *186*
Perfumery   272
Peribsen   31

Persephone   59
Pesesh-Ket knife
  'fishtale lance'   66
Pet lion   *198*
Petrie, Flinders   *185*
PGM - Papyri Graecai Magicae - Magical Papyri   363
Phallus   155, 257
  erect   409
Pharaoh   *182*
Pharmacopoeia   35
Pheneter   62
Philae   *181*, 364, 379
Philosophy   358
Phonemes   170
Photography   227
Piercing   32
Pilgrimage   *186*
Pinch, Margaret
  Magic in Ancient Egypt   *205*
Pitt Rivers museum   72
Pleiades   *14*, 150
Plinthion   139
Pliny
  Natural History   158
Plotinus   57
Plurality   168
Plutarch   *216*
Polaris   *12*
Porphyry   57
Portico
  Second   *201*
Possession   379
Pots
  Black top redware   69
  Broken   65
  Clay   55
  Clay virgin   70
  Red   69
Potter   36
Prayer   386
Priest   100, 382
  Chantress   24
  Heryheb or Lector   57

  kings   *192*
  Prophetess   24
Priestess   372, 382
  Prophetess   373
Prophets   260
Proserpine   *223*
Prostitution   *194*, 372, 377
  Sacred   372–382
Psammetichus/Psamtik   246, 364
Psychology
  Introvert   357
Psychopaths   43
Ptah   170, *203*, 415
Ptolemy   25
Pure   157
Pylon   *198*, 415
  False   *200*
Pyramid   139, 372
  False   *191*
  Giza   *176*
  Of Djozer at Saqqara   136
  Texts   *180*
Pythagoras   90

Q
Qasr el-Aguz (lit. the castle of the old Woman   *217*
Qina   106
Qis   29

R
Ra   26, 28, 38, 159, *206*, 220, 320, 351, 355, 415
  Barque of   369
  Left eye of   94
  Litany   26
  Pre   415
  Pre-Harakhti   415
Ra-Horakhty   *203*, 320
Races   45
Ram   225, 361
Ramesses   94, *196*
Ramesses I   *191*, *196*
Ramesses II   *196*, *198*
Rankine, David and Sorita D'este   123

Red 32. *See also* Pots: Red
  Bull 369
  Crown of the North *182*
  Goddess 358
  Ochre 65, 353
  Redden 368
  Redness 369
  Veil of Nephthys 77
Red Sea 83
Regardie, Israel 88
Reincarnation 27
Rekhyt 100, 358
Religion 56
Rennutet *19*, 300
Resurrection 27, 28
Reversal 32, 65, 67
Rhythm *213*
Ring
  Of power 156
Roman 170
  Egypt 162
Roses *214*
Rudra 344

S

Sacrifice 44, *202*, 361
  Human 64, *202*
Saint Moses *195*
Sais 278, 410, 412, 414
Saitic period *192*
Sakkara 178
Saliva *206*
Sand 32, 65
Satanism 43
SATOR-AREPO 111
Scarab 41
Scepter 250, 414
Sceptre
  Was 79
Scorpion 344
  Charmer 57
Scribes *218*
Seed 98
Sekhmet 72, 365, 415

Selket 78
Semen 38, 53
Semitic *191*, 411
Senwosret I 79
Separation 65
Sepermeru 37
Serpent *222*
Seth 11, 119, *180*, *184*, *209*, *212*,
    214, 226, 241, 245, 264, 289,
    354, 357, 358, *384*, *394*
  and Horus *179*, *201*, *205*
  Benign side 81
  Companions of 101
  Full Moon 239
  Headless 358
  Indigenous god 77
  ladder of 413
  Raging of 352
  Typhon 353
Sethians *16*
Setna 25, 27, 44, 54
Sety *196*
Sety I 29, 94, 101, 104, *174*, *176*,
    191, *194*, *196*, *204*, 225
  At Abydos 144
  Heart's Ease in Abydos *191*
  Own philosophy *201*
  Temple of 34, 42
  Temple of Sethy I at Abydos 405
Sety-mer-en-ptah *201*
Seven *13*, 26, 46, 65
  Charakteres 147
  Creative utterances 33
  Episodes *188*
  Flags *208*
  Greek vowels 122
  Sacred vowels 138
  Sages 33, *137*
  Seals 363
  Serpents 362–364
  Seventh hour 29
  Shamans 28
  Shrines *11*
  Spells 361

Stars   159
Trumpets   155
Vowels   120
72   110
Sex   78, 382
   Anal   53
   Dolphin   54
   Erogenous zones   83
   Erotic texts   40
   Fluids   39
   Love   *213*
   Pudenda   58
"Sexualized" minerals   305
Shabaka Stone   358
Shaitan   *13*
Shaking   *206*
Shamans   33, 70
Shed   44, 416
Shine   26
Shoni   161
Shu   29, 39, 286
   Atmosphere   39
Sickle (Kapesh)   67, 260
Sigils
   The new hieroglyphs   145
Signatures   35
Simon Magus   26
Sin   *184*
Singers   376
Sirius/Sothis   *11*, 75, 107
Sistrum   *213*
Situla   *213*
Sixt   243
Sixteen
   Day of lunar month   239
Skull   64
Sky
   Burial   135
Slaughter   65
Sleep   99, *194*
   Hypnotic   *216*
Smaiut
   N Seth   81
Snake   300, 344, 351, 388

Socrates   *218*
Sokar   *214*, 268, 273, 414, 415
Solomon   50
   Key of   150
   Temple   95, 101
Solstice, summer   *12*
Solstice, winter   *12*
Sopdu (Sirius)
   Heliacal Rising   239
Sound   33, 35, 91
Space   39
Spectacle   356
Speech   35
Spell kit   376
Spit   32, 38
Spitting   346
St Damiana   *195*
St Moses   *195*
Stang   27
Star   150
Statue   98
   Wooden   *188*
Statues
   'splendours'   62
Stele of Revealing   36
Stellar   28
Strabo   *194*, 372
Sudan   25, 64, 66
Suez Canal   117
Sun
   God   245
   Journey   225
   Rise   352
   Set   352
Superposition   32
Swallowing   32, 43
Sweat   39
Sword   57
Sycamore   416
Synesthesia   142

T
T3y   377
Tabernacles or "Booths"

Feast of   116
Taboo   39, 68
Talmud   27
Tanen   278
Tantra   *213*
Tantrism   35, 58, *205*
Taoism   *14*
Tar   275
Taweret   318
Tefnut   39
Tekhy   245
Temenos   *21*, 100, 136, *186*, *197*
Temple   92, 100, *197*, 380
   Library   56
   Of Osiris   *191*
   Rules broken   355
Temple of Sety I   *176*, *181*, *189*, *195*
   First Court   *198*
Temple of Sety I at Abydos   *11*
Tent   368
Terce   243
Teti-sheri   *191*
Thales   90
Theatres of Memory   95
Theban Magical Library   92, 138
Thebes   56, 118, *190*, *217*, 409, 416
Theodosius   56
Theurgy   157, 224
Thinis   *177*, *185*, *187*
Thoth   53, *180*, *217*, 224, 330
   Book of   25, 27, 37, 76
   Hill   106
Thunder magic   *15*
Thunderstorm   342, 352
Tiers   139
Tiye   72
Toad   31
Tomb   377
   Redi-nes at Giza   388
Torah   147
Totality   169
Trampling   32, 54
Trance   379, 380

Transition   341
Trapezoid   415
Tree
   Acacia   46
   Tree of Destiny   *203*
   Tree of Life   164, *203*
Triangle   139
Trigrams   *14*
Tum   159
Turpentine   275
Tutankhamum   45, 54
Twilight language   144
Two Brothers
   Tale of   46
Typhon   *214*, 250, 353, 354
   Or Trident   127
Typhonians   361
Typhonia   339
Tzaddhi   76

U

Underworld   28
Unguent   274
Uninitiated   *216*
Uroz   35
Ursa Major   *12*, 76, 81, *119*, 150, *241*, *363*, *384*

V

Valedictions   386
Valley of the Kings   416
Valley of the Queens   416
Vampires   52
Venomous   300
Venus   67
Vessel divination   289
Vibrating   138
Vision   356
Vizier   *196*
Voce Magicae   141
Voice offering
   Peret kheru   33
Voodoo
   Doll   54
Votary/Votaresses   373

Vowel   122
   Song   120
Vulture   362, 364

W

Wadj
   'to flourish'   33
Wand   79
War
   Total   37
Wax   57, 67, 73
   Bees   65
   Dolls   341
   Image spell   54, 83
Wepwawet   289
Weset   416
White crown of Upper Egypt   *182*
Widdershins   126
Wind   124
   East = Iabet   124
   Jimenet   125
   Meheyet   124
   South = Resey   125
Wing (pterugion)   139
Witchcraft   80, 94, *188*

Witch bottles   68
withershins   9
Wolf   135
Womb   *219*, 374
Word play   33
Wound   369

X

Xeper   26
XIXth dynasty   *196*

Y

Yael   82
Yahweh   50

Z

Zeus   372
Zosimos of Panopolis   123

www.ingramcontent.com/pod-product-compliance
Lightning Source LLC
Chambersburg PA
CBHW061925220426
43662CB00012B/1807